The Wars of the Roses

The Wars of the Roses

John Ashdown-Hill

AMBERLEY

First published 2015

Amberley Publishing
The Hill, Stroud
Gloucestershire, GL5 4EP

www.amberley-books.com

Copyright © John Ashdown-Hill, 2015

The right of John Ashdown-Hill to be identified
as the Author of this work has been asserted in
accordance with the Copyrights, Designs and
Patents Act 1988.

ISBN 978 1 4456 4524 7 (hardback)
ISBN 978 1 4456 4532 2 (ebook)

British Library Cataloguing in Publication Data.
A catalogue record for this book is available
from the British Library.

Typesetting and Origination by Amberley
Publishing
Printed in the UK.

CONTENTS

INTRODUCTION

What were 'The Wars of the Roses'?

The term 'Wars of the Roses' is a relatively modern and in many ways rather regrettable invention, which raises a number of quite complex issues. As we shall see, it is debatable whether the conflict which is now commonly so described was really a single war. It may simply have been a series of different battles and other kinds of clash, not all of which were seen, by those who took part in them, as related to one another. Chronologically, some of the battles were widely separated. Also, not all of them had similar objectives. It is also questionable to what extent the conflict overall had anything to do with roses. Although later parts of the contest may have been related to two competing sides, who were popularly associated with different coloured rose emblems, this relates to the period from 1485 until the 1520s – a period when, according to most traditional versions of the story, the 'Wars of the Roses' had ended!

The sequence of events popularly known as the 'Wars of the Roses' is generally perceived as a kind of civil war. Today, the meaning of 'civil war' is normally seen as a dispute involving fighting between two opposing groups within a single nation state.

In the Middle Ages, though, when the so-called 'Wars of the Roses' took place, the concept of a nation state was only just beginning to evolve. Thus, there was no clear nation state of 'England', in the modern sense of the term (indeed, some people may consider it questionable whether a clear nation state of 'England' exists even now).

Nevertheless, in the fifteenth century a 'realm' certainly existed, which at that period comprised England, Ireland, Wales and a small area of Continental European land in the vicinity of Calais. This realm was ruled by a single king, the realistic parts of whose title were 'King of England and Lord of Ireland',[1] and whose son and heir traditionally bore the honorary title 'Prince of Wales'. It is true that the so-called civil war which is now known as the 'Wars of the Roses' took place within that realm, and that it basically involved English, Irish and Welsh fighters, together with members of the Calais garrison. Thus, in one sense, the contest was mainly an internal, English, Irish, Welsh and Calais struggle. Nevertheless, foreign rulers, including Kings of France, of Spain, and of Scotland, and also the Dukes (and Duchesses) of the semi-independent state of Burgundy, did sometimes become involved in the conflict on one side or the other.

What is more, foreign military forces sometimes took part. Indeed, they occasionally played a significant role in the fighting. As we shall see, the French government backed anti-Yorkist attempts on the throne of England in the winter of 1470, in 1483, and in 1485, and they considered doing so (though, in the end, with no real commitment) in the 1490s. In addition, the campaigns of 1470, 1483 and 1485 all included French men-at-arms. In fact it is almost certainly the case that Richard III would not have been defeated, and Henry VII would never have become king, if

French soldiers had not backed Henry, and opposed Richard. At one level it therefore appears highly misleading to describe the campaign which culminated in the Battle of Bosworth as part of a 'civil war'.

Likewise, the Burgundian government supported the restoration of Yorkist power in 1471. Later, there was also a kind of Burgundian backing for the Yorkist campaigns of 1487 and in the 1490s. As for the government of Scotland, it was not even consistent in its involvement. For although it backed anti-Yorkist movements in the 1460s, James IV supported the Yorkist campaign of 'Richard of England' in the 1490s. This strongly suggests that the prime Scottish motivation focused on the interests of the kingdom of Scotland.

Within the realm of England, Ireland, Wales and Calais, the two opposing sides in the battles were ostensibly focussed around rival members of the late medieval Anglo-Norman royal family – usually referred to as the Plantagenets, though it is questionable how many of them would ever actually have used that surname. Thus the opposing sides are seen as comprising the opposing royal princes, together with their various supporters. In other words, on one level the 'Wars of the Roses' was basically a struggle between royal relatives, who were fighting over which of them should sit on the English throne – and/or wield the power behind the throne.

However, in another sense, the conflict clearly centred upon rivalry in the ranks of the aristocracy and gentry. In this second sense the fighting was only superficially linked to what has recently come to be sometimes referred to as 'the Cousins' War' (though the origins of that term are also extremely vague). Indeed, as we shall see, at least two of the battles within the period usually ascribed to the 'Wars of the Roses' were entirely private battles, completely unrelated to the contest for the throne. And if the period could be widened slightly, a greater number of private conflicts would be seen to form part of the picture.

As for the use of the term 'war' in this context, that also requires some examination. A modern war is normally an armed conflict involving a series of battles which may sometimes be separated in terms of their location and outcome, but which remain fairly closely related in terms of chronology. For example, the First World War lasted for approximately four years and four months (from 28 July 1914 until 11 November 1918). In the Second World War the fighting continued for almost exactly six years.[2] In both cases, although a number of separate battles took place in various locations, the armed conflict was more or less continuous.

But the so-called Wars of the Roses is usually said to have lasted for thirty-two years, from 1455 until 1487. And although, as we shall see, those dates can be disputed, arguably the conflict went on, not for less than thirty-two years, but potentially for a considerably longer period. Moreover, the Wars of the Roses did not simply consist of the continuous fighting of battles, as we would probably expect in the case of modern warfare. In the Wars of the Roses there were sometimes long gaps of time between one battle and the next. Thus, for example, no fewer than four years elapsed between the first battle of St Albans and the battle of Blore Heath.

At some such times there was apparent peace in the realm between the battles. Indeed, it may well have seemed, to those living at that moment, that all conflict had then been resolved. For example, during the five years which elapsed between the battle of Hexham and the battle of Edgecote Moor, it looked as if the crown was now secure upon the head of King Edward IV. However, sometimes, even when there was no fighting of battles and no open warfare, the contest for the throne, or for power within the kingdom, nevertheless continued in other significant ways, despite the lack of military action. For the various people involved, these other ways included a wide and diverse range of activities, from plotting, scheming and changing sides to the making of marriages, legal disputes, the killing (or attempted killing) of rivals, and sometimes witchcraft and magic.

Before attempting to explore in detail the history of the conflict, there are a number of basic questions which need to be raised. These basic questions are:

What caused the contest for the English throne?

Why did that contest take the form of armed conflict?

Precisely who were the royal rivals?

Did the Wars of the Roses constitute the first English civil war?

What were the real dates of the Wars of the Roses (and how do we assess these dates)?

Where does the name 'Wars of the Roses' come from?

In the popular perception, most of these questions are already seen as having very simple and well-known answers. In fact, however, the true picture is much more complex.

What Caused Fighting for the Throne?

Nowadays we are used to the idea that the crown should always be inherited by the previous king's (or queen's) closest surviving royal relative. This basic idea also existed in the Middle Ages. But things were not as simple then as they are today.

For example, when King Edward the Confessor died in 1066, leaving no children, he was not succeeded by a member of his English royal family of that period – the family known as the house of Wessex. Edward the Confessor's closest surviving royal male relation was his great-nephew, Edgar the Atheling. But Edgar did not become king when Edward died. Instead there was a fight for the throne between Harold Godwinson (King Harold II) and William the Conqueror, Duke of Normandy (King William I). Both of these contenders were related to Edward the Confessor in different ways, but neither of them had a genuine blood claim to the English throne. Harold was a relative of Edward the Confessor's wife, and was also a distant cousin of King Edward, being descended from his remote ancestor, the early ninth-century Aethelwulf, King of Wessex. As for William of Normandy, he was related to the Confessor's mother. Ultimately, of course, as his epithet 'the Conqueror' shows, it was William of Normandy who defeated Harold Godwinson and won the contest for the English throne.

In the modern world, a comparable situation might be if, for example, Charles, 9th Earl Spencer, and James Middleton were suddenly to advance rival claims to the throne. Earl Spencer is the maternal uncle of H. R. H. the Duke of Cambridge, and is also of distant royal descent (in illegitimate lines, from both Charles II and James II). James Middleton is the brother of H. R. H. the Duchess of Cambridge and shares her extremely remote royal descent from Edward III. Both men are closely related to the royal family by marriage, but could not be described as royal by birth (in spite of the royal Stuart ancestry of Earl Spencer and the even more remote royal ancestry of James Middleton).

However, it is important to note that the act of seizing the throne by force and then having your rule approved by Parliament, as William I did in the eleventh century, was apparently one acceptable way of becoming king of England in the Middle Ages. This same technique was used again later, both by King Stephen and by King John. During the period of the so-called 'Wars of the Roses', the technique was employed again by three sovereigns: King Henry IV, King Edward IV and King Henry VII. Thus this means of becoming king by the violent seizure of power, followed by Parliamentary endorsement, was one key feature of the 'Wars of the Roses'.

Another issue during the Middle Ages was the right of girls to inherit or pass on the crown. In the early twelfth century, King Henry I had no surviving legitimate sons. He therefore tried to ensure that his daughter, Matilda, should succeed him. Ironically, after Henry I's death, Matilda's right to the throne was contested by her cousin, Stephen of Blois, who was descended from William the Conqueror – but in a female line (on his mother's side). In the end, after years of fighting, the throne was inherited by Matilda's son, King Henry II. This means that, both when Stephen seized the throne and when he acknowledged Matilda's son as the next king-to-be, the results of the contest between Matilda and Stephen confirmed absolutely that in the Middle Ages, in England, girls could pass on a right to the throne. The only problem was that, at that time, the idea of having a girl ruling the country in person had not yet been accepted by everybody. Later, as we shall see, every family which put forward a claim to the throne during the 'Wars of the Roses' actually based its contention on a female line of royal descent.

Why Did the Contest Take the Form of Armed Conflict?

This was because of the wider context within which the contest arose. The basic facts are first, that possession of the English crown had been a matter of armed dispute since before the Plantagenet family ever claimed it; and second, that what is traditionally seen as the period of the 'Wars of the Roses' in England had been preceded – and was overlapped – by a similar contest for the throne of France, known as the 'Hundred Years War', which also involved members of the English royal family and members of the English aristocracy.

In the 'Wars of the Roses', Who Were the Royal Rivals?

The basic problems which resulted in the 'Wars of the Roses' were first, that in the fourteenth century there was one king – Edward III – who had many children. This generated a large royal family, containing numerous cousins who were potential rivals. But the second strand of the problem was that Edward III was ultimately succeeded by his senior grandson, Richard II – who produced no children. This led to quarrels about which of Richard's numerous cousins should succeed him. Edward III and Richard II both belonged to the royal family commonly referred to as the Plantagenets.[3]

The 'Wars of the Roses' is usually said to have been a struggle between two rival branches of the so-called Plantagenet royal family (the house of Anjou), known respectively as the house of York and the house of Lancaster. But this is a huge and essentially hindsighted oversimplification of what actually took place. In fact the early rivalry was between Henry of Lancaster and his young cousin, Roger Mortimer, over which one of them should succeed Richard II. This initial contest was ultimately won by Henry of Lancaster, who simply seized the throne as King Henry IV.

By the late 1440s the struggle had become a contest between Edmund Beaufort, Marquis of Dorset (created Duke of Somerset in 1448), and Richard, Duke of York, each of whom was hoping for recognition as the legal heir of the then childless Lancastrian King Henry VI. At this stage, incidentally, the Duke of York was claiming to be the *Lancastrian* heir to the throne. This would have been principally on the basis of his paternal-line descent (though possibly he was also taking account of his female line descent from Edmund Crouchback and his son, the 1st and 3rd Earls of Lancaster – see below, Family Tree 7).

By 1460 the Duke of York had changed his position. Now, instead of claiming recognition as heir to the Lancastrian king on the basis of his male line royal descent, he was claiming that he himself was the rightful king, based on his female line descent from Roger Mortimer. York was killed, as we shall see, in December 1460. But in 1461 the throne was seized by his eldest son, Edward IV. Ironically, this Yorkist success then led to fighting within the Yorkist ranks – based upon what was perceived in some quarters as Edward IV's inappropriate royal marriage policy. The rivalry which thus emerged was based initially upon a contest for the power behind the throne. This contest was between Edward IV's cousin, Richard Neville, Earl of Warwick (known as the 'Kingmaker'), and Edward's queen, Elizabeth Woodville, and her family.

By 1471, the direct male line of descent of the royal house of

Lancaster was extinct. As a result, approximately 100 years after the initial contest between the rival heirs of Richard II, we find that the 'Wars of the Roses' had developed into a struggle between King Richard III (of the house of York), and Richard's second cousin, Henry, titular Earl of Richmond. Henry is normally given the surname 'Tudor' but, as we shall see, that is also questionable. And Henry pretended to be the heir of the house of Lancaster. However, he was certainly not the legal Lancastrian heir.

So the 'Wars of the Roses' was by no means simply a fight between the princely families of Lancaster and York. Families such as the Mortimers, the Beauforts, the Woodvilles and the 'Tudors' all have to be fitted into the picture. In books and on the internet you will find various complicated family trees showing the relationship of the rival royal lines. These published family trees are not all identical. Moreover, the picture they present can seem quite confusing. But we do need to try to get to grips with them. So here are two royal family trees which give different viewpoints on the contest.

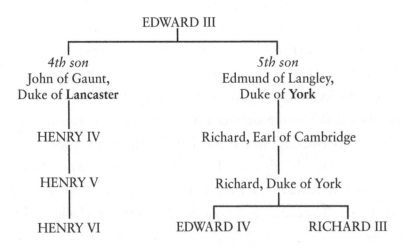

Family Tree 1: The rival lines of Lancaster and York.

This first version of the Lancaster-versus-York family tree is a traditional one. It assumes that what is most important is the descent from father to son. It accurately shows the male lines of descent of both Lancaster and York from their common ancestor, King Edward III. From this family tree, we can see that the house of Lancaster was descended in the male line from Edward III's *fourth* son, John of Gaunt, and the house of York was descended in the male line from Edward III's *fifth* son, Edmund of Langley. This family tree therefore seems to suggest that the Lancasters were the senior royals and had the better claim to the throne.

However, this family tree is misleading for two reasons. First, we should not only look at the male line of descent. Second, as we have already seen, the original contest for the throne was not between the Lancaster family and the York family, but between the Lancasters and the Mortimers. So where does the Mortimer family fit into the picture?

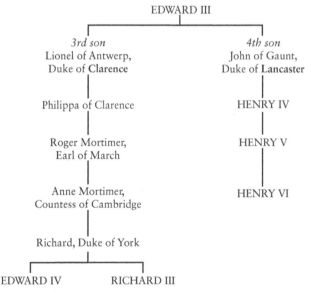

Family Tree 2: The rival lines of Clarence / Mortimer and Lancaster.

This second family tree shows that the Mortimers were also descendants of Edward III. But they were descended from his *third* son. Thus they were higher up in the order of succession than either the Lancaster family or the York family. What is more, as the result of a marriage within the wider royal family, the Mortimers ultimately became the ancestors of the house of York. Therefore, in the final analysis, and through the Clarence-Mortimer line of descent, it was the house of York which possessed the senior claim to the throne. But the Clarence-Mortimer line of descent passed through two women – Philippa of Clarence and Anne Mortimer. This takes us back to the question of whether women had a valid right to the throne in those days.

Nowadays, of course, English women expect to have equal rights to those of men. But what was the position in the fifteenth century? During the Middle Ages women did not have equal rights to men in every respect. But as we have already seen, in England they were definitely able to transmit rights of inheritance to their sons. Both King Stephen (reigned 1135–1154) and King Henry II (reigned 1154–1189) had successfully claimed the English throne via their mothers.

Was This the First English Civil War?

The 'Wars of the Roses' has sometimes been called 'the first English Civil War', but that is clearly nonsense. As we have already seen, England was not then a nation state in the modern sense of the world, and the fifteenth-century fighting also involved Ireland, Wales and Calais. But in any case, the first internal conflict in the realm which expressed itself in terms of battles had taken place more than 300 years earlier – when Henry I's daughter, Matilda, fought with her cousin, King Stephen, over which of them should have the English throne. At that period, the territory held by the house of Normandy included both England and parts of north-western France, and fighting took place in both of those areas. But since the territories in question then comprised the equivalent of a single 'nation state', in one sense the contest constituted the equivalent of a 'civil war'. Subsequently, following the succession of Henry II and the foundation of the house of Plantagenet, further fighting took place between the new king, his wife and their several sons over who should hold which territory in the future. By this time, the Plantagenet[4] equivalent of a 'nation state' was even more extensive and complex (including a great deal of French territory). However, once the parameters of the Plantagenet 'realm' are recognised, this conflict could also be seen as a kind of 'civil war'.

The claim that the 'Wars of the Roses' comprised the first English civil war is therefore ridiculous for more than one reason. But this also highlights a wider problem – the fact that the 'Wars of the Roses' has become surrounded by a great deal of mythology. In this book we shall try to sort out what is myth and what is fact. For example:

What Were the Dates of the 'Wars of the Roses'?

The fighting is traditionally presented as having taken place in the fifteenth century. But, as we shall see, in fact the conflict started towards the end of the fourteenth century and went on into the sixteenth century. Incidentally, before we go any further in the matter of dates, we need to note that, in the Middle Ages, the calendar in England was different from the modern one. In those days the year did not start on 1 January but on 25 March ('Lady Day'). For this reason, in this book, events which took place in January, February or March will usually be given TWO year dates with a stroke between them, thus:

2 February 1460/1

This means that according to our modern calendar the event happened in the second month of 1461, but according to the medieval English calendar it was in the penultimate month of 1460.

Where Does the Names 'Wars of the Roses' Come From?

The names for late medieval 'wars' involving England are not contemporary designations. The records of that period contain no all-embracing names for such conflicts, and the common modern names were only really invented in the nineteenth century. Thus, for example, the appellation 'Hundred Years War', to categorise the very long and often interrupted fourteenth- and fifteenth-century conflict between England and France was only fabricated in the early nineteenth century. And we have already seen that it is disputable whether, in fact, such lengthy and often interrupted late medieval armed conflicts can really be considered single 'wars' in the modern sense of that word.

The contest which forms the subject matter of the present book has been called 'the Wars of the Roses' since the nineteenth century, and the designation has been widely accepted because the white rose is seen as a symbol of the York family, and the red rose as a symbol of the house of Lancaster. But at the time when the fighting took place, no-one had ever heard the phrase 'the Wars of the Roses'. That name appears to have been created about 300 years after the events in question, most probably by the novelist Sir Walter Scott.[5] What is more, as a name it may not be very appropriate. This is because, while the traditional white rose really was one of the badges of the York branch of the royal family and its supporters, the connection between the red rose and the Lancaster family is much more dubious. We shall explore this whole issue, including the real origins of the alleged Lancastrian red rose badge, in greater detail later in this investigation.

For the moment, however, we should note that roses of three colours – white, gold and red – had certainly been used by various kings, queens, princes and princesses of the so-called Plantagenet royal family as badges since the thirteenth century. 'Eleanor of Provence, wife of Henry III, is the first member of the House of Plantagenet to be associated, at least in modern times, with a rose emblem, and is reputed to have used a white rose as her personal badge. Eleanor's sons, Edward I and Edmund Crouchback, are both said to have used rose badges. ... [Edward I's] rose badge is said to have been gold with a green stem ... Five-petalled roses appear on [Edward III's] sixth seal. ...There is also evidence that the rose emblem was used by Edward III's son, the "Black Prince"'.[6] Later, Richard Duke of York and his sons, Edward IV and Richard III all seem to have used a white rose as one of their badges.

So how, and when, did the whole story of the 'Wars of the Roses' really start? And incidentally, for the sake of simplicity, from now on this traditional name will be employed without inverted commas, since hopefully it has now been clearly established that both the name, and many other aspects of the traditional picture of the conflict to which the term is applied, are to be thoroughly re-examined in this present study.

PART I

MULTICOLOURED PLANTAGENETS

I

HOW THE TROUBLE STARTED

The reigns of the kings generally (but, in most cases, retrospectively) referred to as the Plantagenets had always been beset by disputes and contests for the throne. In those days there was not yet any conception within their realm of the 'Divine Right' of the monarch to rule. Although the eldest son of the reigning sovereign was normally allowed to succeed to the throne, if he was weak in any way, or if any of his cousins felt strong and ambitious, or if the sovereign failed to produce male heirs – or produced rather too many male heirs – trouble and contests for power were likely.

Moreover, throughout most of the Plantagenet period of rule, the royal house of England – together with many of its aristocrats, and their followers – was also involved in similar contests in France. At first this was simply a contest over the holding of lands. Later, when the French royal house of Capet died out in the senior male line, leaving Valois younger cousins in France, but living female line descendants (in the person initially of King Edward III) in England, the contest in France evolved into a direct Plantagenet claim to the French throne, leading to the 'Hundred

Years War'. Obviously, if the superior crown of France was a matter for armed dispute, the inferior crown of England could also be fought over.

The first Plantagenet King of England, Henry II, who reigned from 1154–1189, had himself been forced to fight his way to power. As we have seen, Henry II was the grandson of Henry I, but his line of descent was through his mother, the Empress Matilda, who, in spite of her father's efforts on her behalf, had never been generally accepted (and was never crowned) as the reigning English sovereign. As for Henry II, he fathered several sons, who then disputed, both between themselves and with their father, the question of who should succeed him, and in which capacity. And these were disputes which had certainly involved some fighting.

There was one clearly disputed succession in respect of the crown of England, involving the immediate heirs of Henry II, at the end of the twelfth century. Indeed, what then occurred is often perceived as bearing a superficial resemblance to what took place later, in 1483. When Richard I, 'the Lion Heart', died in 1199, he left no children. Richard's closest male-line relative was his nephew, Arthur. This prince was the son of Richard's brother, Geoffrey, who had died in 1186. Prior to his own death, the king had, at one stage, acknowledged Arthur as his heir. But when Richard died, Arthur was passed over. Instead, the surviving younger brother of Richard and Geoffrey was crowned in England as King John. John subsequently imprisoned his nephew, Arthur, in France, and was later said to have murdered him, tied a stone to his dead body and thrown the corpse into the River Seine. This incident emphasises the fact that quarrels and fighting about the succession were always likely when a king had no son.

Later, as we shall see, there was an argument about who had been the rightful successor of King John's son, Henry III. However, there seems to have been no dispute about this at the time. In 1227, Henry III was succeeded by his son Edward I, and at that point Edward's right to the throne appears to have been universally accepted. It was only 150 years later that a story proliferated which cast retrospective doubt on Edward's right to be king.

The reign of Edward I's eldest son, Edward II, witnessed yet another case of what has been described as 'civil war'. This began as a contest between the Despensers (family of the king's second favourite, Hugh Despenser) and Edward II's first cousin, Thomas, 2nd Earl of Lancaster (arguably the first royal rebel of the house of Lancaster), who was defeated at the battle of Boroughbridge and was subsequently beheaded. Hostilitity to the Despensers was later headed by Edward II's own wife, Isabelle of France, and her lover, Roger Mortimer. This time it was Edward II who was defeated. The king was then forced to abdicate in favour of his son, Edward III, in order to prevent the crown being passed to some other candidate.

As the family trees in the introduction showed, the rival claimants for the crown in the Wars of the Roses were all descendants of King Edward III – a long-reigning fourteenth-century king who had a number of children. Edward III died in 1377. However, his eldest son, Edward, Prince of Wales, known as the 'Black Prince', had predeceased him. Therefore Edward III was not succeeded by one of his sons. Instead, he was succeeded by his senior line grandson – the Black Prince's only surviving legitimate child – who became King Richard II. Richard II reigned from 1377 until 1399.

Richard was quite young when he came to the throne. He grew up to be a cultivated man. But he was not always a good king. In some quarters his government proved unpopular. However, Richard II's biggest problem was the fact that, in spite of his marriage to Anne of Bohemia, he never fathered any children. When Anne died, Richard married a second queen – a very young French princess – but still no children appeared. So the big question hanging over Richard II's reign was who would be the next king when Richard died?

The English laws about who can succeed to the throne have never been permanently fixed. The precise rules have varied from time to time. Recently, for example, the laws of the United Kingdom were altered to allow the eldest child of a sovereign to be the heir, irrespective of whether that child is a boy or a girl. In the past, though, male children were always given preference.

Not only did Richard II have no children, but he also had no living full-blood brothers or sisters. Therefore the heir to his throne would have to be one of his royal cousins. Richard's father, the Black Prince, had several younger brothers. The eldest of these brothers who had produced children of his own was Lionel of Antwerp, Duke of Clarence. Logically, therefore, Lionel's descendants should have had the right to inherit the throne when Richard II died, since they were the king's most senior royal cousins.

But, as we have already seen, there was one problem which ultimately led to violence – and to the Wars of the Roses. Lionel, Duke of Clarence, had produced no sons. His only child had been a daughter, Philippa, who had married into the Mortimer family (earls of March). Richard II definitely seems to have

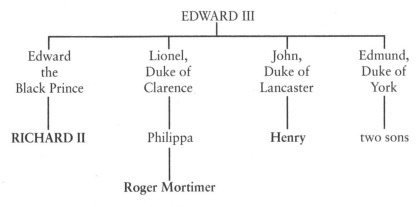

Family Tree 3: Who was Richard II's true heir?

been of the opinion that Philippa's eldest son, Roger Mortimer, should succeed to the throne. However, not everybody agreed with him.

The next surviving brother of the Black Prince, after Lionel, was John of Gaunt, Duke of Lancaster. Unlike Lionel, John had produced a son. In Parliament and elsewhere, John of Gaunt argued strongly that his son, Henry, should be the heir to the throne, rather than Roger Mortimer. This was the origin of the contest between the Lancaster and Mortimer families for the crown of England.

One very strange feature of the Lancastrian argument was the fact that John of Gaunt – a younger son of King Edward III – never claimed to be heir to the throne *himself*. Instead, he claimed this position for his son Henry. Why on earth did he do that? It seems to have been because John was well aware that his elder brother, Lionel, also had living descendants. Lionel was dead, but his grandson, Roger Mortimer had a potentially stronger claim to the throne than John of Gaunt and his family. As we have seen, although no woman had ever yet ruled England in person, the right of female members of the royal family to pass on a claim to the throne had been recognised in England since the twelfth century.

However, John of Gaunt's son, Henry, also had a royal *mother*. John's first wife, Blanche of Lancaster, had been a descendant (the senior descendant) of Henry III's son, Edmund 'Crouchback'. The precise meaning of Edmund's nickname is a matter of dispute. But whatever it meant at the time, it was later interpreted as indicating a physical disability of some kind. John of Gaunt and his supporters therefore put forward a very confusing claim to the effect that Edmund Crouchback had been Henry III's *eldest* son, but had been excluded from the throne in favour of his allegedly younger brother, Edward I, because of his disability. In this way they tried to give Henry a better *female-line* claim to the throne than that of the Mortimer family. Of course, this story effectively claimed that Edward I, Edward II, Edward III and Richard II had all been usurpers. Not surprisingly, that made King Richard II very angry.

Adam of Usk – a chronicler who was born in 1377 and died in 1421 – explains what took place, and also states clearly that the Lancastrian claim which was advanced was incorrect.

> One day in a council ... the point was raised by some that by the right of descent from the person of Edmund, Earl of Lancaster (they declared that the same Edmund was the eldest son of king Henry III, but that on account of his mental weakness, his birthright had been set aside and his younger brother, Edward, preferred in his place) Richard [II]'s succession in the direct line was barred. As to this, see the history in the pedigree, known throughout England, that Edward was first-born son of king Henry, and that after him, and

before Edmund, Margaret, who was afterwards queen of Scotland, was born to the same kin.[1]

Another fact, which Adam does not mention, is that Edmund's 'weakness', whatever it was, was not sufficient to prevent him from attempting, with his father's support, to claim another crown — that of Sicily. Also, William de Rishanger, who was a contemporary of Edmund Crouchback, unquestionably refers to him as '*Dominus Edmundus, filius regis junior*'.[2] Thus, the claim put forward by John of Gaunt was either a deliberate lie or a mistake. Edmund Crouchback had definitely not been Edward I's elder brother. However, both Edward I and Edmund Crouchback had lived a long time ago, and the Lancaster family – or its supporters – obviously hoped that people would simply accept what they were saying.

Meanwhile, during the 1380s Richard II himself became increasingly unpopular. He was considered extravagant and his lavish support of his favourites was resented. In the 1390s the king's second marriage to a French princess was also resented in

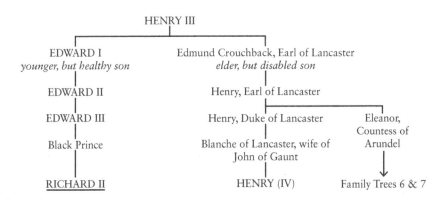

Family Tree 4: The Lancastrian claim as put forward in about 1390.

some quarters, since France had been seen in England as the enemy for the past forty years.

Also, Richard II did something unpleasant. In 1397 he arrested one of his uncles: Edward III's youngest surviving son, Thomas, Duke of Gloucester. Uncle and nephew had been at odds for some time, and Richard II thought Gloucester was trying to oust him. When Gloucester's trial opened, however, the duke did not appear in court. Instead, Richard II's friend the Duke of Norfolk (who had been Gloucester's jailer) announced that unfortunately, Thomas had unexpectedly died. Almost certainly he had been murdered on Richard II's orders. From this point onwards the last two years of Richard's reign were seen in some quarters as a kind of royal tyranny.

In 1398, Richard II's heir, Roger Mortimer, also died. Although he left surviving children, his death probably weakened the position of the Mortimer family in terms of the succession. Mortimer's death was followed, in 1399, by the death of Richard II's last living uncle, John of Gaunt. Gaunt's son, Henry, was abroad at the time, having been banished from England by Richard II. But after his father died, taking advantage of Richard II's absence in Ireland, Henry returned to England without the king's permission. He then gathered supporters and seized control of the kingdom.

To some extent, Henry benefitted from the fact that luck seemed to be on his side. 'If events had fallen out otherwise, it is probable that he would not have dared to seize the throne, but would have stopped short at his original programme of claiming justice for himself.'[3] However, he put his claim to be king to Parliament, and because he was now already effectively in power, he was accepted as King Henry IV.

[The Duke of] Lancaster was in his place, and the throne was left empty. Richard's resignation was accepted, and his deposition voted. The duke [of Lancaster] then read an English declaration, claiming the crown on the grounds of his being in the right line of descent from Henry III.[4]

Thus Richard II was deposed and imprisoned, and the house of Lancaster found itself sitting upon the throne of England.

The claim to the throne which Henry IV had put to Parliament was the claim which had been advanced on his behalf earlier, by his father, John of Gaunt (see above). The full text of Henry's claim reads as follows:

In the name of Fadir, Son, and Holy Gost, I Henry of Lancastr' chalenge yis Rewme of Yngland and the Corone with all ye membres and ye appurtenances, als I y^t am desendit be right lyne of the Blode comyng fro the gude lorde Kyng Henry therde, and thorghe yat ryght yat God of his grace hath sent me, with helpe of my Kyn and of my Frendes to recover it: the whiche Rewme was in poynt to be undone for defaut of Governance and undoyng of the gode Lawes.[5]

A contemporary chronicle, confirms the nature of Henry IV's claim to the throne.

Thanne aros the said duke of Lancastre and of Hereford, and blissid him, and redde in a bill how he descendid and cam doun lynealli of Kyng Harri the sone of King Johan and was the nexte heir male of his blod, and for that cause he chalanged the croune; and alle the lordis and comunez assentid therto.[6]

But the fact that the Lancaster branch of the royal family had seized the crown did not mean that the rights of Richard II and of the Mortimer family were forgotten. 'The moment that the usurpation was complete the inherent weakness of the new ruler's position began to display itself.'[7] To begin with, Richard II was still alive. And although the ex-king was imprisoned, first in London and later at Pontefract, he was by no means without supporters. These included a group of nobles whom Richard had rewarded with new titles – titles which Henry IV had now taken away from them, because he claimed that they had been involved in the murder of his uncle, the Duke of Gloucester.

The deprived noblemen were soon leading a plot against Henry IV. The men involved included John Montagu (or Montacute), 3rd Earl of Salisbury; Richard II's half-brother, John Holland, 1st Earl of Huntingdon (formerly Duke of Exeter), together with his nephew, Thomas Holland, 3rd Earl of Kent (formerly Duke of Surrey); Thomas le Despenser, 4th Baron le Despenser (formerly Earl of Gloucester); Ralph Lumley, 1st Baron Lumley; Sir Thomas Blount, and Sir Bernard Brocas. The group is also sometimes alleged to have included a member of the royal family – Edward 'of Norwich',[8] 1st Earl of Rutland (formerly Duke of Aumale), the eldest son and heir of Edmund of Langley, Duke of York (a surviving son of Edward III, who was then approaching his sixtieth birthday). However, the involvement of the Duke of York's son and heir is far from certain.

The noble plotters met together secretly on 17 December 1399 at Westminster Abbey. There they formulated a plan to capture Henry IV just after Christmas, while the king was at Windsor, celebrating Twelfth Night (the religious feast of the Epiphany). Their scheme was to capture Henry and put him to death. Richard II was then to be restored to his rightful position as king. A French account states that the royal conspirator, Edward 'of Norwich' (or of York), betrayed his companions by warning King Henry IV of what was planned. However, this account is disputed, and there is no evidence to substantiate it.[9] Nevertheless, in some way Henry became aware of the plot. He therefore avoided Windsor Castle. Instead he remained in London, where he summoned an army to back him up. Alarmed, the noble conspirators fled to the West Country, where they tried to start an armed rebellion against the Lancastrian regime but attracted very little support.

In the end, all the noble conspirators involved in the 'Epiphany Rising' were put to death by Henry IV. Lumley had been killed in the fighting, while he was trying to take Cirencester. At the same time Salisbury and Kent were captured. After a brief imprisonment both these men were executed on 7 January 1399/1400, without having been tried. A week later, a similar fate overtook Le Despenser, who had been taken at Bristol. Meanwhile Huntingdon had been captured at Pleshey, and he was also beheaded. Blount escaped at first, and fled to Oxford. However he was captured there, and subsequently hung, drawn and quartered. As for Brocas, he was beheaded at Tyburn. Following these executions, Acts of Attainder were passed in Parliament against all the conspirators.

Meanwhile, the conspiracy to restore Richard II convinced Henry IV that it had now become too dangerous to allow his cousin, the former king, to remain alive. Very conveniently, therefore, Richard died at Pontefract Castle at some time before 17 February 1399/1400. The surviving evidence suggests that he had probably been starved to death. 'His agony is said to have endured fifteen days.'[10] This cruel means of killing him was probably chosen for the simple reason that Henry IV would have to place Richard's body on display in order to secure the advantage of public awareness that the former king was no more. Of course, when the body was displayed to the public, any injuries would have been noticed and would have invited the suspicion that Henry IV had murdered Richard. However, a death by starvation guaranteed that there would not be a single wound to be seen on Richard II's dead body.

Far from solving all of the problems for the usurping Lancastrian, Henry IV, the killing of Richard II actually led to further conflict. To begin with, not everyone believed that Richard II was dead, and an impostor appeared, claiming the ex-king's identity. Also, Henry IV's namesake, and former supporter, Sir Henry 'Hotspur' Percy, son of the Earl of Northumberland, soon turned against him and marched towards Wales with the probable aim of joining forces with the self-proclaimed Prince of Wales, Owain Glyndŵr.

Owain had already included in his propaganda some pretence that he was fighting on behalf of Richard II. However, in reality his programme was essentially nationalistic in terms of Wales, and he had engaged in quite effective guerrilla warfare, causing the usurper, Henry IV a number of problems. These problems were then exacerbated by two invasions of England – by French forces along the south coast and by a Scottish army, under the Earl of Douglas, in the north of England. The Earl of Northumberland initially backed Henry IV against the Scottish invasion. But the Percy family was then dissatisfied with the fact that Henry failed to reward them in the manner they had expected. Therefore, Henry 'Hotspur' decided to recruit former supporters of Richard II to his side. Although 'Hotspur' was basically engaged in a kind of feudal rebellion, he and his supporters condemned Henry IV as a usurper, and as the murderer of the former king.

The outcome was the battle of Shrewsbury (21 July 1403), in which Henry IV very nearly lost both his life and the crown he had seized from his cousin, Richard II. Indeed, his army suffered more losses than that of Henry 'Hotspur', and if the latter had not been killed, he might well have been proclaimed the victor!

Meanwhile, the claim to the throne of the Mortimer family had not been forgotten. After all, the Mortimers had been Richard II's closest living relatives and should arguably have been his legal heirs. Although, after his dubious victory at the battle of Shrewsbury, Henry IV managed to remain on the throne, he was beset by further conflict two years later. In 1405 the Archbishop of York, and the Earl Marshal, Thomas Mowbray (son of Henry IV's former enemy, the Duke of Norfolk) agreed with the father of the late Henry 'Hotspur' – the old Earl of Northumberland – that Edmund Mortimer, Earl of March, should be recognised as King of England. Henry IV dealt with this new problem by offering to meet his enemies under a flag of truce and then seizing and executing them. Not surprisingly, the execution of an archbishop was viewed by many as an example of martyrdom.

Despite yet another rebellion in 1408, Henry IV managed to remain upon the throne until he died naturally in 1413. However, the disease which ultimately killed him – and which first beset him a few days after his execution of the archbishop of York – was seen as a divine punishment for his usurpation, and for all his evil actions. Thus, although the accession of his son, the second Lancastrian king, Henry V, passed initially without any conflict, that still did not make the new royal dynasty acceptable to everyone in England.

As we have seen, Richard II's cousin and heir, Roger Mortimer, had died before King Richard, in 1398. But in 1406 Roger's daughter, Anne Mortimer, had married her royal cousin Richard of York, Earl of Cambridge, the younger brother of Edward 'of Norwich' (or of York), who had allegedly been involved in – but had then betrayed – the 'Epiphany Rising'. This marriage produced one very important son, Richard. He is a key character in the story of the Wars of the Roses, and we shall look at the reason for this in just a moment. Meanwhile, however, the marriage of Anne Mortimer led to involvement of her young husband, the Earl of Cambridge in a movement called the Southampton Plot. This was an attempt to depose the new king, Henry V, and replace him with the then living royal heir of the Mortimer line: Anne Mortimer's brother, Edmund.

Unfortunately, as had been alleged in the case of the earlier 'Epiphany Rising', the new anti-Lancastrian plot was betrayed from within. Edmund Mortimer was a very nervous man. On Wednesday 31 July 1415 he therefore revealed the Southampton Plot to Henry V. As a result, the Yorkist prince – the Earl of Cambridge – was beheaded on Monday 5 August. He was subsequently given a less-than-royal burial in the Church of St Julien, Southampton (then the chapel of the Leper Hospital of St Julien – or 'God's House').

Anne Mortimer, Countess of Cambridge, had died before her husband. However, as we have already noted, between them this interesting royal couple – comprising a wife descended from Edward III's third son and a husband descended from Edward III's fifth son – had produced just one single child who would prove, in the future, to be a major thorn in the side of the house of Lancaster. This little boy was Richard Plantagenet, Duke of York, a very significant claimant to the throne, and destined one day to be the father of the Yorkist Kings, Edward IV and Richard III.

Incidentally, there is no real sign that the surname 'Plantagenet' had actually been used by any members of the English royal family since the thirteenth century, but Richard, Duke of York, and his heirs now definitely readopted it.

2

THE AMBITIONS OF THE BEAUFORTS

Henry IV's eldest son, Henry V, was in one way the most successful Lancastrian king of England. He spent much of his short reign campaigning in France, trying yet again to add the French crown to the English one which he was already wearing. Finally he married Princess Catherine of France, one of the daughters of his French rival, King Charles VI.

But Henry V was short-lived. He died, aged thirty-four, at the Castle of Vincennes in France on 31 August 1422. His young widow, Catherine, had borne him one son just before the previous Christmas, and this little baby now succeeded to the English throne as the very young King Henry VI. If anything were to happen to this infant the next English king would be one of Henry V's two surviving younger brothers: John, Duke of Bedford (1389–1435), or Humphrey, Duke of Gloucester (1390–1447).[1] Meanwhile, these two surviving brothers of Henry V held power during the minority of Henry VI – Bedford, in France, and Gloucester in England. However, both of these two rather different characters found their power as regents somewhat limited. In France, Bedford had to fight to maintain it. In England, Gloucester was only granted the title of 'protector', and was encircled by a council which restricted his actions. On this council, his half-uncle, Cardinal Beaufort (son of John of Gaunt, and surviving half-brother of Henry IV), often led opposition to Gloucester.

Meanwhile, in the wake of Henry V's corpse, his twenty-one-year-old widow, Catherine – now the very youthful Queen Mother – travelled to England. There she lived a quiet life, mostly in retirement – though she made public appearances on ceremonial occasions. But Catherine's mother, the French queen, Isabeau of Bavaria, had a reputation for nymphomania and it is possible that young Catherine inherited her mother's over-riding sexual desires. At all events, within about two years of Henry V's death Catherine was involved in an affair with her deceased husband's young cousin, Edmund Beaufort, who was first given a French title (Count of Mortain – see below) and then raised to the English peerage as Earl of Dorset (1442), Marquis of Dorset (1443) and Duke of Somerset (1448).

After her death (reportedly in childbirth) the following information about Catherine and her relationships was recorded:

In the next year [1437/38], on the second day of January,[2] Catherine, queen and mother of Henry VI died, who had three sons, though in secret, because the lords of the king's council did not want to consent, during the king's youth, to her marriage to anyone. Because she had wanted to have the lord Edmund Bewford, Count of Mortain;[3] but the Duke of Gloucester and many other lords had refused, enacting (contrary to apostolic advice) that whoever should presume to marry her should be punished by forfeiture of all his goods and by suffering death as a traitor against the king. But she, unable to curb her carnal passions completely, took Owen [Tudor] esquire, who owned little property that could be forfeited, and they did this in secret so that they would not claim his life on those grounds.[4]

In his male line of descent, Edmund Beaufort was a kind of wrong-side-of-the-blanket member of the Lancastrian royal house. In fact, he was acknowledged as a grandson of John of Gaunt. Edmund's father, John Beaufort, generally accepted as the half-brother of Henry IV, had been born to Catherine de Roët (Swynford). Since she was then the mistress of John of Gaunt, the latter was widely thought to have fathered John Beaufort – though his paternity was always questioned in some quarters. Indeed, recent DNA testing – which revealed that living male-line descendants of John Beaufort have a different Y-chromosome than the last Plantagenet king, Richard III – could potentially be interpreted as proving that the living Beaufort descendants are not (and perhaps never were) of royal descent.[5] Obviously, one possible explanation for this could be that John of Gaunt was not really John Beaufort's father. But without further evidence the precise meaning of the DNA test results remains somewhat uncertain. Later, John of Gaunt married his mistress – with the result that Edmund's father, and his sister and brothers, were all formally legitimised as children of the Duke of Lancaster. However, they never used the then defunct royal surname Plantagenet. Instead they were given the newly invented name of Beaufort.

When John Beaufort's half-brother became King Henry IV and founded the Lancastrian dynasty, he made it a rule that the earlier legitimisation of his Beaufort half-siblings did not permit them to inherit the throne of England. However, John, the eldest of the Beauforts, made a very significant marriage. His wife, Margaret

Holland, was more royally descended and more royally related than her husband. Margaret's father, Thomas Holland, 2nd Earl of Kent, was the half-brother of Richard II, and a direct and legitimate descendant of King Edward I.

But even more significantly, Margaret Holland's mother, Alice Fitzalan, was a daughter of Eleanor of Lancaster. Thus, if the descendants of Eleanor's niece, Blanche of Lancaster (mother of Henry IV) were to die out, Eleanor's descendants could claim to be the Lancastrian royal heirs.

This important maternal line ancestry of the heirs of John Beaufort has previously been overlooked by most writers, who have always tended to assume that subsequent Beaufort attempts to assert rights to the throne simply depended on the family's putative male line descent from Edward III, via John of Gaunt.

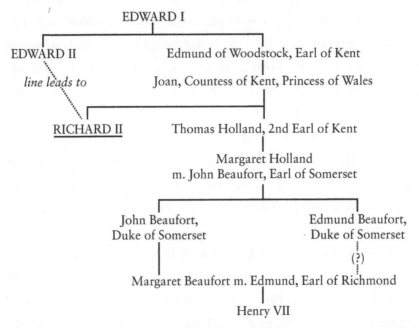

Family Tree 5: The descent from Edward I of the Beauforts & Henry VII (simplified).

The male line descent has always been seen as debatable in terms of the rights to the throne which it conveyed. On the other hand, the female line descent from Eleanor of Lancaster was absolutely unquestionable, and highly significant. However, in assessing the significance of the descent from Eleanor, account has also to be taken of the similar Lancastrian royal descent of the Mortimers and the royal house of York (see below, Family Trees 7 & 8).

John Beaufort died in 1410, but he left several children, and these included his son, Edmund. Edmund was about nineteen years old, and still unmarried and untitled,[6] when he first caught the eye of the young Queen Mother.

After the capture of his brothers at Baugé Edmund had returned to England with his mother, and between then and his departure

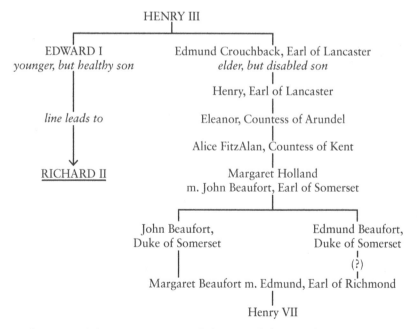

Family Tree 6: The Lancastrian royal descent of the Beauforts & Henry VII (simplified).

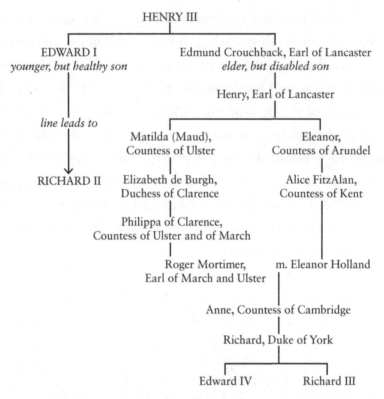

Family Tree 7: The Lancastrian royal descent of the Mortimers & the House of York (simplified).

to France in the company of Bishop [later Cardinal] Beaufort in March 1427 his activities are totally obscure. He is most likely to have lived in his uncle Exeter's household, and thus to have come into frequent contact with the court and the queen mother. By 1425 Edmund was aged 19 and Catherine 24. Her evident desire to marry him threatened to bring the governance of the young king more directly and permanently under the influence of the Beauforts than Gloucester, or perhaps even Bedford, was inclined to contemplate.[7]

As Harriss notes, the surviving sources offer no precise date for the commencement of the love affair between Queen Catherine and the young Edmund Beaufort.[8] He suggests, however, that their relationship was probably 'an undercurrent in the crisis of 1425-6'.[9] This implies that Catherine and Edmund were lovers by 1426 at the latest. As we shall see shortly, there is parliamentary evidence which supports that interpretation.

But Harriss also speculates that the affair between Catherine and Edmund was not of short duration, but continued for some time. Two years later, Edmund Beaufort accompanied his uncle, the Cardinal, on a trip to Hertfordshire which included a pilgrimage to the shrine of St Alban. After praying at the shrine on 22 September 1428, the Cardinal 'visited the nuns at Sopwell [the following morning] and after dinner journeyed to the queen mother at Langley. If Edmund Beaufort was still accompanying him he now had the opportunity to resume his liaison with Catherine, for the cardinal proceeded alone to Walsingham and thence to King's [sic] Lynn.'[10]

At an uncertain date, generally seen as around the year 1430, Queen Catherine gave birth to a second son, who was christened Edmund. 'Her choice of his name for her first-born [sic] may have been mere sentiment, but it must raise the suspicion that the father was Edmund Beaufort.'[11] Nevertheless, this boy has generally become known to history as Edmund Tudor, because after her relationship with Edmund Beaufort, Queen Catherine reportedly had a second love affair, this time with a servant called Owen Tudor. Indeed, it has widely been claimed that Catherine secretly married Owen Tudor – though in actual fact there is no proof of such a marriage.

The date of the alleged marriage between Queen Catherine and Owen Tudor remains as mysterious as the date of Edmund (so-called) Tudor's birth. Various authors have proposed a variety of wedding dates, ranging over the four years from 1428 to 1432. But, as we have seen, during the period 1428-31, Catherine met Cardinal Beaufort on a number of occasions. Since his nephew, Edmund Beaufort, was a member of the cardinal's household during this period, it is possible that Catherine was still seeing her first lover during the period when she is believed to have conceived Edmund 'Tudor'. Moreover, it seems clear that at one point Catherine had hoped to marry Edmund Beaufort.

At the Parliament held at Leicester in 1426 Edmund's uncle, Henry Beaufort, Bishop of Winchester, had tried to get permission for Catherine to remarry if she so desired.[12] Bishop Beaufort was presumably hoping that, if permission was given, the Queen Mother would marry his young nephew – thus advancing Edmund Beaufort's career and position. However, the proposed new law to allow the queen mother to remarry encountered strong opposition, led by Henry V's surviving brothers, John, Duke of Bedford, and Humphrey, Duke of Gloucester. In the end, the proposed bill was dropped.

> It was this that prompted the inclusion of the queen in the solemn articles of mutual trust between the two brothers, and the passage of an act in the parliament of 1427 forbidding her to marry during her son's minority, and imposing penalties of forfeiture on any spouse.[13]

A translation of the text of the 1427 Act is reproduced below, in Appendix 1. This Act meant that Catherine could not marry Edmund. But of course, that did not preclude the existence of their relationship.

Eventually, Catherine's second son, Edmund 'Tudor', became

the father of Henry 'Tudor' – the future King Henry VII, and the founder of the famous royal family known as the Tudors. But since the evidence in respect of who was the father of Edmund 'Tudor' remains inconclusive, we are confronted with the possibility that he and his subsequent bride, Margaret Beaufort, were, in fact, first cousins – in which case the royal house known as 'Tudor' would have been descended via the Beaufort line on both the male and the female sides.[14]

In this context, it is interesting to note that Edmund 'Tudor' never used the real Tudor family's red and white coat of arms. Instead he was granted a version of the royal coat of arms – very similar to the arms of Edmund Beaufort, but with a slightly different blue border.[15] If he was not of English royal descent on his father's side it is impossible to see upon what basis he was thought to be entitled to such a coat of arms. Obviously, if it could ever be proved that the real father of Edmund 'Tudor' was not Owen Tudor, but Edmund Beaufort, it would then be logical to refer to the sixteenth-century English royal family under the surname Beaufort rather than Tudor!

In 1435 Henry VI's senior uncle, John of Lancaster, Duke of Bedford, died. Since 1422 the Duke of Bedford had been the heir presumptive to the English throne, which was then held by his childless nephew, Henry VI. Following the Duke of Bedford's death, Henry V's only surviving brother was Humphrey, Duke of Gloucester (1390–1447). Thus, from 1435 Humphrey was the heir to the throne, given that the young king was still unmarried and childless.

Humphrey – who, together with his elder brother John, had opposed Queen Catherine's marriage to Edmund Beaufort – himself married twice. The more important of his two relationships was the second of these marriages, with a commoner called Eleanor Cobham. Initially Eleanor had been Humphrey's mistress. In 1425 (when he was still married to his first wife) the beautiful and clever Eleanor Cobham caught his eye, and in 1428, after his first marriage had been dissolved, Humphrey married Eleanor. People were very surprised at this relationship, because Eleanor was neither royal nor noble. In fact, she came from a very ordinary family. But the marriage seemed a happy one – though, sadly, it produced no children.

However, the Beauforts had apparently not forgiven Humphrey for his opposition to the marriage of Queen Catherine and Edmund Beaufort. Thus Humphrey and his second wife, Eleanor, both found themselves caught up in the Beauforts' plans for revenge against Humphrey. In fact, to begin with, the Beauforts' main attack was on Eleanor. She was accused of witchcraft and treason.

Her failure to give her husband a son and heir was probably the factor which first led Eleanor in the direction of magic. She hoped that spells and potions might help her to become pregnant. As a result she found herself mixing with the wrong kind of people. The potion maker whose services she used was a woman called Margery Jourdemayne. Margery not only made potions – she also claimed to be able to foretell the future.

It is said that one day, Eleanor thoughtlessly asked Margery how long the young King Henry VI would live. Eleanor must have been well aware that if Henry VI died childless, then her own husband would become the next King of England – with the result that Eleanor herself would then be queen. It is therefore easy to understand why she might have been interested in learning about the young king's life expectancy. But in those days, asking questions of fortune tellers about how long a king would live counted as treason.

Significantly, Margery Jourdemayne had other patrons among the court. We know that one of these was Edmund Beaufort, because Margery gave him an important prophecy, which we shall hear about later. Perhaps through Edmund Beaufort's conversations with Margery, it became known that Margery was also seeing Eleanor Cobham. As a result, questions were asked, and these eventually produced the allegation that Eleanor had questioned Margery regarding the king's life expectancy.

Poor Margery was arrested. Her house was searched, and among her potions and spells, a little wax image was found. The image had been partly melted. It was later claimed that this wax figure represented Henry VI, and that Margery had been melting it slowly, in order to make the king ill. That way he would die, so that Eleanor Cobham would one day be queen.

The result was that Margery Jourdemayne found herself condemned to a cruel death. The poor woman was burned at the stake as a witch on 27 October 1441. Meanwhile, Eleanor had also been arrested. She admitted that she had known Margery Jourdemayne for about ten years, and that she had made use of her services. Eleanor insisted that she had only visited Margery in order to get the potions she needed to help her conceive a child. Nevertheless, despite her denials of the other charges brought against her, Eleanor was judged guilty of treason.

The case against her was pursued strongly because her husband's political enemies – particularly his Beaufort cousins – wanted to destroy him. They hoped that by condemning his wife, they would also bring Humphrey down. Now they had achieved their first aim. Eleanor Cobham was first made to do public penance in the streets of London. After that she was shut up in prison for the rest of her life.

But the aim of the Beauforts and their allies had not simply been to bring down the low-born Duchess of Gloucester. Their real intended victim was her husband, the king's legitimate uncle and royal prince, Humphrey of Lancaster, Duke of Gloucester. Previously Humphrey had been a significant power in the kingdom – particularly since the death of his eldest brother, King Henry V. But now, the disgrace of his wife had destroyed him politically. He no longer had any power or influence. In fact, after Eleanor's imprisonment, Humphrey retired completely from public life. But even this was not enough to satisfy his enemies. They were out to destroy Humphrey utterly. It took them a few more years to achieve this.

Obviously, one way to remove Humphrey from the position of heir to the throne was to ensure that the young king produced a child. Thus, Cardinal Beaufort and his ally the Duke of Suffolk began planning a royal marriage for Henry VI, who was now in his early twenties. That other conflict – the so-called Hundred Years War – had long been going on in France between the French and the English. As we saw earlier, this war had started when Edward III had tried to claim the throne of France. The war had gone up and down, from an English point of view. But Henry V had done well. He had even had himself recognised as heir to the French throne, and his little son, Henry VI, had later been crowned King of France as well as King of England. However, since the death of Henry V, the war had been going badly for the English. So Cardinal Beaufort and the Duke of Suffolk planned a marriage between Henry VI and his cousin, a French princess called Margaret of Anjou. This marriage took place in April 1445.

The marriage did not immediately produce the desired heir to the throne. Nevertheless, about two years after the wedding, on 20 February 1446/7, Henry's uncle, the Duke of Gloucester, was arrested on a charge of treason. Three days later, on Ash Wednesday, Humphrey died mysteriously at Bury St Edmunds in Suffolk. At the time of his death it was widely believed that Humphrey had been murdered – probably by the use of poison. This remains a possibility. However, it is now thought more probable that the stress of the situation in which he had been placed had brought on a stroke, and that this was the cause of Humphrey's sudden demise. His body was carried to St Alban's Abbey in Hertfordshire, and buried there, beside the shrine of St Alban.

The most significant result of this lay in the fact that, apart from his nephew, the young King Henry VI, Humphrey had been the last living male member of the royal house of Lancaster. In spite of his recent marriage, as yet Henry VI had no children; therefore, at the time of his death, Humphrey was still the heir presumptive to the throne. Humphrey's death put the clock back. The situation in England was now ominously similar to the one which had existed in the reign of Richard II. Now once again there was no clear heir to the throne. So if anything happened to the young king, Henry VI, who should inherit his crown?

Given the fact that, with the exception of the young king himself, Edward III's son, John of Gaunt, now had no surviving legitimate male descendants, the legal heir in terms of all-male-line royal descent was arguably the king's second cousin, the young

Duke of York, since York was descended in a direct male line from Edward III's next son after John of Gaunt – Edmund of Langley, Duke of York. It is true that there has been some modern speculation that York's father, Richard of Conisburgh, Earl of Cambridge, was not really the son of Edmund of Langley, 1st Duke of York. But there is no firm evidence in support of this. In any case Richard, Earl of Cambridge was executed when Richard, Duke of York was only a few years old, so York did not really know his father well as a person. He merely knew *of* him on paper (parchment) as the officially recognised younger son of the first Duke of York.

Nevertheless, in spite of their illegitimate descent from John of Gaunt; and in spite of the fact that Henry IV had explicitly banned them from the succession; among the most powerful people in the land – and those closest to the throne – were the Beaufort family and their supporters. What is more, although this key fact has apparently passed unnoticed by most previous historians, as we saw earlier, in their capacity as female-line descendants of Edmund Crouchback, Earl of Lancaster, the Beauforts could now potentially consider themselves – and claim to be – the legitimate heirs of the royal house of Lancaster.

It is essential to emphasise that at this stage, no-one was actually contesting the right to the throne either of King Henry VI himself, or of his royal dynasty – the house of Lancaster. What was in question – given the two key facts that Henry VI remained childless, and that all his male-line uncles were now dead – was who was the rightful heir to his throne. The scene was now set for a contest between Edmund Beaufort, Marquis of Dorset (Duke of Somerset) and Richard Plantagenet, Duke of York. But at this point, neither of these two royal dukes and cousins had any thought of attempting to oust the young king. They were merely quarrelling – and eventually fighting – over which of them had the superior claim to be recognised as Henry VI's heir.

3

BEAUFORT VERSUS YORK

Richard, Duke of York, had been Henry VI's Lieutenant in France since the death of the king's uncle, the Duke of Bedford in 1435. There, York and his friend and ally John Talbot (later 1st Earl of Shrewsbury) had worked hard, and with some success, to maintain the English position. However, after wielding power in France for about ten years, York returned to England, having been superseded in his post as Lieutenant in France by the Duke of Somerset. Back in England, York regularly attended the royal council meetings in the late 1440s. After 1447 – and the death of Henry VI's uncle, Humphrey, Duke of Gloucester – York badly needed to be on the spot in London, in order to protect his interests, and most particularly, to maintain his claim to be the heir presumptive to the throne. He had inherited Baynard's Castle from Humphrey (see below, chapter 4), and that gave him a base in London.

However, in the eyes both of Queen Margaret and of Edmund Beaufort, Duke of Somerset, it was absolutely essential to get the Duke of York out of the way. Only if York was removed would the way become clear for the Beauforts to assert their claim to the throne. But how could York be got rid of? A secret murder was out of the question, because York was far too well-known and popular. Nor could he be attainted in Parliament.

Only one convenient way of removing York from the centre of power presented itself. He was appointed the king's Lieutenant in Ireland. The pretext for this was that Ireland was in rebellion – so a firm governor was required. York was given the Irish royal appointment on Sunday 30 July 1447. Of course, everyone knew that the post was not meant as a compliment. Indeed, people at the time described it as a kind of banishment. Moreover, it was obvious to everyone that the Irish post compared rather badly with the command of France, which had first been taken away from York, and was then handed over instead to his arch-rival, Somerset.

But York's appointment in Ireland did not get him out of the way immediately. Instead of sailing directly to Dublin, York appointed a deputy: Richard Nugent, Baron Devlin. When York did finally set off to Ireland, about two years later, attempts were made by Queen Margaret and her Beaufort allies to prevent York from ever reaching Dublin. Instructions were dispatched in the name of the king to Cheshire, to the Welsh Marches, and to the Welsh ports, requesting that the Duke of York should never reach his destination, and some local landowners did attempt to intercept him. However, York had the strong backing of his own force of retainers. Thus, he evaded his enemies and successfully embarked for Dublin, accompanied by his wife, and probably also by some of his family. When he finally reached the Irish capital, the local population welcomed him very enthusiastically and seemed delighted to see him.

Meanwhile, Cardinal Beaufort had also died in 1447, leaving his former ally, William de la Pole, Duke of Suffolk, as the chief power behind Henry VI's throne. Suffolk held various posts, including those of Chamberlain and Admiral of England. He was also one of the leaders of the English forces in France. Aware of the fact that the English were still doing badly, Suffolk tried negotiating with the French leaders. However, back home in England this was viewed with great suspicion. When English defeats continued, in spite of the negotiations, Suffolk found himself in serious trouble. There was a lot of infighting within government circles, and Suffolk now became the victim. He was arrested in January and imprisoned in the Tower of London. When England experienced yet another defeat, at the battle of Formigny in April 1450, Suffolk found himself banished from his own country for five years.

But an even worse fate was waiting for him. His ship was stopped, and boarded, on its way to Calais. The men who came on board were aiming to finish Suffolk once and for all. A contemporary poem, referring to the Duke under his nickname of 'Jakken-apes', describes his death thus

> In the monethe of Maij, when gresse groweþ grene,
> Flagrant [fragrant] in her floures, wᵗ swete sauour,
> Jac Napes¹ wolde ouer the see, a mariner to ben,
> With his cloge and his cheyn,² to seke more tresour.
> Suyche a payn prikkede hym, he asked a confessour:
> Nicholas³ said, 'I am redi, thi confessour to be'.
> He was holden so, that he ne passed that hour;
> For Jac Napes soule, *Placebo* and *Dirige*.⁴

It is sometimes said that he was beheaded and his body was thrown overboard. Crowland Abbey Chronicle states that a ship came hastening with all speed from an opposite quarter to meet him, and those who were on board shouted aloud, 'Where is that traitor to England? where is the duke of Suffolk? On denial being made, they speedily resorted to force, and compelled the others to drag him forth from a dark corner, and deliver him up to them; upon which, they immediately seized him, and with great outcries and cheers on part of the sailors, beheaded him on the prow of the ship.[5]

However, may Suffolk simply have been thrown into the Channel? His body was later found washed up on an English beach, and it was identified and buried. And it might, perhaps, have been hard to identify the remains if he had no head. At all events, he died. And since one of Suffolk's chief enemies was Richard, Duke of York, it was suggested by some people that York was the man responsible for Suffolk's death.

Having made the trip to Ireland, York only remained there for about a year. One of the reasons for this was the fact that, during the summer of 1450, a revolt known as 'Jack Cade's Rebellion' broke out in Kent and Sussex. Henry VI's weak and corrupt government had become very unpopular, especially in the south east of England. Matters came to a head in the spring of 1450, when a man generally known as Jack or John Cade issued *The Complaint of the Poor Commons of Kent*. This was a long list of grievances against the Lancastrian government. The document also attacked the king himself. In fact, an uprising was threatened unless all the complaints were sorted out.

At the same time the suggestion was put forward by the rebels that maybe Henry VI should abdicate in favour of a better ruler. Since this was connected with requests for the rapid return of the

Duke of York from Ireland it was probably not too difficult to guess whom they had in mind for the new king. Cade's Rebellion certainly seems to have been Yorkist in flavour. In fact, Jack Cade himself sometimes used the name of *John Mortimer*, claiming to be a cousin of the Duke of York.

During May 1450, Cade's supporters had just been holding local rallies in Kent and Sussex. But in June matters came to a head, when about 5,000 men, led by Cade, set off in the direction of London. When they established themselves in a camp at Blackheath, the king and his court left London very rapidly, heading off in the opposite direction. As a result, when they reached London the rebels found no one with whom they could negotiate. So they simply captured and looted London. In the process, they killed a few minor government officials who had not been wise enough to escape in time. Later, however, the royal army advanced on the capital and drove the rebels out. At this point Cade's men were defeated on London Bridge, and lots of them were slaughtered. Cade himself escaped, but he was killed later, near Lewes in Sussex.

But even Cade's death did not end the problems. Campaigning against the government continued in Sussex – still linked with continuing demands for the recall of the Duke of York from Ireland, in order that he could sort out the muddled situation in England. Some contemporaries suspected that York himself had been behind the whole Cade rebellion. But instead of recalling the Duke of York, Henry VI's government decided to appoint York's rival, Somerset, as Constable of England.

In September 1450, the Duke of York therefore made up his own mind to return to England from Dublin. His stated aims were to attack the alleged traitors in Henry VI's government, and to formally assert his own claim for recognition as the rightful heir to the throne. He brought an army of his own with him. Thus Cade's Rebellion and its aftermath can be seen as constituting a kind of prologue to the real fighting of what is generally called the Wars of the Roses.

By Shrove Tuesday, 22 February 1451/2, the Duke of York – now back in England – was in the vicinity of Northampton. The Duke was on his way south, aiming to enter the capital. At the same time King Henry VI was in Northampton. Although he had received assurances from the Duke of York that his only aim was to remove traitors, Henry VI (or his government) clearly did not entirely trust his cousin or his intentions. 'There were certain persons enjoying the royal intimacy, who were rivals of the said duke, and who brought serious accusations against him of treason, and made him to stink in the king's nostrils even unto the death.'[6] Therefore the king reportedly kept York at a distance, informing him that 'when work requires it, or necessity compels, we shall ask for your help'.[7] The king also issued orders that York should not be permitted to enter London. Thus, when the Duke reached the city he was not allowed in. He therefore camped for three days at Kingston-upon-Thames, considering his next move. York held lands in Kent, but Henry VI had hoped to prevent him from moving into that troubled county, which had so recently been the focus of Jack Cade's uprising against him. The king himself therefore headed south.

But although he had succeeded in keeping York out of London, Henry VI was not able to prevent him from marching into Kent. Heading, perhaps, for his own estate at Erith, near Dartford, the Duke of York eventually found himself confronting Henry VI and the royal army at Blackheath. This meeting could very easily have turned into the first battle between the two parties. However, on this occasion fighting was, in the end, avoided. Negotiations took place, and York was persuaded to come and put his complaints against his rival, the Duke of Somerset, to the king in person.

Perhaps somewhat naïvely, York trusted the king and his good faith. But he was mistaken. In the event, Henry VI's invitation proved to be merely part of a plot to arrest the Duke of York. Thus, when he reached the royal camp, York found himself disarmed. He was then carried off to London under guard. In the capital, on Friday 10 March 1451/2, he was forced to swear a solemn oath at St Paul's Cathedral not to rebel again.

York's enemies now seemed to be very much in the ascendant. In November 1452 Henry VI gave noble titles which had previously been held by his two royal uncles, the Dukes of Bedford and of Gloucester, to his two half-brothers, Edmund and Jasper, known as 'Tudor' – the younger sons of his mother, Queen Catherine – fathered possibly by her lover, Edmund Beaufort, now the Duke of Somerset. Almost certainly Somerset himself – the king's chief advisor – was behind the king's decision to ennoble these 'Tudors' and to grant them adapted forms of Somerset's own Beaufort version of the royal coat of arms. As for the 'Tudors' themselves, they may have taken part of the inspiration for their subsequent claims from their alleged Tudor father's Welsh background. For according to Welsh law a son was a son, and he had the right to inherit from his father, whether or not his parents had been married.

A few months later, in March 1452/3, Edmund and Jasper were jointly given guardianship of the ten-year-old Lady Margaret Beaufort, the senior heiress of the Beaufort line. Despite Margaret Beaufort's young age (she was either nine years old or eleven, depending on her disputed date of birth), she was subsequently married to her distant (or perhaps not so distant) cousin, Edmund 'Tudor'. This wedding took place in October 1455. The significance of this marriage – which resulted in the birth of the future King Henry VII – is obvious. The Duke of Somerset was doing his best in every possible way to advance the Beauforts as potential heirs to the Lancastrian throne. Clearly, as he and his family now perceived things, Henry IV's earlier attempt to exclude them from making such claims was no longer relevant. As we saw earlier, this was probably because, irrespective of their questionable descent from John of Gaunt, the Beauforts also had an entirely different, female line claim to be the heirs of the house of Lancaster.

Of course, the essential reason for the Beaufort claim at this stage was the fact that, in spite of his marriage to Margaret of Anjou, Henry VI remained without a son and heir. This situation continued for a number of years. What is more, Henry VI was reported to be totally averse to sexual contact, a fact which did not augur well for the future of his Lancastrian royal line. As we have seen, Somerset and York had both been campaigning for recognition as heir presumptive to the throne. However, it seems that the Duke of Somerset may have had another – and very clever – string to the bow of his ambition, a plan which would advance his bloodline without the Duke of York being able to do anything to prevent it. Having already conducted a love affair with one French-born English queen (Catherine), he had now set his sights upon her successor. Towards the end of 1452 it seems that Somerset became Margaret of Anjou's lover.

In February 1452/3, the queen (whose marriage to the king may never have been consummated) at last found herself pregnant. The real father of her expected child was probably the Duke of Somerset. Significantly, Edmund Beaufort is named in her financial accounts for 1453 as her 'most dear cousin', and in the same document he is also highly praised by the queen for an obviously important – but unspecified – service which he had performed for her.

Margaret's discovery that she was pregnant roughly coincided with the outbreak of further disputes among English magnates. The first of these involved the Earl of Warwick, the Duke of Somerset, and land in Wales. Not surprisingly, perhaps, the royal council favoured the claim of the Duke of Somerset over the rival claim of Warwick. At the same time, Warwick's family, the house of Neville, found itself involved in another territorial dispute with the Percy family. Up until this point, in spite of his close relationship to Cecily Neville, Duchess of York, the Earl of Warwick had shown no sign of particularly favouring the Duke of York. Now, however, that was about to change.

As for Queen Margaret's pregnancy, when the news of that became known, it was greeted with great astonishment. Significantly, even the king himself subsequently described it as a miraculous event. However, at that period no scientific techniques existed which would have made it possible to prove whether or not the child that Queen Margaret was carrying had actually been fathered by the king. Since Henry VI himself subsequently chose to grant the baby his recognition, eventually the little boy had to be accepted and acknowledged as the heir to the throne.

At the end of July 1453 Henry VI set off from London in the direction of Dorset. However, he only reached the royal hunting lodge at Clarendon. There, he suffered a mental breakdown. He was described by the Benedictine Abbot John Whethamstede of St Albans as unable to move about in a normal way, and incapable of remembering who he was or what he was supposed to do. This was perhaps a hereditary condition, derived from his French grandfather, King Charles VI, who had also suffered from mental illness. However, the symptoms described in the cases of these two monarchs appear to have been somewhat different. Whereas Charles VI became violent and foamed at the mouth, Henry VI was reported as being silent, withdrawn and uncommunicative. Some writers, beginning with Henry's contemporary, John Paston, thought that the onset of his mental illness may have been the king's response to the disastrous news of the English defeat at the battle of Castillon.

Attempts were made to treat Henry's condition. John Arundel, Warden of the Hospital of St Mary of Bethlehem, gave the king a mixture of gargles, laxatives, poultices and potions. The sick king was also subjected to bleedings and cauterisations. In addition, he became the object of attempts at exorcism. But none of these remedies appeared to produce any positive results.

At first the queen and the Duke of Somerset tried jointly to conceal the situation. When the king fell ill there was still no direct heir to the throne, and until Margaret gave birth to a living child, that situation would not change. Moreover, if her child then proved to be a daughter, the situation might still be somewhat confused. However, on Saturday 13 October 1453, in the Palace of Westminster, the queen gave birth to her son. One effect of this was that, once Henry VI could be persuaded to formally recognise the baby as his son and heir, there would then be no further dispute as to who was the rightful heir to the throne.

In spite of the king's illness, at first nothing was done openly to change the situation in terms of the government. 'Minor administrative uncertainty was inevitable, but the council at Westminster could and did continue to give effect to measures already generally decided before Henry's departure.'[8] Thus, for some time, the king's incapacity remained concealed.

But finally there came the summoning of a great council meeting, in October 1453. Although both Somerset and the queen may have longed to do so, in the end it proved impossible to exclude the Duke of York from this meeting. At about the same time there was also growing public criticism of the Duke of Somerset. This appears to have been led by York's cousin and nephew by marriage, John Mowbray, 3rd Duke of Norfolk.9 The final outcome was that York was appointed protector of the kingdom, to act for the deranged king. As for the Duke of Somerset, he found himself imprisoned in the Tower of London.

Meanwhile the queen's baby had been baptised and created Prince of Wales. The name chosen for the little boy may have been significant. All the previous Lancastrian kings had been called 'Henry'. But the new baby was not given that name. Instead the name chosen for him was 'Edward'. Possibly this reflected the fact that King Edward III may have been the last English king from whom this new 'prince' was truly descended. It may also be significant that one of the baby's godfathers was none other than his possible biological father – Edmund Beaufort, Duke of Somerset. Because of his birthplace, the baby became known as Edward of Westminster. Of course, he was now the legal heir to the crown of England. In theory his birth had therefore put an end to the dispute over the succession between York and Beaufort.

At around Christmas, Margaret of Anjou's baby was taken to Windsor Castle to be shown to the king.

At the Princes coming to Wyndesore, the Duc of Buk' toke hym in his armes and presented hy, to the Kyng in godely wise, besechyng the Kyng to blisse hym; and the Kyng yave no maner answere. Natheless the Duk abode stille with the Prince by the Kyng; and whan he coude no maner answere have, the Queene come in, and toke the Prince in hir armes and presented hym in like forme as the Duke had done, desiring that he shuld blisse it; but alle their labour was in veyne, for they departed thyens without any answere or countenaunce saving only that ones he loked on the Prince and caste doune his eyene ayen, without any more.[10]

Meanwhile, the Duke of York enjoyed his first period of rule as protector of the realm. However, this proved brief. It ended in 1455, when Henry VI recovered from his mental illness – and was presented with, and finally accepted, his wife's miraculous son. Following the king's recovery not only was York removed from the post of protector, but also the Duke of Somerset was released from his imprisonment in the Tower of London. Thus, despite the fact that the succession question had apparently been resolved, these two rival cousins of Henry VI were once again at liberty to quarrel and fight over which of them was the more important.

Standard attributed to Henry IV as drawn by Sir Christopher Barker, Garter King of Arms, in the 1540s. (Redrawn from BL, MS Harl. 4632, f. 238.)

In the introduction it was mentioned that, while there is plenty of evidence that the royal house of York used a white rose as its badge, there is no contemporary evidence to show that any of the Lancastrian kings used a red rose badge.[11] It is true that the royal banner attributed to Henry IV bears red roses. However this is not *contemporary* evidence, because the earliest image of the banner which survives was drawn by or for Sir Christopher Barker, Garter King of Arms. Thus the illustration dates from the 'Tudor' period – probably from towards the end of the reign of Henry VIII, or from early in the reign of the 'Tudor' King Edward VI. The only contemporary evidence of a rose in association with Henry IV comprises small roses on the morse of the cloak depicted on his tomb effigy. But these roses are not red (see plate 4). There is no surviving contemporary evidence of rose emblems associated with Henry V or Henry VI.

Indeed, a political poem in favour of the house of York, written in about May 1460, refers to the rose badge exclusively in the context of the house of York, and does not even mention, or treat as significant, the colour of the rose in question:

> R for þe Rose, þ[r] fresshe is in euery stede
> Boþe þe rote and þe stalke ben gret of honoure,
> Fro Norway to Normand þeire power wol sprede,
> Fro Ryland [Ireland] to Estland men ioy of þat flowre.[12]

This verse of the poem is surrounded by other verses which focus upon other relevant badges of the house of York and its supporters, including the fetterlock of Richard, Duke of York, the eagle of the Earl of Salisbury, and the ragged staff of his son, the Earl of Warwick.

Incidentally it is also important to note that both here, and also in other contemporary political poems, the Yorkist rose often appears to have been seen specifically as the badge of Edward, Earl of March, eldest son of the Duke of York – the future King Edward IV. With one possible exception (see below), the rose is not explicitly related to Richard, Duke of York, himself. Instead, York's personal badge is generally referred to as the fetterlock. For example, a poem on the battle of Northampton (10 July 1460) speaks of 'certeyne persones þt late exiled were, ... þe Rose [Edward, Earl of March], þe Fetyrlok [Richard, Duke of York], þe Egle [Richard Neville, Earl of Salisbury], and þe Bere [Richard Neville, Earl of Warwick]'.[13]

Nevertheless, in his overall editing and publishing of these poems, Sir Frederic Madden accepted that, although the rose generally appears to be associated with Edward, Earl of March, 'whose cognisance of the white rose was derived from the castle of Clifford', this emblem had also been used by earlier members of the house of York. Indeed, he states that it was 'said to have been first used by Edmund of Langley, fifth son of Edward III'.[14]

A rose emblem certainly seems to have been used by the two generations of the house of York which came between Edmund of Langley and Edward IV.

Seals prove that both Richard, third Duke of York (father of Edward IV and Richard III), and his uncle, Edward, second Duke of York, used a rose badge. Unfortunately the seals do not indicate the colour of the rose. Logic might appear to suggest that it must have been white, but these were not the first Plantagenet princes to employ a rose badge, and the earlier users seem to have used roses of various colours. ... On the other hand the white rose may have been

Rose emblems from the seals of a) Edward, second Duke of York, 1403 (BL, Dept of MSS, Cott. Ch. xxv. 3); b) Richard, third Duke of York, 1437 (BL, Dept of MSS, Add. Ch. 425), and c) Edmund Mortimer, third Earl of March, 1372 (BL, Dept of MSS, lxxxviii.33).

a badge of the house of Mortimer. Edmund Mortimer's seal showed his arms suspended from a rose bush in flower.[15]

Madden tentatively dates the last-but-one of his published political poems to about the time when the Duke of York was recognised as heir to the throne (November 1460), on the assumption that a) its use of 'the epithet of the *Rose*' cannot refer to Richard, Duke of York 'as this epithet is uniformly given to his son Edward Earl of March',[16] and b) Edward would have been too young to figure so prominently in the poem in the other proposed date of 1455. However, this penultimate poem certainly cannot possibly post-date the battle of Wakefield, since it mentions the Earl of Salisbury. Thus, if Madden's conclusion is correct, that 'the Rose' cannot refer to Richard, Duke of York, then the living head of the house of York is nowhere mentioned in the poem. That would seem rather odd. It therefore seems reasonable to accept the wider claim that the white rose was symbolic of the house of York in general, and that in Madden's penultimate poem the rose symbol refers to Richard Duke of York, rather than to his son.

To anyone who takes the traditional view of a fifteenth-century contest between red and white rose badges, it must surely appear amazing – and highly significant – that no specific reference is made in any of the contemporary poems to the fact that the rose of York should be white in colour. The only logical conclusion seems to be that no other rose badge was being used in the 1450s by anyone else involved in the conflict. It is also worth noting that the collar worn by Edward IV's sister, Margaret of York, in the portrait of her painted at about the time of her marriage to Charles the Bold, Duke of Burgundy, in 1468, shows both white and red roses. Also, Margaret's surviving crown depicts large enamelled white roses, but is also decorated with tiny red roses and dark green roses. Therefore in the 1460s it is possible that members of the house of York sometimes used rose badges of various colours, and not always a white rose.

However, a red rose badge was certainly used later, by the first 'Tudor' king, Henry VII. And after he married Edward IV's eldest daughter, Elizabeth of York, Henry VII's red rose was combined with Elizabeth's white rose to create the well-known red and white 'Tudor Rose'. Moreover, Henry VII seems to have acquired the red rose badge from his mother, Lady Margaret Beaufort, because there is evidence that she used a red rose as her symbol too.

So what was the origin of the story of the red rose and its connection with the Lancastrian side in the Wars of the Roses? In his play *Henry VI Part 1*, act 2, scene 4, Shakespeare presents a scene in the Inner Temple Garden in London, where the Duke of York and John Beaufort, Earl of Somerset, are engaged in a serious quarrel.

As presented by Shakespeare, on this occasion the argument became very bitter. As a result the two lords and their followers picked different coloured roses from among those then flowering in the gardens, in order to show which side each person was on. The Duke of York and his supporters picked white roses, of course. As for the Earl of Somerset, he and his supporters picked red roses.

No evidence survives from the fifteenth century to prove that such a quarrel in the Temple Garden ever really happened. However, the story may be based on truth, and there are several interesting points about it. Shakespeare does not give a precise date for the event, and the chronology – as in many of his 'historical' plays – is rather muddled. As presented by Shakespeare, the rose quarrel would seem to have taken place in about 1425. But such a quarrel would, perhaps, have been more likely between the Duke of York and *Edmund* Beaufort, who only became the male head of his family after his elder brother's death in 1444. Therefore, if, in reality, such a quarrel in the gardens did happen, it probably took place much later – in 1455, just before the Wars of the Roses fighting started. If the quarrel did happen in that year, it is logical to suppose that it may have taken place in late April or early May 1455 – because the two sides then went off to start the fighting, and the first actual battle took place on 22 May 1455.

Interestingly, we know that the flower which comprised the Yorkist rose badge was a plant called *Rosa Alba Semiplena*. Unlike modern garden roses, which flower all year round, *Rosa Alba Semiplena*, and all the other medieval garden roses, flowered only for a short time, in late spring and early summer. So the fact is that the rose flowers would have been there in the Inner Temple Garden to be picked at just the right time – a week or two before the fighting began.

The other interesting thing about Shakespeare's version of the story is that it does not claim that the red rose was the badge of the royal house of Lancaster. Instead the red rose is presented as the badge of the Beauforts and their supporters. We have already seen that, while there is no evidence that the Lancastrian kings used the red rose badge, this symbol was undoubtedly used later by Henry VII and by his mother, Margaret Beaufort. Therefore the truth may well be that the red rose was the badge of the Beaufort family – Lancastrian royal cousins of originally illegitimate descent.

One tiny piece of evidence is favour of this theory is the fact that the arms of Cardinal Beaufort included one tiny rose in the upper centre of the bordure (see the illustration of his seal, below). There is also a red rose painted on the Cardinal's tomb at Winchester Cathedral. However, this is part of a nineteenth-century restoration, paid for by the Duke of Beaufort, and is therefore of little value.[17] On the basis of the evidence which has been presented, this present study will not talk about 'the red rose of Lancaster', but will refer henceforth to the second alleged flower badge of the Wars of the Roses as 'the red rose of Beaufort'.

Seal of Cardinal Beaufort.

4

QUEEN MARGARET OF ANJOU
VERSUS YORK

It is in May 1455 that the actual fighting in the so-called Wars of
the Roses is usually considered to have begun. On Thursday 22
May King Henry VI's army was defeated by the Duke of York's
forces at the first battle of St Albans. This battle came as something
of a shock to many people, because although the rival armies had
been manoeuvring, on the whole they had probably expected – and
hoped – that the outcome would be another stand-off, followed
by a peaceful resolution of some kind – rather like the one which
had occurred in 1452, when the rival forces had confronted one
another at Blackheath.

When the battle took place, the king was on his way to Leicester,
and the Duke of York, who had been ousted from political power
and influence, set out to intercept and confront him in order to try
to regain his place in the government. York was now supported by
his Neville relatives and allies, the Earls of Salisbury and Warwick.
The size of their combined forces is a matter of some dispute, but
it was certainly larger than the king's army.

The king, who seems to have feared that York might now be aiming to depose and replace him, reached St Albans first. Before setting out from Watford, he had received a messenger from the Duke of York, in the person of the latter's confessor, William Willeflete, who brought a letter from York affirming his loyalty to Henry as sovereign. However, when Henry and his party reached St Albans they heard that York and his supporters were not far away, at Ware, and that York's men outnumbered his own. Therefore, probably on the advice of the Duke of Somerset, the town of St Albans was prepared for defence.

York, when he arrived, pitched camp in a field on the eastern side of the town. Initially, there were attempts to parley, but the negotiations between the two sides proved ineffective. The Duke of York was insisting on the re-arrest of the Duke of Somerset, and to this Henry VI would not consent. Finally, York decided to seize Somerset by force of arms. Thus a violent clash ensued, right in the market place of St Albans.

On the whole, the first battle of St Albans was quite a small affair. Nevertheless it had some serious consequences. Henry VI, who was present, and armed, found himself slightly wounded 'by the shotte of an arowe in the necke'.[1] Historians have often reported that Henry was taken prisoner after the battle. However, Gregory's Chronicle specifically denies this, reporting that 'the Duke of Yorke brought hym unto London as kynge and not as a presener'.[2] Another serious outcome was the fact that Edmund Beaufort, Duke of Somerset, was killed in the fighting. Somerset had found himself trapped in front of a hostelry called the Castle Inn. Nothing remains of the medieval inn today, but its site is marked by a modern plaque on the corner of St Peter's Street and Victoria Street.

Years before, Edmund Beaufort had been given a prophecy by Margery Jourdemayne, the spell caster and fortune teller whom the Beauforts and their allies had used to bring down the Duchess of Gloucester. Margery had reportedly warned Beaufort that he should at all costs 'avoid the castle'. The story goes that Edmund Beaufort had always wondered which of the many fortifications in fifteenth-century England was his ill-omened fortress. However, it was only in the last moments of his life that he suddenly realised that Margery had been referring to the Castle Inn at St Albans.

There were also other deaths on the Lancastrian side in this first battle. These included the Earl of Warwick's northern rival, the Earl of Northumberland, together with Northumberland's nephew, Lord Clifford. Ironically, both Northumberland and Clifford shared the Duke of York's royal Clarence/Mortimer descent. However, they ranked below York in the line of succession. In any case, there is no evidence that, at this stage, the Duke of York had any thought of advancing a personal claim to the throne, based on his maternal line royal ancestry. Indeed, the precise reason for the fighting (given that, in theory, the question of the identity of the heir to the throne had now been resolved) does require some attention.

The motivation still seems to have been the ongoing enmity between the Duke of York and his family on the one side, and their Beaufort cousins on the other. Superficially, it might appear that his enmity should have been ended by the birth of Edward of Westminster. But Edmund Beaufort was perhaps the father of the new heir to the throne, and in the light of his close relationship with the baby's mother, Queen Margaret (details of whose new personal ambitions will emerge presently) Beaufort was now in a potentially very strong position.

Nevertheless, despite the fact that armed conflict had now started (or, given the earlier fighting in the reign of Henry IV, resumed) in England, it is important not to assume that, at this stage, York was aiming to overthrow Henry VI and make himself king. There is absolutely no evidence for such a simplistic view of events. Indeed, in spite of the fact that the first battle of St Albans appeared to leave the Duke of York in a very commanding position, beyond having himself reinstated in the royal council, he took absolutely no action to change the status quo. And although Henry VI has been described, following the first battle of St Albans, as 'now more or less a puppet in the hands of York and his associates',[3] the Duke certainly made no attempt to dethrone or replace his cousin as sovereign. Indeed, together with his Neville relations, the Earls of Salisbury and of Warwick, York simply escorted King Henry VI back to London, where, the Duke and the two Earls then presented themselves as the king's loyal subjects. As for Henry VI's role as sovereign, that was symbolically reinforced by means of a crown-wearing ceremony at St Paul's Cathedral.

What is more, Henry VI himself appears, at this stage, to have become convinced of their loyalty. In that respect, it was, perhaps, significant that he now found himself separated from his anti-Yorkist queen, and her young son Edward. They had both taken refuge at Kenilworth Castle. The absence of Margaret of Anjou, and the removal (death) of the Duke of Somerset, coupled with the apparently respectful behaviour of the Duke of York after the battle of St Albans may have been the two key factors which combined to modify the mentally unstable king's perceptions.

The Sunday after the battle was Whit Sunday – the Feast of Pentecost. It was on that religious feast day that the crown-wearing ceremony for Henry VI was held at St Paul's Cathedral, on which occasion it was from the hands of his cousin, the Duke of York, that the king received his royal crown. The following day a Parliament was summoned in the king's name.

Following the battle of St Albans – and perhaps partly as an outcome of his first battlefield experience – Henry VI's health seems to have deteriorated once again. On 5 June the physician Gilbert Kemer was asked to come from Salisbury to examine the king at Windsor Castle. York was seeking to ensure that the ailing king would be in a fit state to conduct the business of the realm. As we have seen, Henry VI had received a small wound in his neck during the fighting at St Albans, and there seems to have been some concern that this might also have caused him some lasting mental damage. In fact, throughout the last five years of his first reign the king's mental health appears to have been precarious. However, Henry VI was apparently fit enough to attend the formal opening of the new parliament on 9 July 1455.

Interestingly, the first session of this Parliament made one of its main aims the reinstatement of the late Duke of Gloucester as 'a true subject in life and death'.[4] The fact that the Duke of York was concerned to re-establish the loyal role of his late Lancastrian cousin, opposed and brought down by the Beauforts, is revealing.

The first session of Parliament ended on 31 July 1455. When the assembly was reopened just over three months later, on 12 November, Henry VI was not able to attend. His mental health had deteriorated, and the day before the reopening, the Duke of York was appointed Henry's lieutenant in respect of the opening ceremony. As a consequence of the king's illness and absence, the Speaker of the House of Commons requested that York be re-appointed protector of the realm, and the Lords backed this request. Although initially York said that he was not worthy of the post, and then requested time to formulate specific plans, on 19 November he was formally reappointed protector, with the condition that he could now only be relieved of this post by the king himself, in Parliament.

The following February, Henry VI had apparently returned to health sufficiently to appear personally in Parliament, though it remains doubtful to what extent he can be said to have fully recovered. However, the king then removed York from the post of protector. From March 1456 onwards, Henry's royal sign manual reappears on government papers. Even so, henceforward (despite the opposition of Queen Margaret) the Duke remained the king's chief councillor and lieutenant – though without the title of protector.

The first battle of St Albans was certainly not seen at the time as the opening battle of an ongoing war. Indeed, as we have seen, this so-called 'battle' had actually begun as a violent quarrel in the market place of the town, and those involved seem themselves to have hoped to avoid actual fighting. Four years of somewhat uneasy peace followed the first battle of St Albans. York was now in possession of Somerset's former post of Constable of England. As we have seen, he had also inherited Baynard's Castle in London from Humphrey, Duke of Gloucester, when the latter died in 1446/7. The Duke of Gloucester had rebuilt the castle following serious fire damage in 1428. Thus, in the 1450s it was an up-to-date London residence, in excellent condition. Therefore this is probably where York resided whenever he was in London. Certainly it is on record that he lodged at Baynard's Castle in 1457.[5]

Meanwhile, Henry VI appeared to have lost all practical interest in ruling the country. Instead, his attention was now focussed exclusively on religion. During this period, Henry VI seems to have felt no personal hostility towards the Duke of York. However, York now found himself confronting a new arch-enemy, in the person of Henry's wife, Margaret of Anjou. The queen consort now appeared absolutely determined to dispose of York. She wished to assert a Continental-style role for herself, whereby she would rule England in her disturbed husband's name. This was at variance with the traditional English pattern whereby, when a king was a minor or incapacitated, it was the senior male-line prince of the blood royal who acted as the realm's protector, at the head of a council comprised of the other senior princes of the blood.

In France the picture was different. There, it was normal for a queen consort or queen mother, or a princess of the blood royal, to exercise such authority for a child king or a sickly husband. Following her husband's death in 1060, for six years Anne of Kiev, consort of Henry I of France, had acted as regent for their son, Philip I. She was the first queen consort of France to serve as regent. Later, Blanche of Castile, consort of Louis VIII, acted as regent twice during the reign of their son Louis IX. The first occasion was during Louis IX's minority, and the second, during the king's absence on crusade. Joan the Lame of Burgundy served as regent of France for her husband, the first Valois king, Philip VI, while he was absent on campaigns. During the mental illness of Charles VI, his consort, Isabeau of Bavaria headed the regency council. Later, at the end of the fifteenth century Anne of France (or de Beaujeu), eldest daughter of Louis XI, acted as regent for her brother, Charles VIII from 1483 to 1491, and subsequently Louise of Savoy, Catherine de Medici, and Anne of Austria would continue the tradition, serving as regents of France in the sixteenth and seventeenth centuries.

The only previous occasion on which something similar had taken place in England had been in the fourteenth century, when an earlier French Queen Consort – Isabelle of France, the wife of Edward II – had taken over her husband's authority, leading ultimately to his deposition. Subsequently Isabelle had wielded the regency of England for four years, during the minority of her son, Edward III. However, in terms of English history, that was a rather unfortunate precedent.

On Saturday 25 March 1458 a 'Love Day' was held at St Paul's Cathedral, as a public act of reconciliation between the queen's party and the supporters of the Duke of York. The king wore his crown again, and was preceded in the procession by the Earl of Salisbury and Henry Beaufort, the new young Duke of Somerset. Henry Beaufort was the eldest (legitimate) son and heir of Edmund Beaufort (who had been killed at St Albans) and his wife, Lady Eleanor Beauchamp. The family tree below shows the rather interesting ramifications of some of the new Duke of Somerset's relatives on his mother's side.

Behind the king, in the Love Day procession, the Duke of York walked hand in hand with Queen Margaret. This emphasises the fact that, in reality, this public event was nothing more

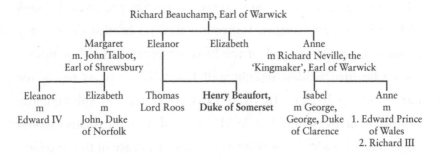

Family Tree 8: The maternal relatives of Henry Beaufort, Duke of Somerset.

than an empty and meaningless ceremony. Beneath the surface the antagonism between the two opposing factions ran very deep. Despite the fact that the legitimacy of the young Prince of Wales was now openly being questioned, Margaret of Anjou was reportedly trying hard to persuade her husband to abdicate in favour of her son. However, the queen herself was now very unpopular in certain quarters.

> That same yere [1458] alle thes lordys departyd from the Parlyment [sic], but they come nevyr alle togedyr aftyr that tyme to noo Parlyment nor conselle, but yf hyt were in fylde with spere and schylde.[6]

Margaret of Anjou was now acting as the reigning sovereign in many respects. It was the queen who received envoys at the Palace of Greenwich in April 1458, despite the fact that the king was then in residence there. As reported by Abbot Wheathamstead and others,[7] by 1459, as a result of the insistent pressure of his wife, Henry VI finally became convinced (or reconvinced) that the Duke of York was not to be trusted. For her part, the queen was now openly preparing for renewed conflict. Weapons were prepared,[8] and all the king's men were summoned to assemble at Leicester in June 1459. Not surprisingly, the Duke of York, together with his brother-in-law, the Earl of Salisbury, and Salisbury's son, the Earl of Warwick, chose not to obey this royal summons.

The Duke of York, accompanied by his wife and their younger children, now installed himself at Ludlow Castle, where his elder sons, Edward, Earl of March, and Edmund, Earl of Rutland, resided. There it was planned that the Earl of Salisbury and his army would join them. But the king – or rather, the queen – was aiming to prevent this at all costs. Therefore Margaret of Anjou dispatched a force recruited under the nominal command of the young Prince of Wales, from his earldom of Chester, to intercept Salisbury and his men.

The real commander of this nominal army of the Prince of Wales was Lord Audley. His forces entrenched themselves on the road to the east of Market Drayton, and there awaited the Earl of Salisbury. The Lancastrian army was holding a very strong defensive position, and when Salisbury arrived, on Sunday 23 September 1459, he had to try to find a way to draw them out. It is thought that he did this by faking a panic and a retreat. Lord Audley's men seem to have broken out in pursuit, only to have their horses killed under them by Salisbury's archers. Finally Audley himself led a troop of infantry against Lord Salisbury's men. The result, however, was that Audley was then hacked down and killed in the ensuing, very bloody fighting. Many Lancastrians – perhaps as many as 2,000 – were killed at Blore Heath, and the battle was theoretically a Yorkist victory. However, the remaining forces loyal to the king were still large in number. Thus York and his allies feared a further confrontation.

The Duke of York, together with the Earls of Salisbury and Warwick, therefore took an oath at Worcester Cathedral, swearing upon receipt of the Blessed Sacrament that they were the king's loyal subjects, and that they were only kept from his royal presence by the malice of others who were bent upon their destruction. This suggests that they were doing their best to avoid an ongoing armed conflict, and that they certainly did not see themselves as taking part in an ongoing civil war. Notification of their solemn oath was sent to the king at Ludlow. However, it produced no response.

The Yorkist victory – of a kind – at Blore Heath was followed on

Friday 12 October by a kind of Lancastrian victory at the battle of Ludford Bridge. It has been claimed that Henry VI personally led his troops on this occasion, displaying his royal standard, and making an impressive speech to his troops, which suitably impressed the royal forces. However, given Henry's state of health, in reality this seems unlikely. Probably the king was simply produced before the army, mounted on a horse, and backed by his royal standard. In any case, the royal army seems to have been much larger, on this occasion, than the forces of the Duke of York and his allies. Gregory's Chronicle reports that Henry's force numbered 'xxx M[l] of harneysyd men, by-syde nakyd men that were compellyd for to come with the kynge'.[9] Numerical superiority was probably therefore sufficient, by itself, to produce a Lancastrian dominance of the field. Initially 'the Duke of Yorke lete make a grete depe dyche and fortefyde it with gonnys, cartys, and stakys',[10] but the much greater size of the king's army gave him no hope of victory. Therefore in the end the Yorkists simply abandoned their camp. At about midnight on 12 October the Duke of York, accompanied by his second son, the Earl of Rutland, fled to Ireland, where, of course, his position was strong. At the same time his eldest son, Edward, Earl of March, accompanied the Earls of Salisbury and Warwick to Calais.

On the following morning the now leaderless Yorkist armies surrendered to the king. However, as a result of the escape of the Yorkist leaders, both Ireland and Calais were now effectively out of government control. Subsequent attempts by the Lancastrians to exercise authority in both areas proved vain. For example, an attempt was made by Henry VI's government to replace the Duke of York as lieutenant of Ireland, and also to replace York's deputies in Ireland. However, these attempts were unsuccessful.

The Irish Parliament confirmed York in his post, authorised him to issue his own coinage in Ireland if necessary, and even provided him with armed forces which he could, if necessary, lead to England.

Meanwhile, as a result of York's defeat and flight, his own wife and their three youngest children: Margaret (future Duchess of Burgundy), George (future Duke of Clarence) and Richard (the future King Richard III), had fallen into the hands of the enemy. Following the Yorkist defeat, Ludlow was pillaged and looted by the Lancastrians. In fact, it was treated just like an enemy town in a foreign country. Thus, its women were raped, while Ludlow Castle was sacked. During this reign of terror, somewhere in Ludlow – either in the castle or in the town itself – the Lancastrian forces came upon Cecily Neville, Duchess of York, and her three youngest children, Margaret, George and Richard. All four of them were taken prisoner, and carried off to Coventry. There,

> the Duchyes of Yorke com unto Kyng Harry and submyttyd hyr unto hys grace, and she prayde for hyr husbonde that he myght come to hys answere and to be ressayvyd unto hys grace; and the kynge fulle humbely grauntyde hyr grace, and to alle hyrs þat wolde come with hyr, and to alle othyr that wolde com yn with yn viij dayes. ... The Duchyes of Yorke was take to the Duke Bokyngham and to hys lady, for they two ben susters, and there she was tylle the fylde was done at Northehampton, and she was kept fulle strayte and many a grete rebuke.[11]

As for the flight of the three Yorkist earls – March, Salisbury and Warwick – to Calais, that meant that Henry VI's government in England was no longer in control of this key enclave on the continent. Lancastrian attempts to recapture Calais were therefore set in motion, led by the new Duke of Somerset (Henry Beaufort). However, these attempts to regain control of Calais failed. Meanwhile, from within the safety of that enclave, the three earls were able to maintain communications with the Duke of York in Ireland. In response to the attempts from England to retake Calais, the Earl of Warwick launched a series of attacks across the Channel in the opposite direction. Eventually Yorkist forces, commanded by Lord Fauconberg and others, occupied Sandwich, thus providing a vital Yorkist base in England. As a result, a full-scale Yorkist invasion was then orchestrated, led by the Earls of March, Warwick, and Salisbury. They and their men landed at Sandwich on Thursday 26 June 1460, and established a firm position there. Publicity was then circulated in Kent and elsewhere, stating that the three earls were loyal subjects of King Henry, and that their only objective was to rid the kingdoms of those traitors who now surrounded the sovereign.

Shortly afterwards, on Wednesday 2 July, Warwick's army took the entire city of London, with the sole exception of the Tower. Meanwhile, King Henry VI (or those who held the reins of power in his name) had established a base in Northampton. Leaving the Earl of Salisbury in London, where he was still besieging the unconquered Tower, March and Warwick set off northwards to attack the king's forces.

Henry VI's army was well-entrenched near Northampton. In effect it had to confront three Yorkist armies, led by Edward, Earl of March, Richard Neville, Earl of Warwick, and Warwick's cousin, Thomas Neville, Lord Fauconberg. In fact, Warwick began with offers of negotiation. However, he was refused access to the king's presence. Indeed the Duke of Buckingham threatened that if Warwick made any attempt to see the king, the Earl would pay for this with his life.

Edmund, Lord Grey of Ruthin, who commanded the Lancastrian vanguard at Northampton, was a female-line descendant of the Lancastrian royal house and also a relative of the Beauforts. Nevertheless, he was suborned by the Yorkists, and agreed to let them through his lines. As a result, the royal army collapsed. In the course of the fighting the Duke of Buckingham, Thomas, Baron Egremont, John, Lord Beaumont and the second Earl of Shrewsbury were all killed, defending their king. Once these lords had been slain, Henry VI was captured in the royal tent by a commoner – an archer called Henry Mountfort. Thus the king found himself once again in the hands of the Yorkists (as after the first battle of St Albans). The Earl of Warwick, Edward, Earl of March, and Lord Fauconberg all then called upon the king in person, and paid him their respects. Once again, absolutely no question was raised regarding his royal status. The monarch was first taken to the nearby Abbey of Delapre. Later he was conducted to London.

Following the victory at Northampton, the Duke of York returned from Ireland, accompanied by his second son, Edmund, Earl of Rutland. However, by this time, York's position and his view of the situation both seem to have changed in a rather fundamental way. He now began to date events by the year of grace, rather than by the regnal year of Henry VI. Also it is reported that he began to use the royal arms without the points of difference which had formally marked his arms as Duke of York. Some years earlier he had also begun to use the appellation 'Plantagenet'. This had been used centuries before, by Geoffrey of Anjou (father of King Henry II), as a reference to his badge of broom seeds. *Planta genista* means 'broom plant'. Since Geoffrey's time, however, no member of the English royal family (including no English monarch) had ever employed the name 'Plantagenet'. Its resuscitation by the Duke of York may therefore have been a sign that he saw himself as in every respect the senior heir of Count Geoffrey and his eldest son, Henry II. It is also a clear and firm statement that, despite some modern speculation to the contrary (see above), the Duke of York had no doubt regarding the legitimacy of his father, Richard of Conisburgh, Earl of Cambridge. Meanwhile, since King Henry VI was now dwelling in his wife's apartments at the Palace of Westminster, York took up residence in the former royal suite.

On 16 October, for the first time, the Duke of York put forward a formal claim to the thrones of England and France, together with the Lordship of Ireland. This claim was submitted to the House of Lords. York stated that he was the senior living descendant of Edward III, via the latter's third son, Lionel, Duke of Clarence. He also showed that he was well aware of the basis on which Henry IV had claimed the kingship, and he took great pains to give the lie to the Lancastrian version of the royal pedigree, protesting against the 'violent intrusyonne of kyng Harry the iiij^the, whyche unryghtefully, wrongfully, and tyrannously usurped the crowne', and declaring 'that the ryghte noble and worthy prince Harry kyng of Englond the iij^de had issew and lawfully gate Edward hys furst begoten sone, borne at Westmynstre the xv kalendis of Juylle in the vygyl of Seynt Marc and Marcellyane, the yere of oure Lorde M^I.cc.xxxix (1239)' . To make his point clear beyond any shadow of doubt, the duke then went on to observe pointedly that Edmund Crouchback was King Henry's 'seconde goten sone which was born on Seint Marcell day, the yere of oure Lord Mccxlv (1245)'.[12]

In one sense this could be described as the real beginning of the Wars of the Roses, since, hitherto, the house of York had never put forward any anti-Lancastrian claim to the throne. Yet even now, as we saw earlier, the rivalry for the throne which had emerged was, in its origins, a 'Clarence versus Lancaster' claim, not a 'York versus Lancaster' claim. The House of Lords was stunned by this unprecedented situation, and tried to avoid giving a specific answer. However, York pressed them for a response. Therefore the Lords temporal and spiritual proceeded to set out all the obstacles to York's claim which they could think of. These included the actual reigns of three Lancastrian kings, and York's oaths of loyalty to the Lancastrian kings. The Lords also cited once again the fact that the original Lancastrian claim had been based on the seniority of Edmund Crouchback, as an elder son of Henry III than King Edward I.

However, on 25 October, through the mouth of the Chancellor, George Neville, the Duke of York was formally recognised as Henry VI's *heir*, thereby excluding from the succession the Prince of Wales, whose legitimacy was considered dubious. The proposal was that King Henry should continue reigning for his natural life-span, but that when he died York, not Edward of Westminster, should succeed him. Moreover, the Act of Parliament of 1406, which had ruled that the succession should be in the person of Henry IV and his heirs, was now repealed. Given his state of health it is not, perhaps, surprising that Henry VI seems to have taken all this quite passively. Indeed, matters appeared to have been resolved as a result of these decisions. York and his sons renewed their oaths of loyalty to Henry VI as the current reigning sovereign, while the Duke of York was now formally endowed with the principality of Wales and the other titles of the heir apparent.

If Sir Frederic Madden's dating of his penultimate published political poem is correct, it would seem that the Duke of York's claim as put forward in parliament was well received outside that legislative body.

> þei seyne in þeire assemble, it is a wondre thyng,
> To se þe Rose in wyntre so fresshe for to spryng.[13]

Naturally, however, the mother of Prince Edward of Westminster, Margaret of Anjou, was furious. She called on the Duke of Exeter, the Earl of Devon, the new Duke of Somerset and his half-brother, Lord Roos, and on John, 9th Baron Clifford, and others, to support her, and together they assembled a new Lancastrian army in the north.

In December, therefore, York and Rutland marched north to deal with the queen's army. However, their vanguard was heavily trounced by the Lancastrians at Worksop. York and the rest of the army managed to reach York's castle at Sandal. But there were no supplies in store there to feed his soldiers, so he had to send out foraging parties. Christmas was now approaching. In the spirit of the festive season, the Lancastrians seemed willing to negotiate, and a truce was agreed.

Subsequently, however, in spite of the truce, a Yorkist foraging party was attacked by the Duke of Somerset's men. York's sortie to confront this Lancastrian attack has often been seen as an unwise move – and of course, in the event it certainly proved to be a serious mistake. However, the Lancastrian victory, which took the Yorkists completely by surprise, was probably largely due to the Duke of York's misplaced trust in one of his relatives by marriage: John Lord Neville (a cousin of the Earl of Warwick). Lord Neville had indicated that he would back York, but when the chips were down he sided with the queen's army.

York and his second son, Edmund, Earl of Rutland, were both killed at Wakefield. York himself was probably killed in the fighting – though the Abbot of St Albans later claimed that York had been captured alive, and mocked as a false king (just as Christ had been before his crucifixion) before being killed. The seventeen-year-old Rutland – 'the Duke of Yorke ys secunde sone, one the beste dysposyd lorde in thys londe'[14] – was slaughtered by his cousin, Lord Clifford, as he was attempting to escape from the battlefield. As for the Duchess of York's elder brother, Richard Neville, Earl of Salisbury, he was captured alive and imprisoned briefly at Pontefract Castle, on the orders of the Duke of Somerset. The duke's intention was to offer Salisbury for ransom, however, on the day following the battle of Wakefield, the earl was killed. This was not, apparently, an officially organised execution. 'The commune peple of the cuntre, whyche loued hym nat, took hym owte of the castelle by violence and smote of his hed.'[15]

As for the Duke of York, after the battle his head, crowned with a mocking paper crown, was sent by Lord Clifford to the city of York. There it was impaled upon a pike and displayed on top of Micklegate Bar. When news of the deaths of her husband, second son, and brother reached the Duchess of York in London, she must have been deeply shocked. However, she took rapid action to safeguard the lives of her two youngest sons, George and Richard (later respectively the Duke of Clarence and King Richard III). Despite the bad weather, she sent the two boys, accompanied by their servants, across the winter sea to Flanders. There they took refuge with the Prince Bishop of Utrecht.

PART 2

THE WHITE ROSE OF YORK

5

THE WHITE ROSE WINS

While his father, the Duke of York, and his younger brother, the Earl of Rutland, had been at Sandal Castle, Edward of York, Earl of March, was near the Welsh border. It was there, early in January, that he received the distressful tidings of their deaths. From that point on his supporters began to refer to Edward as the Duke of York. The Earl of March was still officially in the service of King Henry VI, and under a commission dated 12 February 1460/61, he was supposed to be mustering the king's men in the West Midlands in order to take action against rebels.[1] However, Edward at once began making plans to avenge the killings of his father and brother by leading his own attack against the queen's army. While he was preparing to do so, news arrived that the Earl of Ormonde's son, James Butler, Earl of Wiltshire, together with Henry VI's half brother, Jasper, Earl of Pembroke, had landed in Wales. Edward therefore marched to intercept these two Lancastrian lords. He blocked their route at Mortimer's Cross, near the River Lugg, and on the Feast of Candlemas – Monday 2 February 1460/1 – his own much larger forces easily defeated the Lancastrians.

In the rout which followed the fighting, Owen Tudor (or Tetyr), the putative father of Edmund, Earl of Pembroke was captured. Owen was subsequently beheaded at Hereford. After the execution it is reported in Gregory's Chronicle that 'hys hedde [was] sette a-pone the hygheyste gryce of the market crosse, and a madde woman kembyd hys here and wysche a way the blode of hys face'.[2] She then reportedly set around Owen's head, and lit for him, more than one hundred candles. It appears that she must have been a rather wealthy – and also a young and somewhat agile – mad woman! In this context, it is perhaps important to remember that the account known as Gregory's Chronicle is supposed to have been written by William Gregory, who had been London's Mayor in 1451–52. Gregory lived and worked far away from Hereford. He could therefore only have been reporting rumours which reached him. Incidentally, the author of Gregory's Chronicle also reported that prior to his execution, Owen had said 'that hede shalle ly on the stocke that wass wonte to ly on Quene Katheryns lappe'.[3] This alleged remark has been rather naïvely cited as solid evidence of Owen's marriage to Queen Catherine, the widow of Henry V. But first, if the statement is true, it would merely indicate that a relationship of some kind may have existed between Queen Catherine and Owen. It certainly does not amount to proof of a marriage between them. Secondly, as far as we know, Gregory was not present at Owen's execution. Hence his report of Owen's alleged remark is nothing more than hearsay.

Later Owen's remains were interred in a chapel on the north side of the Greyfriars' Church, Hereford. Perhaps significantly, no action was subsequently taken to commemorate Owen by or on behalf of his alleged significant sons, the Earls of Richmond and

Pembroke – nor by the former's subsequent royal descendants, Henry VII and Henry VIII. In fact, Owen's burial site would have remained unmarked if his *illegitimate* son, David (who was born in Pembroke Castle in 1459 to an unnamed mistress of Owen, and who died in about 1542), had not subsequently commissioned a memorial for him. But later Owen's memorial was lost at the Dissolution, for King Henry VIII did nothing to rescue either the tomb or the remains of his putative great grandfather – perhaps because he knew that, in reality, Owen Tudor and he were not related.

It is said that at dawn on 2 February 1460/1, before the fighting had started, Edward's army had witnessed a curious meteorological phenomenon called a *parhelion*. This means that, because of unusual atmospheric conditions, instead of a single sun, three suns appeared to be rising in the morning sky. Edward himself is reported to have interpreted this as a sign that the Holy Trinity was on his side, and to have adopted the sun behind a white rose (*rose-en-soleil*) as his royal heraldic badge as a result. However, the earliest surviving source for this story is Edward Hall, whose Chronicle was first published around the middle of the sixteenth century, in the year after the author's death (1548). And it is also worth noting that Edward, Earl of March (Edward IV) subsequently claimed to be the legitimate heir of his ancestor, King Edward III, and of Edward III's grandson, King Richard II. Both of those earlier monarchs had also used forms of the sun as one of their royal badges in the fourteenth century. Edward III employed the sun emerging from behind a cloud, while Richard II had used the sun in splendour. Thus the future Edward IV's choice of the sun as his royal emblem, now that he had become the head of the royal house of York, may have been a kind of symbolic statement to the effect that he was the rightful heir of Edward III and Richard II, and thus the true king of England.

It is important to remember that, as we have seen, from 1460 onwards, the Yorkist claim underwent a very significant change. Originally the Duke of York had merely asserted a male line claim (via his father, the Earl of Cambridge, and his grandfather, Edmund of Langley) to be next in line to the throne if the male Lancastrian line died out. But from 1460 onwards, York – subsequently followed by his son, Edward [IV] – asserted a female line claim via York's mother and her Mortimer ancestors, to the effect that they – and not the Lancastrian royal family – were the legitimate heirs of Richard II.

Meanwhile, Margaret of Anjou's army, glorifying in its triumphant defeat of the Duke of York at Wakefield, was marching southwards in the direction of London, with its men wearing the liveries of their own individual lords and also the crimson and black livery of Edward of Westminster, Prince of Wales, together with his badge of ostrich feathers (see below). The Earl of Warwick had been urgently recruiting a large Yorkist force in Kent and in the eastern counties to deflect Margaret's advance. Warwick now assembled his army at St Albans – the site of an earlier Yorkist victory – where he could block the old Roman road known as Watling Street – the main route from the north of England to London. Gregory's Chronicle gives a very intriguing and detailed near-contemporary account of this situation which describes not Warwick, but King Henry VI as leading the army against his own queen at the start of the second battle of St Albans.

Ande the xvij day nexte folowynge [Shrove Tuesday, 17 February 1460/61] Kyng Harry roode to Synt Albonys, and the Duke of

Northefolke with hym, the Erle of Warwycke, the Erle of Arundelle, the Lorde Bouser, the Lorde Bonvyle, with many grete lordys, knyghtys, and squyers, and commyns of an c M^l men. And there they hadde a grete batayle whythe the Quene, for she come ever on fro the jornaye of Wackefylde tylle sche come to Synt Albonys, with alle the lordys a fore sayde; and hyr mayny and every lorde ys men bare hyr lordys leverey, that every man myghte knowe hys owne feleschippe by hys lyverey. And be-syde alle that, every man and lorde bare the Pryncys levery, that was a bende of crymesyn and blacke with esteryge ys fetherys. The substance that gate that fylde were howseholde men and feyd men. I wene there were not v M^l men that fought in the Quenys party, for þ^e moste parte of Northeryn men fledde a-way, and sum were take and spoylyd owte of hyr harnysse by the way as they fledde. And sum of them robbyd evyr as they yede, a petyffulle thynge hit ys to hyre hit.[4]

This time the outcome of the battle was very different. Although the initial Lancastrian attack was driven back, the Lancastrian forces, probably advised of Warwick's position by a prisoner they had captured, then succeeded in outflanking Warwick's army. And although his men fought very bravely, and kept the battle going on a house-to-house basis for some hours, in the end the Yorkist army was driven off. Moreover,

in the myddys of the batayle Kynge Harry wente unto hys Quene and for-soke alle hys lordys, ande truste better to hyr party thenne unto hys owne lordys. And thenn thoroughe grete labur the Duke of Northefolke and the Erie of Warwycke a schapyd a-waye ; the Byschoppe of Exceter, that tyme Chaunceler of Ingelond, and brother unto the Erie of Warwycke, the Lorde Bouser, whythe many

othyr knyghtys, squyers, and comyns fledde, and many men slayne
in bothe partys.[5]

On the occasion of this battle the Lancastrian king is said once
again to have been in an odd mental state. He had reportedly spent
the greater part of the battle sitting under a tree, singing. After
the battle, however, Henry, now reunited with his queen and her
son, pulled himself together sufficiently (or perhaps was organised
by his wife) to bestow a knighthood on Edward of Westminster,
Prince of Wales.

> Ande at the nyght aftyr the batayle the kynge blessyd hys sone the
> Prynce, and Doctor Morton brought forthe a boke that was fulle
> of orysons, and there the boke was oppenyd, and blessyd that yong
> chylde *cum pinguedine terre et cum rore celi*, and made hym knyght.
> And the yong knyght weryd a payre of bregant yerys i-coveryd with
> purpylle velvyt i-bete with golde-smythe ys worke. And the Prynce
> made many knyghtys.[6]

The Prince of Wales was now seven years of age.

Curiously, overall the second battle of St Albans proved to
be not such an effective Lancastrian victory as it might have
been. Although in theory the Lancastrian army should now
have been free to march on to London, in fact their forces were
composed of many Scots and northerners, who had ravaged and
pillaged the 'foreign' country as they marched south. As a result
of their behaviour, these aliens had made the Lancastrian army
very unpopular. Thus, in spite of the fact that 'by the a-vyse
of Docter Morton they sende certayne knyghtys and men unto
London and to Westemyster',[7] the city of London now barred

its gates against the royal envoys. In the end, Henry VI was unable to re-enter his capital, and his northern troops eventually decided to head back for home, taking their plunder with them. Incidentally, it is interesting to note that Dr John Morton – who was later to play a significant role in the Lancastrian and 'Tudor' causes – had now become a noticeable figure in the Lancastrian camp.

Meanwhile Edward, Earl of March, fresh from his triumph at Mortimer's Cross, had also headed for London. On the way he met the Earl of Warwick at Burford ('Burford upon Wolde'), ten miles west of Oxford, and they shared their grief at the deaths of their respective relatives at Wakefield. Subsequently, however, Edward found himself not only admitted to the city of London, but heartily welcomed there.

Then come tydyngys of the comynge of þe[8] Erle of Marche unto London; thenn alle the cytte were fayne, and thonkyd God, and sayde that

He that had Londyn for sake
Wolde no more to hem take,

and sayde, 'Lette us walke in a newe wyne yerde, and lette us make us a gay gardon in the monythe of Marche with thys fayre whyte ros and herbe, the Erle of Marche'.[9]

Edward is usually said to have reached London on Thursday 26 February 1460/61. John Stow dates the arrival of Edward and Warwick on 28 February, but as we shall see, Stow is sometimes mistaken in his recording of dates.[10]

The Earls of March and of Warwick, with a great power of men, but few of name, entered the city of London, where they were of the citizens joyously received; and upon the 3ʳᵈ of March, being Sunday [*sic* for Tuesday. Sunday had been 1 March] the said earl caused to be mustered his people in St John's field, where unto that host was showed and proclaimed certain articles and points wherein King Henry, as they said, had offended; and thereupon it was demanded of the said people, whether the said Henry was worthy to reign as king any longer or not: whereunto the people cried Nay. Then it was asked of them, whether they would have the Earl of March for their king; and they cried Yea, yea.[11]

On Wednesday 4 March, the young Earl of March was formally acclaimed King of England as Edward IV. 'He toke uppon hym the crowne of Inglond by the avysse of the lordys spyrytual and temporalle, and by the elexyon of the comyns'.[12] Arguably, therefore, unlike the later accession of Henry VII, in 1485, the Yorkist takeover may not have been a usurpation. In London's eyes, the Lancastrian period was now at an end. The reign of the house of York had begun, and was apparently well-received in the capital city.

Now of the Rose of Rone [Rouen] growen to a gret honoure,
Therfore syng we euerychone, I-blessid be that floure!

I warne you euerychone, for [ye] shuld vnderstonde,
There sprange a Rose in Rone, and sprad into Englonde;
He þat moued oure mone, þoroughe þe grace of Goddes sonde,
That Rose stonte alone þe chef flour of this londe.
I-blessid be the tyme, that euer God sprad that floure!

Blessid be þᵗ Rose ryalle, that is so fresshe of hewe,

Almighty Jhesu blesse that soule, þᵗ þe sede sewe,

And blessed be þe gardeyne, þer the Rose grewe;

Cristes blessing haue þei alle, þᵗ to þᵗ Rose be trewe!

And blessid be þe tyme, þᵗ euer God sprad þᵗ floure![13]

But of course, the reality was that England now had two rival kings.

Following Edward IV's proclamation as king, there was no time for an immediate coronation. However, some kind of formal recognition of his new rank seemed necessary. Therefore *Te Deum laudamus* was sung in praise of his accession to the throne at St Paul's Cathedral. 'Then was he with great royalty conveyed to Westminster, and there, in the great Hall, set in the king's seat, with St Edward's sceptre in his hand.'[14] On the following day – Thursday 5 March – his cousin, the Duke of Norfolk, rushed off to East Anglia to hastily raise more men in support of the Yorkist cause. 'And on the Saturday next following, the Erle of Warwick, with a grete band of men, departid oute of London northwarde'.[15] Warwick was heading for the Midlands with precisely the same objective in mind as that of the Duke of Norfolk in the eastern counties. 'Then the Friday enswing, the King Edward isswid out of the cite in goodely ordre, at Busshoppisgate, then being the xiiᵗʰ [*sic* 13th] day of Marche'.[16] Together with the Duke of Norfolk's new reinforcements, Edward IV departed northwards in pursuit of the retreating Lancastrian royal army.

Accompanied by her fairly useless husband, and her lively young son, Queen Margaret had meanwhile arrived in the vicinity of York. There she was attempting to canvas support. Some more Scottish troops were obtained for her army. Meanwhile, the majority of the English nobility was still, in theory, supporting

Henry VI. Margaret's immediate aim was that Henry VI and the Lancastrian royal family should remain safely in the city of York while their army dealt with the young Yorkist usurper.

Two weeks before Easter, on Passion Sunday, 22 March, Edward IV arrived at Nottingham. From there he hastened on to Ferrybridge on the River Aire, arriving there on the eve of Palm Sunday (Saturday 28 March). 'When the fore prickers cam to Ferry-brigghe, theire was a grete skarmusshe.'[17] The Lancastrian forces were stationed on the far side of the river, and fierce fighting ensued as they sought to defend the bridge. In the course of this battle the Earl of Warwick was injured by an arrow which hit him in the leg.[18] The Lancastrian troops finally succeeded in wrecking the bridge, thereby preventing the Yorkists from crossing. Initially the Yorkists made an attempt to reconstruct the bridge. However, their working parties were again attacked by the Lancastrian army, so their attempt failed.

Edward IV therefore decided to adopt a different approach. He ordered his vanguard, under the command of Lord Fauconberg, to head upstream about six and a half kilometres (four miles), to Castleford. There, the Yorkist army was able to cross the river. Edward IV's men then found that, fortunately, they had now outflanked Lord Clifford's army. As the Lancastrians fled from them, Lord Clifford himself was killed by a chance arrow, which struck him in the neck at a moment when he had unwisely removed his gorget.

On the following day – Palm Sunday, 29 March 1461 – following his victory at the river crossing, Edward IV prepared for another battle at Towton, just ten kilometres (six miles) north of Ferrybridge. Here the Duke of Somerset had deployed his forces on a ridge. He had also concealed an ambush party in the nearby Castle

Hill Wood. The Lancastrian army was considerably the larger of the two forces and theoretically had the advantage. Interestingly, it included Edward IV's brother-in-law, Henry Holland, third Duke of Exeter (who by 1447 had married Anne of York, Edward's eldest sister), and also Lord Rivers – Edward IV's future putative father-in-law. It was a cold morning and, as the battle began, so too did the snow.

For the first time in the dynastic conflict, two rival kings of England were now confronting one another. Gregory's Chronicle highlights this strange situation by referring explicitly both to 'Kynge Edwarde' and to 'Kyng Harry'.[19] But although in principle the battle was between these two men who now claimed the crown of England, only one of them was actually present on the field, for the other – King Henry VI – was safe behind the walls of the city of York, together with his wife. It was Henry Beaufort, Duke of Somerset, who commanded the Lancastrian forces at Towton.

As was often the case at this period, initially there was an exchange of fire from the archers on the two sides. The Yorkist arrows were helped in reaching their targets by a strong wind from the south. On the other hand, the Lancastrian arrows, which had to fly into the wind, tended to fall short of their targets. The infantry battle which followed was one of the longest and bloodiest ever fought on English soil, possibly because Edward IV had commanded that there should be no quarter. Indeed, a later account says that the Earl of Warwick, who had recently been wounded, killed his own horse, as a sign that, however the battle went, he would not attempt to fly from the field, but would, if necessary, fight on until he died.

The Yorkist army had now been reinforced by the arrival of the Duke of Norfolk and his men. The bitter fighting went on until dusk, when finally the Lancastrian army broke ranks and fled. Though modern historians have suggested that the figures may be an exaggeration, the Yorkists claimed at the time that 28,000 men lay dead on the battlefield – of whom only 8,000 were their own men. Some of the warriors had been forced into the icy river in the course of the fighting, and there they had drowned. As for those men who had been captured alive, after the battle they were all put to death. Forty-two Lancastrian knights are reported to have died in this way. Among the noble victims were Thomas Courtenay, Earl of Devon,[20] and James Butler, Earl of Wiltshire and Ormond, who were captured and then beheaded. The Earl of Wiltshire was executed at Newcastle, and his head was then dispatched to London to be displayed upon London Bridge. 'And Docter Morton, the Prynces chaunceler, was take with hym [the Earl of Wiltshire] and put in the Towre, but he schapyd a way longe tyme aftyr, and ys [1469?] by yonde the see with the Quene, &c.'[21]

Recent analysis of the bones discovered in a mass grave near the site of the battle has revealed that the soldiers who fought at Towton came from many different walks of life. Their average age proved to be about thirty, and several of the men had signs of earlier wounds, showing that they were veterans of earlier battles.

On the day after the battle of Towton – Monday 30 March – Edward IV entered the city of York. There he found that King Henry VI, his queen, the Duke of Somerset and the Prince of Wales had already fled to Newcastle. Initially Edward tried to pursue them. However, since Henry and his supporters ultimately took refuge in Scotland, Edward IV finally abandoned the pursuit in order to return south to London for his coronation. Although Henry VI's supporters were subsequently attainted, generally, Edward really preferred not to kill or imprison his former opponents, but to win them over. Thus, in the end, those noblemen and gentry who proved willing to change sides were treated leniently.

Edward IV's much younger brothers, George and Richard, were now able to return to England from their brief exile in the Low Countries. Both the young Yorkist princes had suddenly become very important boys. In fact, George had now become the heir presumptive to the throne of England, with his younger brother, Richard, the second in line. They were therefore fêted by the Duke of Burgundy (who had hitherto rather carefully avoided meeting them) prior to their departure from his territory.

Meanwhile, at some stage during his campaigning, possibly during the summer of 1460, Edward IV had encountered (or perhaps re-encountered) a very beautiful young widow – the wife of a young Lancastrian knight who had been the heir to the lordship of Sudeley. The lady's name was Eleanor Talbot. The beautiful Eleanor was the daughter of the late, but very famous warrior, John Talbot, first Earl of Shrewsbury, who had been one of the key supporters of Edward's late father, the Duke of York, during his service in France. The young Edward must have known Lord Shrewsbury during his childhood in that country, therefore it is just possible that he had first encountered Eleanor when they were both children, prior to her marriage to (Sir) Thomas Boteler. Apparently, when the teenaged Edward and the young, widowed Eleanor met – or re-met – Edward found Eleanor extremely attractive and desirable.

No historian has ever questioned the existence of a relationship between Edward and Eleanor. However, most earlier writers have followed the official 'Tudor' position, promulgated by Henry VII from 1485 onwards. According to this point of view Edward and Eleanor were never married. Thus Eleanor was nothing more than the youthful king's mistress. However, clear evidence exists which shows that Eleanor was a very religious young lady.²² Her morals, together with her high rank (for she was of royal descent), and the fact that she was a young widow (and therefore readily available for a second marriage), made Eleanor decline to become Edward's mistress. As a result, Edward IV now decided to marry her in secret. The evidence of this secret marriage, presented by the priest who had officiated at it (see below), was formally accepted by the three estates of the realm in June 1483, and by Parliament in 1484.

Thus, as the new young King of England returned south from Towton, heading towards London and his coronation, he chose to pass through the county of Warwickshire. There, Eleanor Talbot owned several manors. It was probably either at Eleanor's manor of Fenny Compton or at her manor of Burton Dassett, that the king's first secret wedding took place, on or around Monday 8 June 1461. The secret marriage between Edward IV and Eleanor Talbot was celebrated by Canon Robert Stillington, a well-educated priest with special expertise in the canon law of the church, who was a former government servant of Henry VI, but who had now changed sides and entered the service of the new king.

Obviously the first objective behind Edwards IV's secret marriage with Eleanor Talbot was to enable him to have sex with her. That objective would rapidly have been fulfilled in June 1461. Probably at that point the new, young and inexperienced king had not thought very far beyond achieving his prime objective. But if Eleanor had become pregnant as a result of their sexual relationship, presumably he would then have acknowledged his marriage contract with her – and acknowledged also the resulting child (or children). Significantly, however, Eleanor's first marriage to Sir Thomas Boteler had remained childless. Moreover, her sister, Elizabeth, wife of John Mowbray, fourth Duke of Norfolk, also experienced difficulties in conceiving – leading her to make a series of pilgrimages to the shrine of Our Lady of Walsingham.[23] In addition the first cousin of Eleanor and Elizabeth Talbot, Anne Neville, wife of Edward of Westminster, Prince of Wales, and later of Richard, Duke of Gloucester (Richard III), had no children by her first husband and only one son by her second. It therefore seems possible that Eleanor may have inherited a problem of some kind, and that she had difficulty in producing children.

She was also a rather gentle lady, who apparently placed no pressure on Edward (unlike his second secret wife, Elizabeth Woodville, who was a much more determined character). Although, Eleanor seems to have persuaded the young king to treat her former father-in-law, Ralph Boteler, Lord of Sudeley, with some kindness while she was around – an aspect of the king's conduct which subsequently underwent a dramatic change, after Eleanor's death – and although the young king appears to have given royal land and other gifts both to Eleanor and to members of her family,[24] during his lifetime Edward IV never publicly acknowledged his commitment to her. Later, however, when both Edward and Eleanor were dead, their marriage was formally authenticated by an Act of Parliament, thereby posthumously acknowledging Eleanor's right to the title of Queen Consort of England.

Incidentally, at this point it is, perhaps, also worth saying something about the fact that the 1484 act of Parliament which officially recognised Eleanor Talbot as Edward IV's legal wife and consort was subsequently repealed. For the past five centuries most historians seem to have considered Henry VII's repeal of the original act much more significant than the original act of parliament of 1484. But that is a very strange way of looking at things, particularly since the repeal offered no evidence whatsoever regarding the marriage question, whereas the 1484 act was the result of direct evidence offered by the priest who claimed to have officiated at the exchange of the marriage vows.

Moreover, in the previous chapter, we witnessed an intriguing parallel – which, however, seems to be evaluated quite differently by historians. In 1460 Henry VI's Parliament had repealed the act of Parliament of 1406 which had established the inheritance of the crown of England by Henry IV and his heirs. Yet no historian ever seems to have considered the 1460 repeal significant, in terms of whether or not one accepts Henry IV, Henry V and Henry VI as valid kings of England. Therefore where is the logic behind arguing that Henry VII's subsequent repeal of the 1484 act means that Eleanor Talbot was not Edward IV's legal consort?

Of course, since Edward IV had claimed the throne of England as the rightful and legitimate heir, his conduct, both in 1461 and in 1464, was very ill-advised. It was obviously unwise and short-sighted of him to enter into secret marriage contracts. In the long run, the effect of Edward's clandestine relationships with Eleanor Talbot and Elizabeth Woodville was to undermine the legitimacy of his own children by his second secret wife. Inevitably, this led to further problems about the succession to the throne of England. Thus, as we shall see, Edward's actions subsequently gave rise to further fighting and to more killings, and it ultimately led to yet another change of royal dynasty. It is therefore utterly ironic that, at the very moment when the house of York had finally succeeded in establishing itself upon the English throne, Edward IV thoughtlessly did something which was eventually destined to wreck his own family's future, and which would lead to the deaths of a number of his closest relatives.

Meanwhile, however, the house of York now appeared to be firmly seated on the throne of England. And could some people possibly have heard rumours of the new king's secret marriage?

> The Rose wan þe victorye, þe feld and also þe chace,
> Now may þe housband in the southe dwelle in his owne place;
> His wife and eke his faire doughtre,[25] and al þe goode he has,
> Soche menys haþ the Rose made, by vertu and by grace.
> Blessid be the tyme, þat euer God sprad that floure!

> The Rose cam to London ful ryally rydyng,
> ij. erchebisshops of England þei crouned þe Rose kyng;
> Almighti Jhesu save þe Rose and geue hym his blessing,
> And al the reme of England ioy of his crowning,
> Þt we may blesse þe tyme, þᵗ euer God sprad þᵗ floure![26]

Edward IV triumphantly re-entered his capital on Friday 26 June 1461. He was crowned in the traditional manner at Westminster Abbey just two days later, on Sunday 28 June. He created his younger brothers respectively Dukes of Clarence and of Gloucester. For the moment everything seemed well, and England appeared to have the hope of a peaceful future.

But the new situation was not good for everyone. John de Vere, 12th Earl of Oxford, had inherited his title as a minor. He was brought up under the guardianship, first of Thomas Beaufort, Duke of Exeter, and later of John of Lancaster, Duke of Bedford. However, when conflict started to emerge in England, Oxford had tried very hard to avoid committing himself to either the Lancastrian or the Yorkist side for many years. Unfortunately, he had finally taken the momentous decision to commit himself to

Margaret of Anjou and to the cause of Henry VI, in December 1459, just over a year before the battle of Towton. Given the subsequent Yorkist success and the defeat of the Lancastrian cause, his decision was to prove rather ill-timed; a piece of rather bad luck for him and his family.

After the Yorkist victory at Northampton, in 1460, John de Vere had kept away from all the fighting on the ground of illness. It is not clear whether this was a genuine illness or just an excuse. At all events, the Earl of Oxford did not long survive the final Yorkist victory. For reasons which are not entirely clear, and in spite of the fact that he had been trying hard to appear not to be causing trouble, in February 1461/2 he and his eldest son and heir, Aubrey de Vere, were arrested and imprisoned in the Tower of London. The Earl was then tried for high treason before the Yorkist Constable of England, John Tiptoft, Earl of Worcester. Both Oxford and his son were condemned to death. The Earl was beheaded on Tower Hill on Friday 26 February 1461/2, and his body was then buried at the church of the Austin Friars in Old Broad Street. His eldest son had also been put to death, six days earlier.

Edward IV's court was now established. The new king's widowed mother lived at her late husband's London home, Baynard's Castle. Her three younger children, Margaret of York and the brothers George, Duke of Clarence, and Richard, Duke of Gloucester, dwelt at Greenwich Palace. There were still occasional disturbances in some parts of the country. For example, we know from a letter she wrote at the time that a lady called Margaret Paston, concerned at disturbances in Norfolk, asked that the young Duke of Clarence and his brother-in-law, the Duke of Suffolk, should come to Norwich to sort things out.[27] Nevertheless, on the whole there seemed to be peace for a time.

But in various ways, new troubles were brewing. Edward IV's cousin, the Earl of Warwick, believing the new king to be still unattached, was trying to persuade him to commit himself to a continental arranged royal marriage. At the same time the deposed King Henry VI and his family were still loitering in Scotland. There the exiled Lancastrians had concluded an offensive alliance with the government of the young King James III. As a result, there were some disturbances in the north of England in 1461, when the Lancastrians and the Scots besieged Carlisle, and threatened Durham. However, the new Yorkist government was gradually establishing itself, even in the extreme north of the country. One interesting outcome of this was that Henry Beaufort, Duke of Somerset, abandoned Henry VI's cause and sought to make peace with Edward IV. As a result, on 10 March 1461/2 Edward IV pardoned Somerset and restored his lands to him. For about a year Somerset then seemed to be very close to Edward IV. Indeed, he was even reported to have slept with the king, who was about six years younger than the very handsome Duke, and who seems, at this stage in his life, to have had a preference for slightly older partners. Somerset himself never married, though earlier he had produced one illegitimate son, by Joan Hill. From this son (called Charles Somerset), the present Duke of Beaufort is said to be directly descended. Unfortunately, however, a recent examination of the Somerset family's Y-chromosome has raised some doubts about its biological descent from the medieval royal family.

The remaining Lancastrians also explored the possibility of causing trouble in Wales. Meanwhile Queen Margaret was talking to her (and her husband's) cousin, King Louis XI of France. As a result, the French king agreed to allow the exiled Lancastrians to try to recruit French mercenary support. Following this, the Duke of Somerset changed sides yet again. Deserting the court of Edward IV he made his way north and rejoined the Lancastrian forces.

Using the forces they had assembled, the Lancastrians tried to seize control of Northumberland. Despite French and Scottish help, overall, the attempt was not successful. However, in 1464 they pushed into Yorkshire and captured Skipton Castle. Next they tried to ambush the Earl of Warwick's brother, John Neville, Lord Montagu(e), who was escorting a group of Scottish ambassadors to York. Although the ambush failed, Lord Montagu(e) found himself fighting a Lancastrian force, commanded by the Duke of Somerset, his half-brother, Lord Roos, Lord Hungerford, and Sir Ralph Percy, at Hedgeley Moor, near Alnwick, on Wednesday 25 April 1464. The Lancastrian lords quickly perceived that the odds were against them, and they withdrew. However, Sir Ralph Percy carried on fighting, and paid for this with his life.

After his withdrawal from the battle of Hedgeley Moor, the Duke of Somerset regrouped his men and tried hard to recruit additional supporters. Even so, the army with which he confronted the Yorkist forces at Hexham, on Tuesday 15 May 1464, was still noticeably inferior in size. In fact it has been claimed that Montagu(e) had eight times as many men as Somerset. Certainly the Lancastrian army panicked, and began to run away at the earliest opportunity. As a result, most of the Lancastrian leaders were captured.

The Duke of Somerset himself escaped from the battlefield, and sought to take refuge in a barn. The many-chimneyed 'Dukes House' at Hexham is said to occupy the site of that barn nowadays. At all events, the Duke was caught in his hiding place, and he was beheaded later that same day, together with his half-brother, Lord Roos. His body was buried at Hexham Abbey.

6

WARWICK VERSUS THE WOODVILLES

Even allowing for the fact that it may have stemmed from an initial meeting which took place in or before 1460, Edward IV's marriage to Eleanor Talbot seems, in practical terms, to have proved a relatively short-term relationship. Although the couple had married privately in June 1461, by the end of that year Edward IV, no doubt taking full sexual advantage of his new position as king, seems to have become involved in another relationship, which may have produced an illegitimate child.[1] The fact that other girls could rapidly conceive by the king – whereas Eleanor Talbot had never conceived a child, either by Edward IV, or by her previous husband – may have proved rather significant for the future of Edward IV's relationship with his secret bride. As we have seen, if Eleanor had become pregnant, Edward IV would presumably have publicly acknowledged their marriage. In fact his subsequent secret marriage with Elizabeth Woodville may well have followed precisely that pattern (see below).

In the meanwhile, however, as far as the general public was aware, the king was still available as a potential royal bridegroom.

Thus his cousin Richard Neville, the 'Kingmaker', Earl of Warwick, was busy negotiating for an official royal marriage between Edward and Bona of Savoy, the sister-in-law of the King of France. At this period, of course, the Earl of Warwick was one of Edward's strongest supporters. Warwick was obviously completely unaware, both of the fact that the king had contracted a secret marriage with the niece of his own wife (the Countess of Warwick was the younger half-sister of Eleanor Talbot's mother), and also of the subsequent existence of a *second* secret 'marriage' – uniting Edward with a woman called Elizabeth Woodville. It is blatantly obvious that Warwick only found out about the Woodville marriage when Edward IV publicly announced it.

This occurred in mid to late September 1464, when the royal council was meeting at Reading. Warwick had decided to make use of this opportunity to urge the king to agree to his plan for a dynastic alliance with Bona of Savoy. To Warwick's astonishment, however, not only did the king reject Bona, he also announced that he was already married. This announcement flabbergasted the entire council. It also insulted and infuriated Warwick, who had been working hard for the proposed diplomatic alliance.

Edward IV had probably first met Elizabeth Woodville late in 1463 or early in 1464. She was the eldest child of Jacquette of Luxemburg, dowager Duchess of Bedford. Jacquette had been married first to one of Henry V's brothers. However, her children (including Elizabeth) were not fathered by that Lancastrian prince. After her first husband died, Jacquette made a second – and secret – marriage with a young man of no account, called Richard Woodville. It was this second husband (created Baron Rivers by Henry VI in 1448, and upgraded to Earl Rivers by Edward IV in 1466) who fathered Elizabeth, together with Jacquette's numerous other children. Incidentally, the fact that Jacquette's marriage to Woodville was secretly contracted proves very clearly that such conduct was by no means unknown in the English royal family in the fifteenth century. Nor is Jacquette's Woodville marriage the only documented example of such conduct.

Just like Eleanor Talbot, Jacquette's eldest Woodville daughter, Elizabeth, was an attractive young widow, a few years older than Edward IV. Unlike Eleanor, however, Elizabeth Woodville already had two sons by her first husband. She was therefore known to be fecund. She was also a much more determined young woman than Eleanor Talbot. Incidentally, the Crowland Chronicle gives the following account of Edward IV's marriage

> King Edward, prompted by the ardour of youth and relying entirely on his own choice, without consulting the nobles of the kingdom, privately married the widow of a certain knight, Elizabeth by name.[2]

While emphasising the fact that the ardour of Edward's youth was in control of his sexual activity, this account shows how, even if some people had heard whispers of the secret Talbot marriage, they might very well have confused those earlier rumours with the king's subsequent announcement, in 1464, of his secret marriage to Elizabeth Woodville. After all, each of the two women involved was 'the widow of a certain knight'. Also, both of their Christian names began with the letter E.

Elizabeth Woodville first met Edward IV as a result of a bitter ongoing dispute between herself and her mother-in-law over some property which belonged to the Greys – the family of Elizabeth's late husband. As had happened earlier with Eleanor, it is reported (for example, in the later account written by Sir Thomas More) that the king was captivated by Elizabeth's beauty. 'When the king beheld [Elizabeth] and heard her speak – as she was both fair, of a good favour, moderate of stature, well made, and very wise – he not only pitied her, but also waxed enamored on her. And taking her afterwards secretly aside, began to enter in talking more familiarly. Whose appetite when she perceived, she virtuously denied him'.[3] Thus, in this case, as also in the case of Eleanor, Edward apparently began his courtship by asking the young lady whom he found so attractive to become his mistress. Like Eleanor before her, Elizabeth refused. Thus, once again Edward found that the only way for him to get what he wanted was by means of a secret marriage.

The great similarities between Edward IV's two secret marriage stories are obvious – making it rather hard to understand why so many historians seem to have found it difficult to accept that the first secret marriage took place. As in the case of his marriage to Eleanor Talbot, Edward's marriage to Elizabeth Woodville was contracted not at a church, but privately, at her family's manor house. In this case the manor was that of Grafton Regis, in Northamptonshire. The celebrant of the Woodville secret wedding is reported to have been Thomas Eborall, a Dominican priest, and the ceremony is said to have taken place on Tuesday 1 May 1464. Since at that time Eleanor Talbot was still alive, the Woodville marriage would have been bigamous, and therefore illegal in terms of the law of the Church, which governed marriage at that time. However, there is, of course, no reason to suppose that Elizabeth Woodville had any idea that such a problem existed. Indeed, if she had been aware of the situation she would almost certainly have taken action to circumvent the problem in some way.

The obvious solution would have been for Elizabeth to insist on a public marriage. At a public wedding, in those days, as now, the people present were asked if they knew any reason why the marriage should not take place. That would have been the right moment for Eleanor Talbot – or her representatives – to speak out. Had they failed to do so, they would then have had no right to contest the second marriage at a later date. However, the key point was that the Woodville marriage was conducted in secret. Thus, no opportunity to object to it was ever offered to the world at large. It was the *secrecy* of the second, Woodville marriage which ultimately played the greatest role in undermining its legality.

Like the earlier Talbot marriage, the Woodville marriage continued to be a secret – at least for a time. In the case of Elizabeth Woodville, Edward IV only recognised his union with her publicly several months after it had happened. Possibly Edward's reason for speaking out on that occasion was partly that he was then under pressure to agree to another marriage (with Bona of Savoy). However, it may also have been partly because Elizabeth had by then informed him that she was pregnant. A pregnancy on the part of Elizabeth Woodville at this period might also account for the delay which occurred in her coronation as queen consort (see below). However, if she really was expecting a child at this point, the pregnancy clearly did not run successfully to full term, since Elizabeth's first living child by Edward IV was not born until 11 February 1465/6.

When the Earl of Warwick first heard of the Woodville marriage, he may well have been furious. The royal family – that is, Edward IV's widowed mother, and his brothers and sisters – certainly seem to have been very unhappy about it, and so were the aristocracy as a whole. 'The nobility and chief men of the kingdom took [the marriage] amiss, seeing that he [Edward] had with such immoderate haste promoted a person sprung from such a comparatively humble lineage'.[4] Nevertheless, in spite of their anger and disapproval, the king's cousin, the Earl of Warwick (together with Edward's younger brother, George, Duke of Clarence) was forced by Edward IV to formally present Elizabeth Woodville to the nation as its queen. It seems that the young king was now flexing his muscles. He probably felt that he was making a show of strength by compelling Warwick and his own brother, the heir presumptive to the throne, to act as Elizabeth Woodville's official patrons and sponsors.

However, in the long term this was to prove a serious mistake. Edward appeared, to other members of the house of York, and also to his cousin, Warwick, to be pursuing a policy which was not in the interests of his royal dynasty. Subsequently they and the king were split apart as a result.

> The reason of this was, the fact that the king, being too greatly influenced by the urgent suggestions of the queen, admitted to his especial favour all the relations of the said queen, as well as those who were in any way connected with her by blood, enriching them with boundless presents and always promoting them to the most dignified offices about his person: while, at the same time, he banished from his presence his own brethren, and his kinsmen sprung from the royal blood, together with the Earl of Warwick himself, and the other nobles of the realm who had always proved faithful to him.[5]

Also, while the house of York had recently asserted its claim to the throne on the grounds of the strict legitimacy of the family's royal descent, Edward IV was now potentially undermining that claim. Even for those who were not aware of the earlier

Talbot marriage, and the consequent bigamy, the marriage of the young king to a person of no consequence – a marriage conducted in secret and without the approval of Parliament – made that marriage questionable. To other members of his family, Edward now appeared to have deviated seriously from the Yorkist official line. Nevertheless, the immediate outcome of Edward's acknowledgement of his Woodville union was that at Reading Abbey, on Michaelmas day (29 September) 1464, Elizabeth Woodville was formally presented to the nation's representatives as the new Queen of England by the Earl of Warwick and the young Duke of Clarence.

None of the surviving sets of letters dating from the 1460s mentions the revelation of Elizabeth Woodville as queen of England, or reactions to that surprising news. The surviving household accounts of John Howard (later Duke of Norfolk) refer in passing to the queen's subsequent coronation, but only in a purely practical way. However, Elizabeth was not crowned as queen straight away. Possibly this was because in September 1464, when her marriage was acknowledged, she was pregnant. But if so, then she must have either had a miscarriage or produced a still-born child. At all events, it was eight months after the public acknowledgement of her marriage to Edward IV that her coronation was celebrated in Westminster Abbey. On that occasion the king's senior brother, George, Duke of Clarence, was once again required to play an important role as the Steward of England.

As we saw highlighted by the second continuator of the Crowland Chronicle (see above), Edward IV's treatment of members of his own royal family – and particularly of his younger brother – seems in some ways to have been extraordinarily insensitive. Since 1461, George, Duke of Clarence, had been not only the king's brother, but also his heir. However, he was now about to be displaced from that position by any children produced by Elizabeth Woodville. Perhaps inevitably the long-term effect of this was ongoing animosity between Clarence and Elizabeth. As we shall see, this animosity was only finally to be brought to an end, after years of bitterness, by the execution of the Duke of Clarence, probably at Elizabeth Woodville's instigation. Thus, from the end of 1464 the royal house of York, which had formerly been united, had effectively become split in two by Edward's acknowledgement of Elizabeth Woodville as his wife and queen.

Another direct outcome of Elizabeth's recognition as queen was the growth of an alliance between Edward IV's cousin, the Earl of Warwick, and the king's brother, George, Duke of Clarence. These two found now themselves united in their opposition to the entire Woodville family. By pushing Warwick and Clarence together in this way, Edward IV had in effect encouraged them to form a united front, aimed at maintaining the legitimist Yorkist position. As a result, Warwick and Clarence become the joint opponents of Edward's new commitment, and the joint enemies of his *parvenu* queen and her upstart Woodville family. To cement their alliance, Warwick proposed that Clarence should marry his elder daughter, Isabel. The Duke of Clarence was keen to accept. However, his brother the king was initially vehemently opposed to the idea of such a marriage.

As for Elizabeth Woodville, she proved to be unpopular as queen of England in various quarters. First, as we have seen, the English nobility as a whole rather resented her, because her family was not truly aristocratic in its origins. Thus she seemed to them to be a kind of interloper. The aristocracy also resented the fact that Elizabeth did everything in her power to advance her numerous brothers and sisters, arranging wealthy marriages for them (sometimes with key members of the English aristocracy's own families), and also arranging for the king to grant them lands and titles. In addition, Elizabeth Woodville was resented for the alleged witchcraft which had reportedly secured her marriage with the king. In the longer term, she was also blamed for the fact that she used her new power and influence to take revenge on certain persons who had offended her, or who had, in her view, got in her way. As we shall see, two key examples of such manoeuvring on the part of the queen were the executions of the Earl of Desmond and of the Duke of Clarence. It is interesting to note that the king's younger brother, Richard, Duke of Gloucester (Richard III), in his mind's eye, saw these two executions as clearly connected.[6] Moreover, he attributed the basic responsibility for both of them to Elizabeth Woodville. It is unlikely that Richard was the only member of the court to make such a connection.

After his acknowledgement of his own, non-royal, Woodville marriage, the king began negotiating for a more proper royal marriage for his youngest surviving sister, Margaret. Her proposed bridegroom was the son and heir of the Duke of Burgundy. However, as we have seen, Warwick favoured an alliance with France. Since France and the duchy of Burgundy were often enemies, Warwick was opposed to Edward IV's Burgundian marriage proposal. Thus, curiously, in two different ways, marriages, which are supposed to bring people together, were now proving rather divisive within the house of York. Meanwhile, Warwick's brother, the Archbishop of York, who had been Edward IV's chancellor, suddenly found himself dismissed from his post. As for Warwick himself, when the Burgundian royal marriage took place, in 1468, he once again found himself compelled by Edward IV to publicly accept and endorse it.

Possibly Elizabeth Woodville was responsible for inciting the king's ongoing quarrel with his cousin. Her character seems to have been rather vindictive. As we have already noted, one alleged example of her revenge was the execution of the Earl of Desmond, while a second, and even more dramatic example, which we shall deal with later, was the execution of Warwick's son-in-law, and the king's own brother, George, Duke of Clarence.

It was on 15 February 1467/8, that Thomas Fitzgerald, 7th Earl of Desmond, the former deputy governor of Ireland, and a friend and ally of Edward IV, was beheaded at Drogheda by Edward IV's new governor of Ireland, the Earl of Worcester. In political terms, Desmond's execution was a bad mistake, which caused consternation in Ireland, and sent the Earl's family into immediate armed rebellion.

Various reasons have been cited for Desmond's execution. At the time no clear public statement was made on the subject. However, sixteenth-century sources attributed the earl's death to the fact that he had reputedly told Edward IV that the king's marriage with Elizabeth Woodville was a serious mistake and that he should have chosen a more suitable bride. This remark reportedly earned Desmond the undying hatred of the queen, who thereafter sought revenge upon him. And although the written account of Elizabeth Woodville's involvement dates from more than half a century after the event, its source is the Earl of Desmond's own family. Thus it appears that there must have been a continuous oral version of the story handed down among his many children. In addition to the oral tradition within the Fitzgerald family, there is also a significant fifteenth-century written implication of Elizabeth

Woodville's involvement in the Earl of Desmond's death, from a very important English source, namely Edward IV's younger brother, King Richard III.

The royal house of York was itself descended via the de Burghs from the Anglo-Irish aristocracy, of which (thanks to its tenure of the earldom of Ulster) it formed part. Thus the Yorks were generally well-regarded in Ireland. As for King Edward IV, he had always been on friendly terms with the Fitzgerald family – which included the earls of Desmond. When James, 6th Earl of Desmond, had died in 1462, his son and successor, Thomas, enjoyed the Yorkist royal favour in his turn. Thomas attended Edward's court in England on occasions, and received rewards for his loyalty directly from the king.

Normally, of course, Earls of Desmond would have been resident in Ireland. Significantly, however, owing to a disagreement between Thomas, Earl of Desmond, and the Bishop of Meath, it so happened that this particular Earl of Desmond had found himself in England, reporting in person to Edward IV, at precisely the time when the king's marriage to Elizabeth Woodville became public knowledge. Thus it is by no means impossible that the king, who trusted Desmond, and who must have known that his secret marriage was being widely discussed and debated, may have asked Thomas Fitzgerald what people were saying about it, and what his own opinion was.

Although some historians have dismissed the allegation that Elizabeth Woodville was behind Desmond's subsequent execution, rejecting it as a later invention, the story certainly seems to have been believed by some people in the fifteenth century. In the 1480s, Richard III, who had been only a young prince at the time of the execution, wrote to Desmond's son, sympathising with him over his father's execution, and linking that event specifically with the death of his own brother, the Duke of Clarence – an execution in which Elizabeth Woodville had undoubtedly played a key role.[7] There is therefore every reason to believe that the Earl of Desmond's execution was (at least in part) one example of Elizabeth Woodville's vindictiveness.[8]

There is absolutely no doubt that Elizabeth Woodville was power-hungry. This is proved absolutely by her conduct in 1483, following the death of Edward IV. On that occasion, as we shall see, instead of accepting that she was now merely the queen mother, and allowing the senior living prince of the blood royal to assume regency powers on behalf of her young son, in accordance with English precedents, Elizabeth attempted to stage a *coup d'état* to maintain herself and her family in power at the expense of the royal family itself. This evidence alone is sufficient to prove that we are dealing with a highly ambitious and power-hungry woman.

It is therefore not surprising that the behaviour of Elizabeth Woodville, coupled with her mediocre birth and her ambitious relatives, combined to provoke the hostility of a significant portion of the English nobility. Moreover, the fact that the king's announcement of his marriage to her had made the 'Kingmaker' Earl of Warwick look a fool over his negotiations for a diplomatic marriage to Bona of Savoy absolutely ensured that Warwick himself became one of the new queen's leading opponents.

Warwick undoubtedly aimed to bring the new queen and her family down, and to try to force Edward IV back onto what he saw at the correct path of Yorkist policy. His chief ally in this was Edward IV's brother, George, Duke of Clarence. Clarence had been heir to the throne until the king married and began to produce children. But by 1469 both Warwick and Clarence were in Calais – the continental fortified town which Warwick had used earlier as the base for the Yorkist conquest of England from the Lancastrians. Now, Warwick was planning to use Calais as his base for opposition to Edward and his policies. And it was in Calais, in 1469, that Warwick's elder daughter, Isabel, married the Duke of Clarence, thus cementing the alliance between her new husband and her father.

Meanwhile, in England, Warwick's plans included the inciting of a rebellion against Edward IV in the north. This rebellion – the idea of which had first been mooted by Warwick the previous year, prior to his departure for Calais – was led by a figurehead known as 'Robin of Redesdale' (probably Sir William Conyers of Marske). The false name of the leader was derived from the earlier legendary English figure of 'Robin Hood'. Although later mythology purports to connect 'Robin Hood' with Sherwood Forest and the Midlands, actually the original of the 'Robin Hood' figure – like Sir William Conyers – probably came from further north.[9]

Given Warwick's backing for the rebellion, it is not surprising to find that one of the chief demands of the rebels was that the new queen's Woodville family should be completely removed from all positions of power. Since Warwick and Clarence were the orchestrators of the Robin of Redesdale rising, the openly voiced aim of the rebels also makes the principal objective of Warwick and Clarence themselves crystal clear.

What is often misunderstood or misinterpreted by historians is the fact that at this stage the 'Kingmaker' and his new son-in-law had absolutely no intention of actually dethroning Edward IV. All they wanted to achieve was to oust the Woodville family from power, thereby bringing Edward IV back into the true Yorkist fold. The natural sequel of the removal of the Woodvilles would presumably have been for Warwick and Clarence themselves to take over the role of the king's chief advisors. Thus they would jointly have become the dominant (and politically correct) power behind Edward IV's throne.

The king himself took no direct action against 'Robin' and his uprising. At first Robin of Redesdale's rebellion was opposed, on behalf of Edward IV, by Warwick's own brother, John Neville, Earl of Northumberland. As a result of John Neville's action the first 'Robin of Redesdale' was killed. However, a second 'Robin' (probably Sir William Conyers' brother, John) took over both the pseudonym and the leadership of the uprising, and the rebellion continued.

Since the Battle of Hexham on 15 May 1464, Henry VI (who had then been captured) had been a prisoner in the Tower of London. Meanwhile, Margaret of Anjou and her son, Edward of Westminster, were in exile in France. Thus, the Lancastrian cause in England seemed finished. Indeed, the only sign of Lancastrian activity had been when Jasper 'Tudor', the Lancastrian Earl of Pembroke, ignited a brief revolt in Wales during the summer of 1468. By a curious twist of fate, therefore, the greatest threat to Edward IV now came not from the defeated Lancastrians, but from his own former supporters. This development was the direct outcome of the conflict between the politically correct Yorkists, Clarence and Warwick, on one side, and the Woodvilles and their supporters – the family of Edward IV's now acknowledged queen – on the other side.

In 1469, following the marriage of the Duke of Clarence to his daughter Isabel Neville in Calais, the Earl of Warwick, together with his new son-in-law, publicly sided with the ongoing 'Robin of Redesdale' uprising in the north of England. This was achieved by the issue of a joint manifesto of their own against the Woodville family. This document publicly lashed out against the Woodvilles for their 'deceivable covetous rule' of England.[10] Following the issue of this manifesto, Clarence and Warwick set sail from Calais and crossed the Channel to the favourite Yorkist port of Sandwich. From there, they rode on to the city of Canterbury, where they invited the men of Kent to rally to them in support of their cause.

Edward IV was now growing anxious about the situation. He therefore asked his counsellors whether he should himself take up arms against the rebels. Reportedly, Lord Hastings, Lord Mountjoy, Sir Thomas Montgomery and others all advised the king to do nothing. This is extremely interesting. Presumably these noblemen all clearly saw the uprisings merely as movements against the Woodville family – not against the king himself. Presumably they also understood that the aim of Warwick and Clarence was simply to bring the king back to the correct path of Yorkist policy. Evidently the removal of the Woodvilles from political power was an objective which by no means alarmed or offended any of them. Indeed, the king himself may have understood the situation better than subsequent historians! For Edward also stated that he could not believe that his brother, George, and his cousin, the Earl of Warwick, meant any harm to him personally.

On around Tuesday 18 July, Warwick and Clarence left Canterbury and rode on to London. Later, they continued their journey in the direction of Coventry. On Tuesday 25 July 1469 Clarence and Warwick found themselves near the village of Banbury, and a battle (the battle of Edgecote Moor) with forces loyal to Edward IV ensued on the following morning. Clarence and Warwick were camped on one side of the river Cherwell, while the royal army was on the other side.

The royal army was led by the Yorkist Lord Pembroke and Herbert,[11] and it included Elizabeth Woodville's father, Richard, Lord Rivers, together with his second son, John Woodville. The Yorkist Lord Pembroke and Herbert had expected the support of Humphrey Stafford, 1st Earl of Devon. But at some point, and for reasons which are not absolutely clear (possibly as a result of a quarrel with Lord Pembroke and Herbert), Devon decided to withdraw, leaving the royal army in a rather weak position. As a result, they lost the battle. After the king's forces had been defeated, a number of important captives were taken. Lord Pembroke and Herbert was captured, together with his younger brother, and both the Herberts were executed the following day in Banbury. The Earl of Devon was captured in Somerset and beheaded. In addition, the two members of the Woodville family were captured at Chepstow. They were given a speedy show trial, after which Earl Rivers and his son, John, were both executed at Kenilworth on 12 August 1469.

The battle of Edgecote Moor has one rather curious tale attached to it. About twelve years before the battle, Jasper's nephew, Henry 'Tudor' – the future Henry VII – had been born at Pembroke Castle on 28 January 1456/7. His father, the Earl of Richmond, had died three months prior to the little boy's birth. Thus, when Edward IV seized the throne, the little boy's wardship had been granted to Lord Herbert, who had then just been promoted by Edward IV to the Earldom of Pembroke – the very same title which had formerly been held by young Henry's uncle. In 1469, Henry – then twelve years of age – accompanied his guardian to the battle of Edgecote Moor. Of course, his guardian was commanding the royal army. Therefore, ironically, young Henry 'Tudor' found himself present at the battle on the *Yorkist* side, as a nominal supporter of King Edward IV.

Following Lord Pembroke and Herbert's defeat and subsequent execution, young Henry returned to the care of the widowed Lady Pembroke and Herbert. Meanwhile his mother, Margaret Beaufort, together with her second husband, Henry Stafford, began campaigning to secure the boy's return to his own family. In the end they achieved this aim as a result of the Lancastrian Readeption of 1470. From that time onwards the young Henry 'Tudor' passed into the hands of the Lancastrian Earl of Pembroke – his uncle, Jasper.

Another sequel to the defeat of Lord Pembroke and Herbert, – followed by the subsequent execution of the lord, together with his brother, Richard – was the capture of Edward IV, who was staying at Olney when he found himself suddenly made a prisoner.

The king heard the news of this, which greatly displeased him, he felt that he had been betrayed, and prepared all his men to go and confront his brother the Duke of Clarence and his cousin of Warwick, who were coming before him. They were between Warwick and Coventry when they received the news that the king was coming to see them. ... it was not then to be believed that his brother of Clarence, nor his cousin of Warwick would think of treason when meeting him in person; wherefore the king proceeded to a village nearby and there he lodged all his men not far from the place where the Earl of Warwick was staying. At about midnight the Archbishop of York came to the king with a large party of armed men. He went right up to the king's lodging, saying to those who guarded his person that he needed to speak to the king, to whom they announced him; but the king sent him a reply that he was resting and that he should come in the morning when he would be happy to receive him. Which response did not please the archbishop, so he again sent his messengers to the king a second time, to say that he had to speak to him. When they did this the king ordered that he should be allowed in, in order to hear what he wanted to say, for he had no doubts regarding his loyalty. When the archbishop had entered the chamber, where he found the king in bed, he quickly said to him 'Sire, get up', from which the king wished to excuse himself, saying that he hadn't yet had any rest. But the archbishop, false and disloyal as he was, said to him a second time: 'You must get up and come to my brother of Warwick, for you cannot resist this'. And the king, thinking that nothing worse could happen to him, got dressed, and the archbishop led him without making much noise to the place where the said earl and the duke of Clarence were, between Warwick and Coventry.[12]

Edward IV subsequently found himself living under constraint at Warwick Castle. As for the Earl of Warwick and his son-in-law the Duke of Clarence, the two of them had now become the effective power in the realm.

7

PRIVATE WARS

Meanwhile, the disruptive and lawless situation prevailing in England caused disturbances to spread. There were personal conflicts which had no direct link with the question of who should be wearing the crown of England. For example, it is reported that early in the reign of Edward IV, John Howard had become involved in violent activity which was in no way connected with the king's service. In May 1461, Sir John Howard's men attacked Thomas Denys, a servant of John de Vere, Earl of Oxford. The Earl of Oxford was married to John Howard's cousin, Elizabeth, and the attack on Thomas Denys seems to have been part of an ongoing conflict between Howard and Oxford over possession of the ancestral Howard manor of Winch, in Norfolk.[1] In August 1461 the attack on Denys was followed by a violent attack by Howard's men on John Paston I. This included an attempted stabbing.[2] As a result of these incidents, Sir John Howard found himself in trouble with the king. According to the surviving accounts written by the Pastons, Howard was reportedly arrested. Indeed, early the following year the Pastons were spreading rumours of his impending execution![3] In the event, these rumours came to nothing, but it is clear that there had been some conflict involving Howard's men, Oxford's men and the Pastons.

The Paston family also found themselves caught up in several other disputes. They were probably by no means unique in this, but the fortunate survival of so much of their correspondence means that we know more of their involvement than that of other contemporary families. For example, Drayton Lodge, just outside Norwich on the left hand side of the road which runs northwards to the shrine at Walsingham, had been inherited by John Paston I from Sir John Fastolf. However, the lodge was also claimed by Edward IV's brother-in-law, John de la Pole, Duke of Suffolk. On Tuesday and Wednesday 15 and 16 October 1465, some 500 men of the Duke of Suffolk sacked the lodge, leaving it in ruins which, ironically, still survive today.[4]

The Pastons also found themselves involved in another dispute over part of the Fastolf inheritance, this time with Sir John Howard's cousin, the Duke of Norfolk. Norfolk was a very high-ranking nobleman, but unfortunately his income was rather small, since his estates had to support not only him and his wife, but also two dowager duchess of Norfolk – his mother and his grandmother. Norfolk coveted Caister Castle, a property which his family had originally expected to inherit. This castle had been built by Sir John Fastolf, who died there in November 1459. On his deathbed, Fastolf changed his will. As a result, Caister Castle passed not to the Norfolk family, but to Fastolf's close friend, John Paston I (1421–66). But the late change in Fastolf's will gave rise to subsequent disputes.

Ten years after the death of Fastolf, the Duke of Norfolk decided that the troubled times in England might offer him a very opportune moment to use force to remove the Paston family, who were then living at the castle. Thus, in August 1469 Norfolk besieged Caister. His army was a large one, said to number 3,000 men (though this may be a slight exaggeration). On the other hand, the Paston defenders of the castle numbered less than 30.

For two months Norfolk was solely preoccupied with taking Caister Castle. He therefore took no part in the wider conflict then going on in England – though he does seem to have been in close touch with the Duke of Clarence, and with the Earl of Warwick's brother, Archbishop George Neville. Indeed, Norfolk apparently sought the support of his cousin, the Duke of Clarence.

As we have seen, Clarence and Warwick were then the leading power in the kingdom. King Edward IV had not, of course, been deposed. He was still king in name, but since August 1469 he had been, in effect, the prisoner of his cousin and his younger brother, who now wielded real authority. In September 1469, the Paston defenders of Caister Castle clearly understood the realities of the situation, because they also sought the help of the Duke of Clarence. By this time it was obvious that they would not be able to hold out against Norfolk's forces.

As a result of the Pastons' request, on Tuesday 26 September 1469 the Duke of Norfolk granted them a safe conduct, which permitted all the surviving defenders to leave Caister Castle unmolested. Although this safe conduct was issued by the Duke of Norfolk himself, he told the Pastons publicly that it had been granted at the request of the Duke of Clarence. One thing which probably encouraged the Duke and Duchess of Norfolk to see their cousin Clarence as a potential friend was the fact that Earl Rivers, father of Elizabeth Woodville, had been executed by the Earl of Warwick at Kenilworth on 12 August 1469.

As the younger sister of Eleanor Talbot, the Duchess of Norfolk had absolutely no reason to like the Woodville family. As for her husband, his fight for Caister Castle was linked with his precarious financial situation, which in turn was due to the fact that his estate was split up to support his widowed mother and grandmother. Norfolk was therefore probably delighted when he heard that, together with the Queen's father, her much younger brother, John Woodville had also been put to death after the battle of Edgecote Moor. In 1465 an extraordinary marriage had united the young John (then aged about 20) to the Duke of Norfolk's aged grandmother, Catherine Neville, the senior dowager Duchess of Norfolk and sister to the Duchess of York, who at the time of this marriage had been about forty-five years old. John Woodville's marriage had been arranged by his sister, Elizabeth, and as a result of this bizarre union, young John had become the Duke of Norfolk's step grandfather – and yet another potential drain on his meagre resources.

From the point of view of Clarence and Warwick – and perhaps also of a number of other English noblemen – the deaths of Lord Rivers and John Woodville were just the first two Woodville executions. It was hoped that many more would follow. Exterminating the Woodville interlopers offered a good start to the process of cleaning up Edward IV's administration. But of course there was still a long way to go.

Thus, in September 1469 the queen's mother, Jacquette, Duchess of Bedford and Countess Rivers, also found herself in trouble. One of the Earl of Warwick's followers, a man named Thomas Wake, produced a damning piece of evidence against her. This was his discovery of a lead figure, broken in the middle and ensnared in wires.[5] Such figurines – made of wax or of lead – were often used in the casting of spells. Indeed, it was just such a figurine which had been a key piece of evidence, twenty years previously, against Jacquette's sister-in-law, Eleanor Cobham, Duchess of Gloucester.

In the new case against Jacquette, the surviving evidence does not state explicitly whom the lead figurine was meant to represent. However, the implication appears to be that the spells associated with it were targeted against the Earl of Warwick. When coupled with the already current gossip which alleged that Jacquette had also used spells to enable her daughter, Elizabeth Woodville, to ensnare Edward IV in a secret marriage, it became clear that Jacquette was now in a dangerous position. It was said that the Duchess of Bedford's involvement in magic to ensnare the king could now be proved. John Daunger, a parish clerk from Northamptonshire, could apparently present evidence to show that the Duchess of Bedford had fashioned images, both of her daughter, Elizabeth Woodville, and of Edward IV. This implied that Edward IV had been entrapped into his secret Woodville union by sorcery.

Unfortunately the precise evidence presented in the original court hearings – which condemned Jacquette for sorcery – is not now preserved. The only surviving accounts we have of the case against Jaquette date from the period some months later, when the king had freed himself from the hands of Warwick and Clarence, and had re-established his own personal authority. At that stage, of course, both Jacquette and the king wished to demolish the case against her. For Edward it was particularly important to demonstrate that there was no black magic underlying his union with Jacquette's daughter. As a result, the case against Jacquette was ultimately set aside.

Many historians have rather naïvely concluded from this that

Jacquette was innocent. This is a rather simplistic view of the situation. As we have already seen, witchcraft certainly does seem to have been used at this period – even in the royal court of England. Thus, it is by no means impossible that Jacquette and her daughter, Elizabeth Woodville had resorted to magic in the hope of ensnaring Edward IV and of winning – and keeping – a crown for Elizabeth.

Meanwhile, the inheritance dispute between Sir John Howard and the Earl of Oxford (involving also Sir John Paston), the fight between the Pastons and the Duke of Suffolk over the ownership of Drayton Lodge, and the Paston conflict with the Duke of Norfolk over Caister Castle, were by no means the only examples of private warfare in England at this rather disturbed period. There had also been a long history of dispute among the potential heirs of the Berkeley family in Gloucestershire. This dispute dated back to the 1440s, and was focussed chiefly on three manors: Wotton, Simondshall and Cowley. Lady Eleanor Talbot's mother, Margaret, Countess of Shrewsbury (eldest granddaughter of the late Lord Berkeley) had been granted these manors for life in 1448, but in 1450 her cousin, James, then the current Lord Berkeley, had seized the manors by force of arms. Apparently not expecting to be able to retain them, James had then simply sacked and wrecked the manor house at Wotton. As the Countess of Shrewsbury herself reported, Berkeley and his men

riotously came to the said manor of Wotton, and entered into the same, and the gates and doors of the said manor they brake, and all to hewe and cut the great and principal timber of the roofs and galleries, and other necessaries sawed and cut in two, the walls, vaults, quines of doors and windows they razed and tore a-down, the ferments of iron in the windows, hinges for doors and windows, gutters and conduits of lead, as well upon the houses as under the earth, they brake and beare away; And the said manor of Wotton in all that they could defaced and destroyed, insomuch that the reparations thereof cost the said earl, countess, John Viscount Lisle, and their servants then there being, to the value of four thousand marks.[6]

The Countess of Shrewsbury had retaliated by sending her eldest son, John Talbot, Lord Lisle, to besiege her enemy at Berkeley Castle. One of Lord Berkeley's men – captured by Lord Lisle – had agreed to help the Talbot family and their army gain entry into Berkeley Castle. As a result, Lord Berkeley and his four sons had been captured when the Talbots had seized the castle. The ensuing renewed legal dispute had then initially appeared to be going in favour of the Talbot family. However, it had finally attracted royal attention, with the result that Henry VI had intervened and the Crown had taken charge of the entire Berkeley estate.

Eleanor Talbot's immediate birth family (she herself, her mother, and the latter's other children) had all sided with the Yorkists by about 1460, despite – or perhaps because of – the fact that Eleanor's elder half-brother, the second Earl of Shrewsbury, and his heirs, were Lancastrians. Hoping, perhaps, to placate Eleanor's relatives for the fact that his own relationship with her had not been publicly acknowledged, Edward IV had then favoured the Yorkist Talbots in terms of their land disputes.

By 1469 both Eleanor and Lady Shrewsbury were dead. The key Talbot player in respect of the disputed Gloucestershire manors was now Eleanor's nephew and legal heir, Thomas Talbot, 2nd Viscount Lisle.[7] His opponent was William, 2nd Baron Berkeley.

On 20 March 1469/70 the battle of Nibley Green was fought between them and their respective retainers. This was the last private battle of the Wars of the Roses.

Viscount Lisle was the heir-general of Thomas, 5th Baron Berkeley, while William was the heir-male. On 19 March 1469/70, Lord Lisle, an impetuous young man at the best of times, challenged Lord Berkeley to a duel. However, Lord Berkeley replied that a duel would not solve the issue. He suggested that they should fight a battle instead. He also proposed that the battle should be fought at Nibley Green, early in the morning, on the following day.

Unwisely, Lord Lisle agreed, despite the fact that he had very little time to put an army together, whereas Lord Berkeley already had an existing force at his disposal, based at Berkeley Castle. In the end, Lisle appeared with about 300 men, while Lord Berkeley was backed by at least 1,000. Thus Lord Berkeley had the clear advantage. However, he concealed most of his men in woodland, and only about 250 of them were visible as the fighting started. Had he not done this, Lord Lisle would probably have withdrawn and sought a different solution.

The battle opened with a charge, led by Lord Lisle, who was mounted on his horse. However, the charge was halted by the arrows rained down by Berkeley's men. Unwisely, Lord Lisle, though in full armour, had not closed his visor. One of the Berkeley arrows pierced his left temple. As he fell from his horse, he was finished off by cruel dagger thrusts through the joints of his armour. His army, deprived of its leader, broke and fled. Many of them were hacked down as they struggled uphill, hoping to claim sanctuary at St Martin's Church. In the end, many of the dead were buried in St Martin's churchyard.

After the battle, Lord Berkeley's forces advanced once again upon Lisle's manor of Wotton-under-Edge, and sacked it. Viscountess Lisle was pregnant at the time, but the shock of her husband's defeat and death, and the destruction of their home caused her to miscarry, and she lost the child who might otherwise have been the next Viscount Lisle.

As for Lord Berkeley, unfortunately Edward IV now needed his support, so he was not punished for what he had done. In fact, Edward IV created him a viscount in 1481. Later, when Richard III was dividing up the Mowbray inheritance, Lord Berkeley (whose mother was one of the Mowbray co-heiresses) was given the earldom of Nottingham. Ironically, after the Battle of Bosworth, Berkeley was also favoured and promoted by Henry VII.

8

'KINGMAKING'

According to a nineteenth-century story, the name of the battle of 'Losecoat Field' was based on the fact that many former Lancastrians, who fought in this battle under Lord Willoughby, were wearing livery of either the Earl of Warwick or of the Duke of Clarence. The story goes that, when they saw they were losing the fight, they took off this livery, not wanting to be caught by the victors wearing the wrong colours. In reality, however, just like the name 'Wars of the Roses', this 'Losecoat' story is probably merely a nineteenth-century invention. The real explanation is probably that the battle took place near a pigsty cottage (or 'Hlose-cot' in old English).

The battle known as Losecoat Field (with various possible spellings) – also sometimes called the battle of Empingham – brought about the reassertion of Edward IV's personal authority and the flight of the Earl of Warwick and his son-in-law (Edward IV's brother), George, Duke of Clarence. For about a year – ever since the battle of Edgecote Moor – Edward IV had been in the hands of his cousin, Warwick, and his younger brother,

Clarence, as a virtual prisoner. Indeed, it has often been asserted that Warwick had been seeking to dethrone Edward IV and place George, Duke of Clarence, on the throne. In reality, as we have seen, there is absolutely no evidence of this. Indeed, the fact that Edward was NOT actually deposed argues conclusively against it. The real aim of Warwick and Clarence at this stage was simply to control Edward and the government – and also, of course, to remove their Woodville enemies from power.

Now, however, with the support of his youngest brother, the loyal Richard, Duke of Gloucester, Edward IV had regained his liberty and his royal power. On Tuesday 6 March 1470 the Duke of Clarence met Edward at Baynard's Castle, the London home of their mother. Everything seemed friendly between the two brothers at this meeting. Indeed, at the end of it the two of them left their mother's house and went together to the nearby St Paul's Cathedral to make a joint offering.

In the background, however, there was still conflict between the two brothers and both of them continued to seek support for their respective causes. Clarence and his father-in-law, Warwick, courted the Welles family. Sir Robert Welles, Lord Willoughby was a former supporter of Henry VI. He now decided to take advantage of the situation arising from the Earl of Warwick's earlier actions against Edward IV to side with Warwick and Clarence against the Yorkist King. He therefore began assembling an army in the north and in Lincolnshire. Meanwhile, the king summoned Lord Willoughby's father, Richard, Lord Welles, to London, where he was ultimately arrested and imprisoned.

At first Clarence and Warwick claimed in public that they were supporting Edward IV against the rebellion of Lord Willoughby. Initially, the king apparently believed them and authorised them to recruit forces to aid his cause. However, when Warwick, Clarence and Willoughby were all found to be heading for Leicester, it became evident to Edward IV that they were not to be trusted. He therefore ordered Lord Willoughby to disband his army, warning him that otherwise his father, Lord Welles, would be put to death. Willoughby therefore retreated to Stamford, and his planned meeting with the forces of Warwick did not take place. Edward himself then confronted Willoughby near Stamford, and on 12 March, before the fighting commenced, the king had Lord Welles executed in the sight of both armies.

The furious rebels then advanced on Edward IV's forces, crying 'a Warwick, a Clarence'. However, the king's cannon-fire broke up the enemy advance, and when his own men began a counter charge, the rebel forces broke ranks and fled. Lord Willoughby and others were captured. Another outcome of the battle was that the second 'Robin of Redesdale' (probably Sir John Conyers) submitted to Edward IV.

After the battle Sir Robert Welles, Lord Willoughby, now a prisoner of Edward IV, was taken to Doncaster. There he broke down and made a confession, in which he named Warwick and Clarence as his partners in the rebellion. Documents he produced backed up his claim. Meanwhile, news had reached Edward IV that Clarence and Warwick were at Austerfield just ten kilometres to the south east. Having been confronted, as a result of Willoughby's confession, with clear evidence that they were still engaged in plotting against his independent interests, on Sunday 18 March Edward IV summoned his brother and his cousin to appear before him and answer certain charges. Their nervous response was to ask the king for safe conducts. Their request was probably rather naïve. At all events, it certainly failed to elicit safe conducts from the king. Fully aware of the potential danger which now confronted them, Clarence and Warwick therefore refused to obey the royal summons.

On the following morning, Monday 19 March, Sir Robert Welles, Lord Willoughby, was executed at Doncaster. His body was buried at the Carmelite priory (Whitefriars). Meanwhile, Edward had mustered his army in preparation for another possible armed conflict. However, the battle which he expected did not take place. Instead, of openly confronting the king and his army, Clarence and Warwick fled in the direction of Manchester. The brother and cousin of the king were now desperately hoping to gain the support of Lord Stanley. However, no such support materialised.

On Sunday 25 March, having arrived in the city of York, Edward IV restored to the Percy family their ancient earldom of Northumberland. The king had previously granted this title to Warwick's brother, John Neville, who had remained impeccably loyal to him throughout. However, Edward felt that he now urgently needed to win over the Percys to his support. Thus, rather insultingly, John Neville suddenly found himself deprived of his Northumberland title. In theoretical compensation for the loss of the earldom of Northumberland, the king granted John a newly invented marquisate. But the long-term result of this action proved to be that Edward had now forfeited John Neville's loyalty.

Meanwhile Warwick and Clarence had reached the West Country, where they found themselves in a very weak and perilous position. They therefore decided to flee the country. The two lords embarked at Exeter and sailed off in the direction of Calais, taking with them their wives, children, and as many of their supporters as they could. Warwick's daughter, the Duchess of Clarence was nearing the end of her first pregnancy and it was a bad time for her to be travelling, but, of course, she could hardly be abandoned in England.

Warwick was still the captain of Calais. As we have seen, he had profited from this fact on earlier occasions, using Calais as his base when things were not safe for him in England. In his absence, of course, the Calais garrison was commanded by his lieutenant, Lord Wenlock. Naturally, Warwick now expected Wenlock to welcome his lord's return. However, Lord Wenlock became known – not without some justification – as 'the prince of turncoats'.

The problem was that Edward IV had sent an urgent message to Lord Wenlock, commanding him not to allow Warwick and Clarence to land in Calais. This message had managed to reach Wenlock just a short time before Warwick's ship was sighted. Thus, despite the fact that Warwick was his lord, Wenlock decided that he had no option other than to obey the king's instructions. As a result, Warwick and Clarence and their party found themselves not allowed to land. Indeed, warning cannon shots were fired from Calais in the direction of their ship.

Meanwhile, the unfortunate Duchess of Clarence had gone into labour on board the ship. There she eventually gave birth to her first child. Appeals to Lord Wenlock persuaded him to send two flagons of wine to the young duchess to ease her labour. However, her little baby had a difficult birth, and died in the process, or very shortly afterwards. Since the party was not permitted to land in Calais, the baby's body then had to be buried at sea.

Having failed to gain entry to Calais, Warwick and Clarence considered the possibility of returning to England. But despite his cannon shots at their ships, Lord Wenlock was still, in a way, the friend of Warwick. He therefore had different advice to offer to his lord.

When the Earl of Warwick stood off Calais, hoping to enter the town as his principal place of refuge, Lord Wenlock, who was very clever, sent him word that if he entered he would be lost, for he had all of England against him as well as the duke of Burgundy, the people of the town and several of the garrison in Calais, including my lord of Duras [Gaillard de Durfort], the king of England's Marshall and some others, who all had men in the town. The best thing he could do was to withdraw to France. He told him that he should not worry about Calais because he would give him satisfaction at the right time.[1]

Following Wenlock's advice, the Earl of Warwick and his party therefore sailed westwards along the French coast to Normandy. This was part of the territory of Warwick's friend, King Louis XI of France, and here, at the port of Honfleur, Warwick and his family finally landed. Shortly after their arrival in his kingdom, they were greeted by King Louis XI in person. The Earl of Warwick 'was very well received by the King, who gave him large sums of money for his troops'.[2] Indeed, the French sovereign apparently had a lasting and genuine regard for Warwick.

Meanwhile, Warwick had obviously been thinking hard, during his sea voyages and his frustrating reception at Calais, about the possible ways forward. As a result he had now come to a truly astonishing conclusion. What he now proposed to the French king was a campaign to oust his cousin, Edward IV, and to restore to the English throne the Lancastrian, King Henry VI.

Of course, Henry VI himself was Edward IV's prisoner, held in the Tower of London. However, Henry's wife, Margaret of Anjou, together with her son, Edward of Westminster, had sought refuge with Margaret's cousin, King Louis. The French king was probably amazed, at first, to hear Warwick's new plans. Nevertheless, he sent to his cousin Margaret, inviting her and her son to come to Amboise to discuss what the Earl was now proposing. Margaret hated the Earl of Warwick, whom she saw as her implacable enemy. Her initial response to Louis XI's invitation was therefore very unenthusiastic. However, the French king persevered, and eventually Margaret agreed to come and meet her former enemy.

It is absolutely clear from the evidence of their actions that, up to this point, Warwick and Clarence had at no previous stage been campaigning to dethrone Edward IV. Their objective had simply been to remove the upstart Woodville family from power, and to ensure that King Edward had the right advisors – namely themselves. Warwick may also have hoped to oust Elizabeth Woodville's children from the English succession and reinstate the Duke of Clarence as heir, so that one day his own grandson – the child of his daughter Isabel and of George – would be able to sit upon the English throne.

However, now the situation had changed dramatically, and Warwick was planning to dethrone Edward IV and restore Henry VI. Thus, new plans were also needed for the future of Warwick's own family. The obvious way of now ensuring that his own descendants would one day wear the English crown was for Warwick to propose a marriage between his younger daughter, Anne Neville, and Margaret of Anjou's son, Edward of Westminster, Prince of Wales – and this is what he did. As soon as a new marriage contract between Anne Neville and the Lancastrian prince had been agreed, a papal dispensation to allow these cousins to marry was requested. Their wedding could not be celebrated until such a dispensation was obtained from Rome, because the new bride and groom were both great-great-grandchildren of

John of Gaunt. They were therefore related to one another in the prohibited fourth degree of consanguinity.

Meanwhile, however, Warwick had not forgotten the potential future of his elder daughter and her husband, the Duke of Clarence. On their behalf, he also negotiated with Margaret of Anjou an important agreement to the effect that Clarence should now become the Duke of York. Moreover, he was also to be acknowledged as the next in line for the crown of England if Edward of Westminster should die without leaving any children. Thus Clarence now found himself granted that same acknowledgement which his late father had sought for so many years, namely that he was a *Lancastrian* heir to the throne. It is evident, therefore, that Warwick, who had no sons of his own, was still doing his best to secure the future of his son-in-law, cousin, and long-term close ally, Clarence.

But for his part, Clarence himself now seems to have felt that there was a growing gulf between him and his father-in-law in terms of their political goals. At the same time, back in England, Edward IV had also become aware of the growing gulf between Clarence and Warwick. The Yorkist king now sought to take advantage of the situation by making the gap between them greater. For this purpose, Edward sent a lady to France with a secret message. The name of his secret envoy is not recorded, but we know that she had been in the service of the Duchess Isabel – and would therefore be welcomed by the exiled Clarences. Her purpose was to win Clarence back to the side of his brother, Edward IV, and to the support of his own family – the house of York. As subsequent events show, this mysterious lady – one of the earliest recorded English female diplomats – obviously carried out her appointed task very well.

She won over the duke of Clarence, who promised to join his brother, the king, as soon as he came back to England. This woman was not a fool and she did not speak lightly. She had the opportunity to visit her mistress and for this reason she was able to go sooner than a man. And however cunning Lord Wenlock was this woman deceived him and carried out this secret assignment which led to the defeat and death of the earl of Warwick and all his followers.[3]

As we have seen, although a marriage between Anne Neville and Edward of Westminster had now been agreed, because of their blood relationship it could not actually be celebrated until the Pope's permission for the union was received. Meanwhile, preparations were under way for Warwick's return to England. On Sunday 9 September accompanied by the Duke of Clarence, the Admiral of France, the 'Earl of Pembroke' (Jasper 'Tudor'), and the Earl of Oxford, Warwick embarked for England. He left his wife and daughters in France. There, as soon as the Pope's dispensation for Anne Neville's wedding arrived, she was to be married to Edward of Westminster. This marriage was indeed celebrated, after Warwick's departure. However, Margaret of Anjou was obviously not fully committed to her new alliance with the Neville family – for she seems to have ensured that her son's union with Anne Neville was never consummated.

Meanwhile, Warwick and his Lancastrian invaders had landed in the West Country on the night of Thursday 13 September. There they issued a joint proclamation naming Henry VI as king. As their forces moved northwards and eastwards, 'a great number of men joined [Warwick] and he was in a strong position'.[4] Among those noblemen who now united with Warwick were Lord Stanley and the Earl of Shrewsbury.

Since Warwick himself was in the West Country, it is often stated in modern accounts that it was Warwick's brother, Archbishop George Neville of York, who went to the Tower of London and freed King Henry VI from his rather grubby prison. Other versions of the story claim that Henry was eventually released by Warwick in person. However, John Stow – who wrote his report about a century after the event but who was a citizen of London, and may therefore have known the truth – states that

> in the year 1470, the Tower was yielded to Sir Richard Lee, mayor of London, and his brethren the aldermen, who forthwith entered the same, delivered King Henry of his imprisonment, and lodged him in the king's lodging there.[5]

The Earl of Warwick himself reached the capital on Saturday 6 October.

At the time when Warwick landed, Edward IV had been in the north of England. His brother-in-law, 'the duke of Burgundy had informed King Edward clearly about the port where the earl would land ... but he paid no attention to him and only continued his hunting. No one was closer to him than the archbishop of York and the marquis of Montague, brothers of the earl of Warwick, who had given him a very solemn undertaking to serve him against their brother and all others. He had confidence in this.'[6]

But once Warwick had landed, and gained support, Edward IV 'recognised the danger [and] began to look to his own affairs, although it was too late. He sent to the duke of Burgundy imploring him to keep his fleet at sea so that the earl could not return to France. On land, he said, things would turn out well.

These words did not please the duke very much because he thought that it would have been better to have prevented the earl from landing in England than to be forced to bring him to a battle.'7

Marching southwards, Edward summoned Warwick's brother, John Neville, to his support. At first the marquis dutifully set out. But he obviously felt himself to be in a state of turmoil. In the end he halted his men and gave them a speech in which he said that Edward IV had treated him badly, depriving him of the earldom of Northumberland. He then announced his support for his brother, Warwick, and asked his men to shout, 'Long live King Henry!' Most of his men accepted what he said, and changed loyalty with their lord.

Edward IV was now in a panic. 'There were several good knights and esquires who all recognised that things were going badly.'8 Accompanied by his youngest brother, Richard, Duke of Gloucester, his brother-in-law, Anthony Woodville, Earl Rivers, his friend, Lord Hastings, and a few other loyal supporters, he fled to the north coast of East Anglia. 'By divine providence the king was camped close to the sea and some ships were following him, bringing victuals. These included two flat-bottomed merchant ships from Holland. He just had time to take refuge in them.'9 Edward and his party thus embarked and sailed from Bishop's Lynn (the modern King's Lynn) to Flanders.

Meanwhile, Elizabeth Woodville was still in the English capital. She had not accompanied her husband on his journey north because she was eight months pregnant. Now she too panicked and fled into sanctuary at Westminster Abbey, accompanied by her mother and her children.

When the Duke of Clarence arrived in London he took up

residence at the Erber, a property previously owned by the Earl
of Warwick's father. (Cannon Street Station now stands upon
the site.) But Clarence had no real role to play in the restored
Lancastrian regime, and was able to exert very little influence over
the new government. Moreover, as we have seen, before leaving
France he had heard from the mysterious female messenger sent
to him by Edward IV. Thus, when his mother and his eldest sister,
the Duchess of Exeter, quietly contacted him, aiming to win him
back to the Yorkist side, their words fell on very receptive ears. At
the same time in Flanders his youngest sister, Margaret, Duchess of
Burgundy, was also busy persuading Edward IV to be reconciled
with George.

Edward IV's flight to the Low Countries had not gone easily.

He fled straight to Holland. At this time the Easterlings were
enemies of both the English and the French and had several
warships at sea. The English were very frightened of them and
not without cause, for they were good fighters. ... The Easterlings
espied the ships in which the king was fleeing from a great distance
and seven or eight ships began to give chase. But he was too far
ahead of them and reached Holland or rather a little further up
the coat because he landed close to a small town called Alkmaar
in Frisia [just north of Amsterdam]. He anchored his ship because
the tide was out, and they could not enter the harbour, but they
came as close to the town as they could. The Easterlings did the
same, anchoring close to him with the intention of boarding him at
the next tide. ... [But] by chance my lord of Gruthuse, the duke of
Burgundy's governor in Holland, was then at the place where King
Edward wanted to disembark. He was immediately told about this,
for they had landed some men, and about the danger they were in

from the Easterlings. Straight away he sent word to the Easterlings forbidding them to attack Edward, and went aboard the ship the king was in to welcome him. Edward then landed together with fifteen hundred men, including the duke of Gloucester, his brother, who later became King Richard.[10]

Edward IV and his brother Richard, Duke of Gloucester, had embarked on 29 September 1470, and they were in The Hague by 11 October.[11] They had been accompanied by a number of loyal supporters, probably including the Portuguese Jew, Duarte Brandão, who had settled in England in 1468 and converted to Christianity under the patronage of Edward IV, with the name Edward Brampton (or Brandon). Brampton was later to play a significant role in the Low Countries on behalf of Edward IV and his heirs.

The two Yorkist royal brothers spent the winter of 1470 in exile in the Low Countries, as the guests of Louis de Gruuthuse, governor (*stadtholder*) of The Hague. Gruuthuse, whose family came from Brugge, and who had helped to arrange the wedding of Margaret of York and Charles the Bold, was related by marriage to the Scottish and French royal families.

Richard, Duke of Gloucester, was still unmarried. As for Edward IV, he now found himself separated from his usual spouse. It is therefore conceivable that either (or both) of the royal brothers might have sought for themselves a local mistress in Gruuthuse's household during this exile. The most likely brother of the two to have done so, given what we know of their characters in this respect, would probably have been Edward IV. If Edward had engendered a pregnancy as a result of such a relationship, around the middle of his exile in the Low Countries (i.e. in about

December 1470), an illegitimate child of his might subsequently have been born after the Yorkist king's return to England, in about September 1471. This speculation is of possible relevance to the wider story of the Wars of the Roses, and we shall return to explore its potential significance in greater detail later (see below, chapter 12).

In the meantime, however,

In the yere of grace 1471, after the comptinge of the churche of Englande,[12] the ij. day of Marche, endynge the x. yere of the reigne of our sovereign Lord Kynge Edwarde the IV. by the grace of God Kynge of England and of Fraunce, and Lord of Irland, the sayde moast noble kynge accompanied with ij thowsand Englysshe men, well chosen, entendynge to passe the sea and to reentar and recovar his realme of England, at that tyme usurpyd and occupied by Henry, callyd Henry the VI., by the traitorous meanes of his greate rebel Richyard, Erle of Warwicke, and his complices, entred into his shipe, afore the haven of Flisshinge, in Zeland, the sayde ij. day of Marche; and forasmoche as aftar he was in the shippe, and the felowshipe also, with all that to them appertained, the wynd fell not good for hym, he therefore wold not retorne agayne to the land, but abode in his shipe, and all his felowshipe in lyke wyse, by the space of ix days, abydynge good wynde and wether; whiche had the xj. daye of Marche, he made saile, and so did all the shipps that awayted upon hym, taking theyr cowrse streyght over [towards] the coste of Norfolke, and came before Crowmere, the Tuesdaye, agayne even, the xij. day of Marche; whithar the Kynge sent on land Ser Robart Chambarlayne, Syr Gilbert Debenham, Knyghts, and othar, trustinge by them to have some knowledge of how the land inward was disposed toward hym.[13]

The knights discovered that Edward's cousin and supporter, the Duke of Norfolk, was a virtual prisoner in London, and that the hostile Earl of Oxford was controlling the eastern counties. Therefore obviously Cromer was not a safe landing place. 'natheles, the sayd ij Knyghts, and they that came on land with them, had right good chere, and turned agayne to the sea. Whos report herd, the Kynge garte make course towards the north partyes'.[14]

Despite storms and tempests, on 14 March the ships were at Humberhead, and by 18 March Edward had reached York. He then marched south towards Coventry. The Earl of Warwick withdrew as Edward approached. Unable to bring the Earl to battle, Edward IV took control of the town of Warwick. It was there, towards the end of March, that he met once again with his brother, the Duke of Clarence.

> By right covert wayes and meanes were good mediators, and mediatricis, the highe and mighty princis my Lady, theyr mothar; my lady of Exceter, my lady of Southfolke, theyre systars; my Lord Cardinall of Cantorbery; my Lorde of Bathe, my Lord of Essex; and, moste specially, my Lady of Bourgoigne ... a parfecte accord was appoyntyd, accordyd, concludyd and assured betwixt them; wherein the sayde Duke of Clarence full honourably and trwly acquitted hym.[15]

George duly made his peace with Edward, and his men added the Yorkist white rose badge to the Clarence gorget badge which they were wearing on their liveries.

Incidentally, in the wider context of the so-called Wars of the Roses, this raises an interesting and very significant point. It is generally assumed that all members of the house of York used the white rose badge. Actually, however, there is absolutely no evidence to that effect. Indeed, it would have been rather impractical. Badges were meant to be individual – and were then worn by the people in the individual's service, to indicate whom they served. The fact that men serving the Duke of Clarence normally wore his own gorget badge – or possibly his alternative black bull badge – and that in March 1470/1 they had to add the white rose emblem to show they were now also serving King Edward IV – reveals the reality of the situation.

Essentially the white rose was the badge of King Edward IV. His younger brother, Richard Duke of Gloucester is also unlikely to have used it, at least, while Edward was alive. The evidence we have shows that the badge associated with Richard was the white boar, not the white rose. After succeeding Edward IV as king, Richard may have adopted the white rose badge as a secondary emblem, but the evidence relating to the Battle of Bosworth appears to show that the white boar definitely remained his chief personal symbol. Later, the white rose badge was certainly adopted by whoever saw himself as the Yorkist heir. But there is no evidence to suggest that it was used as a heraldic emblem by *every* descendant of the house of York.

The news was spreading that Edward IV had returned to his kingdom and was moving southwards in the direction of the capital. In the Eastern Counties Lord Howard emerged from Colchester Abbey, where he had been hiding in sanctuary, and publicly proclaimed Edward as king once more. Meanwhile, in spite of his return to his Yorkist allegiance, Clarence had not deserted his father-in-law, the Earl of Warwick.

The Duke of Clarence, beinge right desyrows to have procuryd a goode accorde betwixt the Kynge and th'Erle of Warwyke; not only for th'Erle, but also for to reconsyle therby unto the Kyngs good grace many lords and noble men of his land, of whom many had largly taken parte with th'Erle ... made, therefore, his mocions, as well to the Kynge as to th'Erle, by messagis sendynge to and fro, bothe for the well above sayde, as to acquite hym trwly and kindly in the love he bare unto hym, and his blood, whereunto he was allied by the marriage of his dowghtar.[16]

Sadly, however, Clarence found that his father-in-law could not be won over.

On Saturday 6 April Edward IV reached Daventry. There, the following morning, he attended the celebration of Palm Sunday in the parish church. 'The Kynge went in procession and all the people aftar, in goode devotion, as the service of that daye askethe, and, whan the procession was comen into the churche, and, by order of the service, were comen to that place where the vale shulbe drawne up afore the Roode, that all the people shall honor the Roode,'[17] a miracle happened. During his exile, Edward IV had been praying to various saints for help. But his most particular devotion had been to the mother of the Blessed Virgin Mary, St Anne.

In the parish church at Daventry,

aforne the place where the Kynge knelyd, and devowtly honoryd the Roode, was a lytle ymage of Seint Anne, made of alleblastar ... and this ymage was thus shett, closed and clasped, accordynge to the rules that, in all then churchis of England, be observyd, all ymages to be hid from Ashe Wednesday to Estarday in the mornynge.[18]

However, when the king knelt before the Holy Cross, the doors which enclosed the nearby image of St Anne 'gave a great crak and ... openyd all abrod',[19] revealing the statue. The king rejoiced, taking this as a sign of the saint's blessing to him and his cause. Unfortunately the church in which this incident took place does not survive, having been rebuilt in the sixteenth and in the eighteenth centuries.

Meanwhile, from a distance, the Earl of Warwick desperately tried to stir up Londoners to support the Lancastrian King Henry VI. On his instructions his brother, the Archbishop of York, arranged a royal procession around London on Tuesday 9 April. Archbishop Neville 'cawsed Henry, callyd Kynge, to take an horse and ryde from Powles thrwghe Chepe, and so made a circuit abowte to Walbroke, as the generall processyon of London hathe bene accustomyd, and so returned agayne to Powles, to the Bysshops Palays, where the sayd Henry at that tyme was lodged, supposynge, that, what he has shewyd hym in this arraye, they shuld have provokyd the citizens, and th'enhabitants of the citie, to have stoned and comen to them, and fortified that partye'.[20] However, Henry VI reportedly appeared so feeble that he attracted very little support.

Edward IV spent the night of Tuesday 9 April at St Albans. The following day, his forces secured the Tower of London. The Earl of Warwick himself had been shadowing Edward IV's march on London in the hope of tackling him at some point. But no suitable opportunity had arisen, and Warwick was dismayed to observe the speed with which Edward IV repossessed his capital city. On Maundy Thursday Edward IV rode to St Paul's Cathedral and took charge of his rival, Henry VI. He then rode to Westminster to extract his consort, Elizabeth Woodville, from the sanctuary there, discovering in the process that 'she had browght into this worlde, to the Kyngs greatyste joy, a fayre sonn, a prince, where with

1. Richard II. Nineteenth-century engraving after the fourteenth-century portrait at Westminster Abbey.

Left: 2. Lionel of Antwerp, Duke of Clarence, 3rd son of Edward III and ancestor of the royal house of York. Nineteenth-century engraving from the effigy on his father's tomb at Westminster. *Right:* 3. Thomas, Duke of Gloucester, the uncle whom Richard II had killed. Thomas may have used a white rose as his emblem. In this picture he is wearing a rose badge on his shoulder. Nineteenth-century engraving after BL MS Cotton Nero D VII.

Left: 4. Henry IV, first king of the house of Lancaster, and his second wife, Joan of Navarre, from their tomb effigies at Canterbury Cathedral.

Right: 5. Henry V, redrawn from a fifteenth-century portrait at the National Portrait gallery. © M. Hanif.

6. Catherine of France, consort of Henry V. A reconstruction combining her funeral effigy features with contemporary female costume. © M. Hanif.

Right: 7. Cardinal Beaufort, from a stone effigy at his palace of Bishop's Waltham. © Historic England.

Below: 8. Cardinal Beaufort, from the Coventry Tapestry, courtesy of St Mary's Guildhall and Coventry City Council.

Left: 9. The Church of St Julien, Southampton, where Richard of York, Earl of Cambridge, was buried after his execution in 1415. © Peter Anderson.

Below: 10. Edmund Beaufort, later Duke of Somerset, from the tomb of his father-in-law, Richard Beauchamp, Earl of Warwick.

Left: 11. Richard, Duke of York, redrawn after his only surviving authentic contemporary portrait, a fifteenth-century MS in the British Library.

Right: 12. Humphrey of Lancaster, Duke of Gloucester, redrawn after a fifteenth-century sketch at Arras. © M. Hanif.

13. Henry VI, redrawn from a contemporary image in the diary of Jörg von Ehingen, who met him in the late 1450s. © M. Hanif.

Above left: 14. Margaret of Anjou praying, redrawn after the London Skinners' Fraternity of the Assumption Guild Book, 1475. © M. Hanif.

Above right: 15. Edmund 'Tudor', Earl of Richmond, from the nineteenth-century restoration of his tomb brass.

Below: 16. A modern reproduction of one version of the *rose-en-soleil* badge of Edward, Earl of March (Edward IV).

17. Dr John Morton, based on the depiction of his head in the roof of Bere Regis Church, Dorset.

18. A facial reconstruction of Eleanor Talbot, based on what may be her surviving skull from the Norwich Carmel. © M. Satchwill.

19. Richard Neville, Earl
of Warwick, from the
tomb of his father-in-law,
Richard Beauchamp, Earl
of Warwick.

20. Edward IV, courtesy of
the Society of Antiquaries
of London.

21. Elizabeth Woodville. © The President and Fellows, Queens' College, Cambridge.

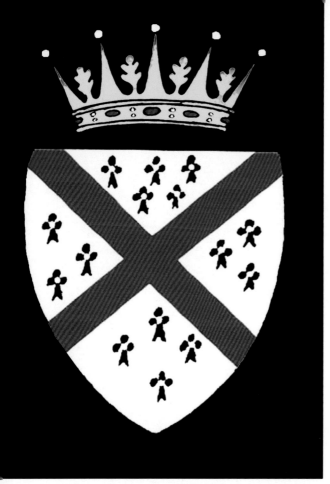

22. The arms of Thomas Fitzgerald, Earl of Desmond.

23. Isabel Neville, daughter of the Earl of Warwick and wife of the Duke of Clarence. Nineteenth-century engraving after the Rous Roll.

Above left: 24. The young Edward of Westminster, Prince of Wales, redrawn from the Rous Roll. © M. Hanif.

Above right: 25. George, Duke of Clarence, from the Coventry Tapestry, courtesy of St Mary's Guildhall and Coventry City Council.

Below: 26. Possible skull of George, Duke of Clarence, showing a healed sword cut to the front of the head. Clarence Vault, Tewkesbury.

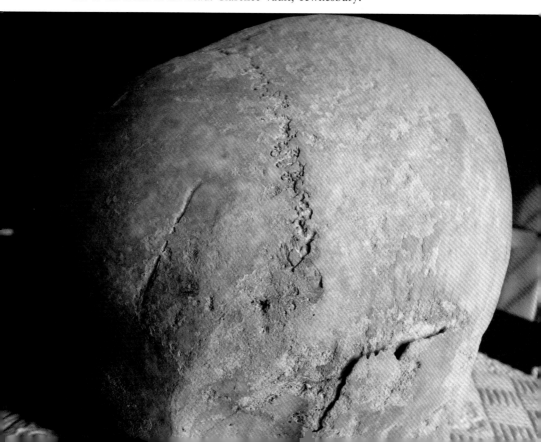

27. Edward of
Westminster, Prince
of Wales, from the
Coventry Tapestry,
courtesy of St
Mary's Guildhall
and Coventry City
Council.

Left: 28. Anne Neville, younger daughter of the Earl of Warwick, and later
Princess of Wales and Queen of England. A nineteenth-century engraving of an
image from the Rous Roll. *Right:* 29. Edward V.

Above left: 30. Elizabeth of York. Nineteenth-century engraving.

Above right: 31. Richard III, from the Coventry Tapestry, courtesy of St Mary's Guildhall and Coventry City Council.

32. Margaret Beaufort, Countess of Richmond and Derby. Nineteenth-century engraving.

Above left: 33. Margaret of York, Duchess of Burgundy, a copy of her marriage portrait of 1468. Note that this Yorkist princess is wearing both white and red roses on her collar – an indication that, while the rose was definitely a Yorkist emblem, the rose *colour* may not have been particularly significant in the 1460s.

Above right: 34. The great seal of 'King Edward VI', courtesy of the National Library of Ireland.

Left: 35. Henry VII, courtesy of the Society of Antiquaries of London.

Left: 36. 'Richard IV', redrawn from the contemporary image at Arras.

Right: 37. Emperor Charles V. Nineteenth-century engraving.

38. Philip II of Spain.
Nineteenth-century
engraving.

WARD COURTNEY Earl of DEVONSHIRE.

an Original by Sr Antonio More, at the Duke of Bedfords at Woburn

Left: 39. Edward Courtenay, Earl of Devonshire, great-grandson of Edward IV. Eighteenth-century engraving.

Below: 40. The tomb effigy of Philippa of Lancaster, Queen of Portugal, Monastery of Santa Maria da Vitoria (Capela do Fundador), Batalha, Leira, Portugal. © Conway Library, The Courtauld Institute of Art, London.

she presentyd hym at his comynge'.[21] They then joined Edward's mother at Baynard's Castle, where they heard the Mass of the Last Supper, and where presumably Edward washed the feet of the poor.

Meanwhile, the Earl of Warwick camped a few miles to the north of London, at Barnet. He was unable to advance further. Indeed, on Holy Saturday, 13 April, Warwick's outposts were driven back by the king's advancing forces. Having secured possession of his capital, Edward IV was now planning to deal with his cousin. The king was supported by just under 1,000 men, while Warwick had a slightly larger army, which he had disposed on the plateau which runs from Hadley Green to Barnet. The two forces camped very close to each other during the night of 13–14 April. Indeed, at one point Warwick ordered his cannon to fire on the king's troops. However, his gunners missed their mark.

On the morning of Easter Day, Sunday 14 April, the battle began in earnest, soon after 4 a. m. It was a very misty morning. Thanks to the mist the visibility was rather poor and it was not easy to see clearly. One result of this was that the two armies were not accurately aligned. Warwick's right flank, led by the Earl of Oxford, was too far too the west, while the king's right flank, commanded by the Duke of Gloucester, was too far to the east. Nevertheless, Oxford's men made contact with Edward IV's left flank, under Lord Hastings. In fact they succeeded in driving Hasting back. But as a result of this, Oxford's men found themselves in the town of Barnet, where they gave up serious fighting in order to start looting. The Earl of Oxford had trouble getting them back together. When at last he had done so, he led them back in a northerly direction. Unfortunately, in the morning mist, his colleague, Edmund Beaufort, whom the Lancastrians now called 'Duke of Somerset', thought that Oxford's approaching force must be Yorkists and therefore fired upon them. As a result of this, many of Oxford's men then fled the battlefield crying 'treason'.

The most intensive hand-to-hand fighting was in the centre. There, many men were wounded either in the head or in the legs. Among the injured was George, Duke of Clarence, who suffered a wound, traces of which are possibly still discernible on a surviving skull at Tewkesbury which may perhaps be his (see plate 26). Clarence's younger brother, Richard, Duke of Gloucester, also suffered a slight injury. As for George's father-in-law, Richard Neville, the 'Kingmaker', Earl of Warwick, was killed in the battle as he struggled to remount his horse. His brother, John Neville, Marquis of Montagu(e) was also killed. The battle had lasted for about three hours. When the fighting ended, it was still very early in the morning.

> On the morrow aftar, the Kynge commandyd that the bodyes of the dead lords, th'Erle of Warwicke, and hys brother the Marques, shuld be browght to Powles in London, and in the churche there, openly shewyd to all the people; to th'entent that, aftar that, the people shuld not be abused by feyned seditiows tales, which many of them ... would have made aftar that, ne had the deade bodyes there be shewyd, opne, and naked.[22]

Meanwhile, as we have seen, in September 1470, the ladies of the Neville family had not sailed back to England with Warwick and Clarence. Instead, they remained in Normandy with Margaret of Anjou and Edward of Westminster. Initially, the young Anne Neville was waiting for the papal dispensation which was required before her marriage to Edward of Westminster could be formalised. The marriage of Anne and Edward was finally celebrated at Bayeux, on about 13 December 1470. However, Margaret of Anjou would not allow the marriage to be consummated. Before firmly committing her son to a union with Warwick's daughter, she wanted to see what Warwick would do for her cause in England.

In the spring of 1470/1, after the celebration of his marriage with Anne Neville, Edward of Westminster set sail, with his mother and his bride, for England. But the Countess of Warwick – probably accompanied by her elder daughter, the Duchess of Clarence – did not travel with the royal party. She sailed in her own separate ship. Unfortunately, there were problems with the weather. In particular, the winds were against them. Thus it took them two weeks to make the short voyage across the Channel. On the way the winds had separated the two vessels, which then followed different routes and sailed at different speeds. In the end it was the Countess of Warwick who reached England first. Originally, both ships had planned to land at Weymouth, in Dorset, but the ship bearing the countess ultimately ended up further east, at Portsmouth in Hampshire.

Meanwhile, the ship carrying the Lancastrian queen and Prince of Wales took longer to make its landfall. However, their vessel did finally succeed in reaching the planned destination port of Weymouth. There the party of Henry VI's queen landed on the evening of Easter Sunday (14 April). This was, of course, the very day on which the battle of Barnet had been fought. Early that same morning, the Earl of Warwick had been defeated and killed. But of course, when the Lancastrians landed, news of the day's battle had not yet reached the West Country. Thus Margaret of Anjou, her son and her daughter-in-law spent the night not far from the port at which they had landed, at Cerne Abbey. Then the following morning Edmund Beaufort, the titular 4th Duke of Somerset, brought them tidings of the Barnet defeat.

As for the Countess of Warwick and her party, soon after they had landed at Portsmouth, they had set off north-westwards towards Southampton. The plan was for them to meet up with Margaret of Anjou's group. But the meeting never took place, for it was at Southampton that the Countess heard that her powerful husband had been defeated and killed. Panic then set in, and she gave up any idea of seeking Margaret of Anjou. Instead, she dashed to Beaulieu Abbey, where she claimed sanctuary.

Left to herself, on receiving news of the defeat at the battle of Barnet, Margaret of Anjou might also have given up, and been inclined to get straight back on her ship and sail off to France and safety. However, her young son argued strongly that they should keep up their struggle for the crown of England. Edward was hoping to meet up with his 'Tudor' relations, and gain their backing. Therefore he and his mother headed towards Wales. They were still accompanied by Edward's young theoretical wife, Anne Neville, though the girl's chances of ever having her marriage accepted and consummated must, by this time, have become rather slim.

Forces loyal to Edward IV prevented the Lancastrians from crossing the River Severn at Gloucester, therefore they made for Tewkesbury. However, they were now being very closely shadowed by Edward IV and his troops. The Yorkist army finally forced the Lancastrians into battle just outside the town of Tewkesbury. Once again, Margaret of Anjou was initially inclined to avoid a battle at all costs. However, the 'Duke of Somerset' urged her to confront the enemy. Thus the disastrous battle of Tewkesbury was fought.

'Somerset' and Edward of Westminster were both killed as a result. 'Somerset' was captured after the battle, when he was found hiding in the town of Tewkesbury together with the Prior of St John's (Sir John Langstother) and a number of other knights and squires. These captives were tried by the king's brother, Richard, Duke of Gloucester, Constable of England, and his cousin John Mowbray, 4th Duke of Norfolk, Marshall of England. The Lancastrians were sentenced to death and 'were executyd in the mydste of the towne, upon a scaffold therefore made, behedyd evereche one, and without eny other dismembringe, or settynge up, licensyd to be buryed'.²³ There are various later accounts of what happened to Edward of Westminster, but according to the contemporary evidence, it seems that he 'was taken, fleinge to the towne wards, and slayne, in the fielde'.²⁴ The grief-stricken Margaret of Anjou sought refuge in a nearby convent, where she was found three days later.

Within about a month of the battle of Tewkesbury, King Henry VI died in his prison at the Tower of London. He was forty-nine years old – quite a good age for a male member of the house of Lancaster. In fact, Henry VI lived longer than his father, Henry V, his uncle, John of Lancaster, Duke of Bedford, and his grandfather, Henry IV. Of the immediate male members of his family, only one of his uncles, Humphrey, Duke of Gloucester, lived longer than he did, dying at the age of fifty-six. Nevertheless, according to later accounts, Henry VI was reported to have been murdered, and his death is usually stated to have occurred on the night of 21 May 1471.

Actually, neither of these points is certain. His death certainly occurred at quite a convenient moment from the point of view of Edward IV. But Henry VI's health had been rather indifferent for a number of years. As for the date, only *one* fifteenth-century source claims that Henry died on Tuesday night, 21 May. Another fifteenth-century source – the *Arrivall* – says the death occurred on 23 May, while other fifteenth-century sources which give no specific date nevertheless suggest that Henry died a week or two later (towards the end of May or possibly early in June). One modern historian has argued that he died on morning of Wednesday 22 May, while another has shown that payments for Henry's keep at the Tower of London continued until at least 24 May. Therefore Henry VI's generally accepted death date of 21 May should actually be treated with very great caution.

Of course, thanks to later (hostile) propaganda, Henry's death has frequently been attributed to Richard, Duke of Gloucester, (later Richard III). Indeed, it is one of the many alleged deaths which are supposed to show that Richard was a serial killer. But in reality there is absolutely no evidence that Richard was in any way involved. If Henry was killed, the most likely person responsible for his death would have been King Edward IV.

However, the account given in the *Arrivall* states specifically that the death of Henry VI was natural. It says that when Henry learned of the loss of his putative son and heir, the capture of his wife, and the complete defeat of his partisans 'he toke it to so great dispite, ire, and indingnation, that, of pure displeasure, and melencoly, he dyed the xxiij. day of the monithe of May. Whom the Kynge [Edward IV] dyd to be browght to the frieres prechars [Blackfriars'] at London, and there, his funeral service donne, to be carried by water, to an Abbey upon Thamys syd, xvj myles from London, called Chartsey, and there honourably enteryd.'[25]

Although Henry VI was initially buried in a private grave at Chertsey Abbey, in 1484 Richard III had the body moved and gave Henry VI a royal tomb in the Chapel Royal of St George's in Windsor Castle. This was an honourable royal fate which, ironically, was recently denied to Richard III's own remains.

The death of Henry VI, closely preceded by the death of the Lancastrian Prince of Wales, raises a highly significant question. Who was now the Lancastrian heir to the English throne? Of course, this role was later claimed by Henry 'Tudor' (King Henry VII), but his claim was nothing more than a myth – the latest, and weakest example of the earlier Beaufort claim to the throne. The reality was very different. But it is open to two possible interpretations.

First, as we have seen, according to the terms of an agreement made between Margaret of Anjou and the Duke of Clarence – an agreement later confirmed and endorsed by Henry VI himself – George, Duke of Clarence, had been formally recognised and acknowledged as the next Lancastrian heir to the throne after Edward of Westminster. This legal claim was not subsequently forgotten. It was to prove significant at two later stages of the ongoing conflict, in 1476 and in 1485 (see below, chapter 9 and chapter 11).

Second, in terms of the Lancastrian royal bloodline, in 1471 the senior living descendants of John of Gaunt and his first wife, Blanche of Lancaster comprised the Portuguese royal family. This family was very well aware of its Lancastrian royal descent. But despite this, no attempt to claim the English throne was heard from Portugal following news of the death of Henry VI. However, one Portuguese princess in the Low Countries – Isabel of Portugal, dowager Duchess of Burgundy, the mother of Charles the Bold and the mother-in-law (and friend) of Margaret of York – did formally register a claim with the English Parliament on 17 June 1471.[26] Isabel's claim requested that *she* should be regarded as the heir of her late cousin, Henry VI.

Isabel's action was somewhat strange. Her eldest brother, King Duarte (Edward), had died many years earlier, in 1438, but her nephew, King Alfonso V of Portugal, was still living and reigning in 1471. Alfonso was thus the senior living descendant of the royal house of Lancaster, and therefore the rightful Lancastrian heir to the throne of England in terms of bloodline.

But although Alfonso himself did nothing about this in 1471, other descendants of the Portuguese royal family asserted their Lancastrian claim to the throne of England in the sixteenth century. As we shall see, this claim was initially put forward on behalf of King Alfonso's great nephew, Emperor Charles V, in the 1530s. At that point no military action ensued. However, half a century later, in 1588, Charles V's son, Philip II of Spain, reasserted the claim to the English crown. This resulted in what must, in one sense, be regarded as the last battle of the Wars of the Roses – namely, the Spanish Armada. We shall return to that story later.

9

NEW SUCCESSION PROBLEMS

With Henry VI and Edward of Westminster both dead, and with the house of Beaufort now extinct in the legitimate male line, in terms of lineal descent from John of Gaunt, or from Edmund Crouchback, no obvious Lancastrian claimant to the throne remained alive in England. The only possible contender would have been Edward IV's brother-in-law, Henry Holland, 3rd Duke of Exeter. Henry Holland was a grandson of Henry IV's sister, Elizabeth of Lancaster. However, he had never been taken seriously as a potential Lancastrian claimant to the throne because of his unpopularity and his unpredictable temper. The Duke of Exeter survived until 1475. He is then thought to have been put to death by drowning, on the orders of King Edward IV. However, in the aftermath of the battle of Barnet (at which he had commanded the Lancastrian left flank) he had, in any case, been imprisoned by Edward.

In this situation, and given the fact that Richard, Duke of York, had previously claimed to be the potential Lancastrian heir to the throne if and when the legitimate line of John of Gaunt died out, one possible point of view in 1471 was that the Duke of York's eldest son – King Edward IV himself – was now not only the senior Yorkist claimant, but also the senior Lancastrian claimant.

But another possible viewpoint, based on the enactment of Henry VI in 1470 (see above, chapter 8) was that the Duke of York's second surviving son, George, Duke of Clarence, was the legitimate Lancastrian heir.

The said Duke [of Clarence] continuyng ín his false purpose, opteyned and gate an exemplificacion undre the Grete Seall of Herry the Sexte, late in dede and not in right Kyng of this Lande, wherin were conteyned alle suche appoyntements as late was made betwene the said Duke and Margaret, callyng herself Quene of this Lande, and other; amonges whiche it was conteyned, that if the said Herry, and Edward, his first begoton Son, died withoute Issue Male of theire Bodye, that the seid Duke and his Heires shulde be Kyng of this Lande; which exemplificacion the said Duke hath kepyd with hymself secrete, not doyng the Kyng to have eny knowlegge therof.[1]

The existence of this Clarence claim undoubtedly raised important issues later.

As for the Yorkist position in 1471, on the surface the future of the house of York as the English royal family now appeared assured and certain. After all, during the Lancastrian Readeption, Elizabeth Woodville had finally given birth to a living son by Edward IV. As a result, England once again had a Prince of Wales, bearing the name of Edward. But although, superficially, the future of the house of York seemed secure, in fact there were significant flaws beneath the surface. The irregularity of Edward IV's marriage to Elizabeth Woodville, and the unpopularity of Elizabeth and her family, had not gone away. Also, while Edward IV's middle brother, George, Duke of Clarence, had apparently returned to the Yorkist fold, he had only recently been openly opposing the king and his politics. Thus, there was no certainty that George's future loyalty could be counted upon.

One key factor in this respect was that if doubts were publicly expressed about the validity of Edward's Woodville marriage – and the legitimacy of the children of that marriage – then George was the prince with the best claim to be the rightful Yorkist heir to the English throne. When coupled with the fact that in 1470 Henry VI had recognised George as the legitimate Lancastrian heir if Edward of Westminster died, leaving no children, it was therefore arguable that the person with the best overall right to the crown – from both the Yorkist and Lancastrian points of view – was George, Duke of Clarence.

There is absolutely no reason to believe that, in 1464, at the time of her secret marriage with Edward IV, Elizabeth Woodville had any suspicion that her royal marriage might be invalid. If she had suspected that it is more or less certain that she would have insisted, at some point, upon a different (and more public) form of marriage ceremony. Nevertheless, one contemporary writer, Domenico Mancini, tells us that by 1477 doubts had been publicly voiced regarding the validity of her marriage to the king. What is more, this questioning had obviously come to the ears of Elizabeth Wooodville herself, and she was seriously concerned about it, because 'the queen then remembered the insults to her family and the calumnies with which she was reproached, namely that according to established usage she was not the legitimate wife of the king'.[2] The surviving records do not tell us specifically who had publicly questioned the royal marriage. But the target of Elizabeth Woodville's subsequent revenge and counter-attack was the king's brother, the Duke of Clarence. It therefore seems that Clarence himself must have been the man who had begun asking the awkward questions.

Moreover, this fits very well with the fact that one of Clarence's retainers, a man called Thomas Burdet, is known to have published in Holborn, and in Westminster, verses which openly questioned the future of Edward IV's royal family. The texts of these verses do not survive. However, it seems possible that they may have included public questioning of the validity of Elizabeth Woodville's marriage. Indeed, Burdet himself might perhaps have been Clarence's source of relevant information in this respect, because, as a young man, Burdet had been in the service of the Boteler family of Sudeley – the family of Eleanor Talbot's first husband.[3] What is more, it is possible that Burdet's political poems and songs were also the original source for the so-called 'prophecy of G'. Burdet's subsequent trial and execution linked him specifically with two astrologers from Oxford. These two Oxford magicians and fortune tellers were then executed by Edward IV, together with Burdet, for whatever it was that they had all been doing.

The story of the 'prophecy of G' mainly survives today in sixteenth-century accounts. But the earliest extant source dates from about 1490. This recorded the prophecy as one of the reasons behind the subsequent execution of the Duke of Clarence. It is therefore clear that the prophecy must have been current in 1477. The earliest record of it states that 'there was a prophecy that after E., that is, after Edward the fourth, G would be king – and because of its ambiguity – George Duke of Clarence (who was between the two brothers, King Edward and King Richard) on account of being Duke Ġeorge, was put to death'.⁴

If this prophecy formed part of Burdet's campaign, the intention behind it must have been to encourage the people of England to look upon George, Duke of Clarence, as the rightful heir to the throne.⁵ At all events, both the king and Elizabeth Woodville clearly came to the obvious conclusion that the letter 'G' in the prophecy referred to George. Elizabeth Woodville therefore decided that the Duke of Clarence now had to be eliminated, otherwise her royal son might never become king.

Clarence was arrested in 1477, on various grounds, including his potential claim to be the Lancastrian heir (see above), and he was tried before Parliament in January 1477/8. Curiously, one of the most significant charges against him was that he had been attempting to smuggle his son and heir, the young Edward, Earl of Warwick, out of England, either to Flanders or to Ireland. That charge has a very deep potential significance which will be explored later. Meanwhile, George was declared guilty of treason and was sentenced to death. And, significantly, at about the time when he was sentenced, the Bishop of Bath and Wells (who later claimed publicly to have married Edward IV to Eleanor Talbot) was also arrested, 'on account of some dubious action on his part connecting him with the treason of George, Duke of Clarence'.⁶

One more or less contemporary account tells us that initially George's sentence was that he should be dragged through the streets, then hung, drawn and quartered. However, perhaps partly on the supplications of their joint mother, the dowager Duchess of York, Edward IV finally ordered that the execution should be carried out privately, and that royal blood should not be shed.

Clarence was ultimately executed out of sight, in the Tower of London. Contemporary accounts report that the death sentence was carried out by drowning, using a wine barrel.[7] By exterminating the Dukle of Clarence, Elizabeth Woodville had done her best to ensure that her eldest son by the king, Edward, Prince of Wales, should succeed his father. But since her action had had led to the death of a Yorkist prince, she had potentially once again incited the enmity and opposition of the rest of the royal house of York.

A few years later, Edward IV rather unexpectedly fell ill and died. The Prince of Wales was still a minor. Therefore, following the precedent of Margaret of Anjou, Elizabeth Woodville urgently set plans in motion to take power into her own hands until her son came of age. The boy was proclaimed king as Edward V, and Elizabeth ordered her brother, Earl Rivers, to bring him quickly from Ludlow Castle to London, so that he could be crowned. Meanwhile she herself, backed by her family, proposed to take on the role of regent.

It cannot be stressed too strongly that in England, at this period, Elizabeth Woodville's plan was illegal, and contrary to all custom and tradition. The norm, when a boy was king, was for power to be exercised by his closest surviving male-line relative, the senior prince of the blood royal, who would be given the title of protector (not regent). On the continent, the pattern which Elizabeth Woodville now sought to introduce in England was the norm. In France, queen-mothers acted as regents for their young sons. But in England this was an alien idea, and Elizabeth Woodville had no authority for what she was trying to do. Her actions, following the death of Edward IV, amounted to an attempted Woodville coup, aimed at retaining power in the hands of herself and her parvenu family. According to the standard English custom and practice, the person who should hold power for the young King Edward V was his only surviving paternal uncle, Richard, Duke of Gloucester.

But when Edward IV died, Gloucester was in the north of England, far away from the centre of power. Taking advantage of his distant location, Elizabeth Woodville did her best to keep this senior royal prince out of things. Thus, Gloucester did not even attend his own brother's funeral. Indeed, it was only because his cousin, the Duke of Buckingham, together with Lord Hastings, sent him information, that Richard, Duke of Gloucester, had any knowledge of what was taking place in London.

The absence of the Duke of Gloucester from London was probably by no means accidental. Despite later political propaganda which has accused him of always aiming for the crown, there is actually no evidence that Richard ever wanted to sit upon the throne. He had always been a loyal servant of his brother, Edward IV. However, he had been deeply shocked by Edward's execution of their middle brother, George. Richard's own later correspondence as king shows clearly that he held Elizabeth Woodville responsible for Clarence's death. Following that event, Richard therefore showed a tendency to keep away from the capital, and appeared to be increasingly wary of the Woodville family.

Since he was both George's brother and a member of the House of Lords, the Duke of Gloucester must have had some awareness of whatever issues the Duke of Clarence had raised in 1476-77. Thus, if George's propaganda at that time had included assertions that Elizabeth Woodville was not the rightful queen, and that her children by Edward IV were not the legitimate heirs to the throne, Gloucester must have heard something of this. Nevertheless, in 1477 (as previously) Richard chose to remain loyal to Edward IV and avoided any involvement in the Duke of Clarence's anti-Woodville manoeuvres. Subsequently, the Duke of Gloucester kept himself away from the centre of power, and quietly fulfilled his duties in the north of England.

In 1483, when news reached him of the death of Edward IV, Richard of Gloucester summoned the nobles of the north to York to take oaths of allegiance to his nephew, the new king, Edward V. Then, warned by the Duke of Buckingham and Lord Hastings that Lord Rivers was taking the new king to London, and that Elizabeth Woodville was, in effect, claiming the role of regent, Richard moved south and met his nephew's party at Stony Stratford. Later that day, Buckingham joined them. Probably it was Buckingham who then encouraged Richard to arrest and execute Lord Rivers. Henry Stafford, Duke of Buckingham, is a new, but significant character in the story. He was a descendant of Edward III's youngest son, Thomas, Duke of Gloucester, and hence a distant cousin of the Yorkist kings.

Accompanied by the Duke of Buckingham, Richard and his nephew then continued en route to London, where the young king was initially housed in the Bishop of London's Palace. Later, however, Buckingham suggested that the most appropriate residence for the boy-king in the lead-up to his coronation would be the Tower of London. Not only was Buckingham the first to propose that Edward V should be lodged at the Tower; he was also a leading member of the delegation which later persuaded Elizabeth Woodville to allow her younger son, Richard, Duke of York, to join his brother there. As we shall see presently, he was also regarded by some contemporary continental sources to be the person responsible for the subsequent fate of the two 'princes' (whatever that fate really was).

Meanwhile, since the Woodville coup had failed, Elizabeth

Woodville had once again claimed sanctuary at Westminster Abbey. Richard, Duke of Gloucester, was now officially the protector of the realm during the minority of the new king. Initially, plans went ahead for the coronation of Edward V. But at one of the meetings of the royal council where the coronation plans were being discussed, a spanner was thrown into the works by the Bishop of Bath and Wells. This bishop publicly questioned Edward V's right to the throne by stating that, technically, he was illegitimate, owing to the fact that the bishop himself had married Edward IV to Eleanor Talbot prior to the late king's secret marriage to Elizabeth Woodville.

Since the late Duke of Clarence may have attempted to raise this issue earlier (in 1477) the contents of Bishop Stillington's speech probably did not come as a complete surprise to the members of the royal council. However, Clarence's evidence regarding the validity of Edward IV's Woodville 'marriage' may have been slight. That, together with his subsequent execution, had probably persuaded most people to give the illegitimacy of Edward IV's children as little credit as the contemporary French legend of Edward IV's own illegitimacy.

Now, however, the situation had changed dramatically. For the person now recounting the story of Edward IV's earlier Talbot marriage was none other than the priest who, before he became a bishop, claimed to have actually married Edward and Eleanor. In addition the bishop was an expert in marriage law. Thus, when he told the council that Edward IV's subsequent Woodville marriage was bigamous and that the children born of it were illegitimate, he had to be taken seriously.

Nevertheless, initially the royal council was divided in its response. Some, led by Lord Hastings, thought that the whole question should be hushed up and that the coronation of Edward V should go ahead. Indeed, hitherto, Richard, Duke of Gloucester (insofar as he was aware of the disputability of Edward IV's Woodville marriage), himself seems to have adopted that point of view. But others, led by the Duke of Buckingham, thought that the opportunity to now remove the half-Woodville child-king was too good to be missed. They therefore urged very forcefully that Edward V should be set aside as a bastard, and that the crown should pass to Richard, Duke of Gloucester.

Unbeknown to Richard, Buckingham may already have had his own axe to grind in all this. As a young orphan of royal descent, he had been brought up by Elizabeth Woodville and her family, and had been married off to one of Elizabeth's younger sisters. But despite this, the Duke of Buckingham by no means favoured the Woodvilles and their cause. While he may have been prepared to accept Edward IV's son as king (and indeed, his later policy suggests that he was), Buckingham was totally opposed to government passing from the hands of the princes of the blood royal (among whom he counted himself) into the hands of the upstart Woodvilles. As we have seen, he had already firmly opposed Elizabeth Woodville's regency claims by supporting Richard, Duke of Gloucester, for the role of protector. Now he perceived the setting aside of Edward IV's bastard children by Elizabeth Woodville as the best and most permanent means of ensuring that the Woodvilles would never again hold power in England. He therefore campaigned for the throne to be offered to Richard, Duke of Gloucester. In this, he found himself in direct opposition to Lord Hastings.

That, too, was probably no accident on Buckingham's part. Earlier, Edward IV had allowed – and indeed encouraged – Lord

Hastings to establish himself as the leading magnate in Staffordshire. This was a role which, in Buckingham's eyes, rightfully belonged to his own family, the Staffords. Thus, it was probably Buckingham who pushed Richard to execute Lord Hastings in June 1483. Although Hastings had certainly taken what ultimately proved to be the wrong side, politically, over the question of whether or not Edward V should be set aside, and had also been involved in plotting with Bishop John Morton, Richard's final decisive action against him may well have been influenced by Buckingham who had interests of his own in this affair. Of course, the immediate outcome, for Buckingham, of Hastings' execution, was that he – Buckingham – was then able to re-establish his own position in Staffordshire.

Meanwhile, nothing was done in secret. The evidence regarding Edward IV's Talbot marriage was publicly presented to the 'three estates of the realm'. This was a kind of informal Parliament comprising the secular nobility, the church leaders, and the representatives of the commons, who had come to London to constitute the first Parliament of the new king's reign. Since no king had yet been crowned, a formal parliament had not yet received its state opening. That would have taken place after the coronation. But now, with the identity of the king himself in question, there was no head of state available to open a formal parliament.

Nevertheless, the informal 'parliament' of 1483 assembled at the Guildhall and considered the evidence presented to it. There, both the lords spiritual and temporal, and the commons, decided that Edward IV had indeed been married to Eleanor Talbot; that Edward's subsequent Woodville marriage had been bigamous, and that all the children of that marriage were therefore illegitimate. In consequence of this, the estates of the realm then concluded that the throne must be offered to Richard, Duke of Gloucester. He, 'being elected by the nobles and commons in the Guildhall of London, took on him the title of the realm and kingdom, as imposed upon him in ... Baynard's Castle'.[8] Thus it was in the London home of his late father, and of his living mother, that he was duly proclaimed King Richard III. The following year, a full and official Parliament repeated the 1483 decision of the three estates of the realm, enshrining it as an official Act of Parliament.

As we have seen, there is no evidence that Richard III had ever wanted to be king. Indeed, he may have found his new position uncomfortable in many ways. However, a splendid coronation was celebrated for him, after which he and his wife, Queen Anne Neville – the younger daughter of the dead Earl of Warwick, and the former bride of the Lancastrian prince, Edward of Westminster – began a royal progress through parts of their kingdom. But they then found themselves confronted by an attempt to extract the two sons of Edward IV from the Tower of London, and re-enthrone the elder of them. The latter was the initial public object of 'Buckingham's Rebellion'. Overall, the event known under that name is something of a mystery. The Duke of Buckingham certainly took part in the rebellion, but it seems highly unlikely that he can have been the orchestrator of the entire movement, which, in the end, comprised at least three different – and mutually incompatible – aims.

When he became king, Richard III had rewarded Buckingham for his support by returning to him and his family lands formerly held by the Lancastrian kings. Richard then set off on his royal tour of parts of his kingdom on Monday 21 July. He, the queen and their party rode first from Windsor to Reading. Three days later they were in Oxford. By the beginning of August, they had reached Gloucester, and it was in Gloucester that the Duke of Buckingham last saw his cousin, the king, face to face.

One key factor in the events of July 1483 was that, during Richard III's absence from the capital, attempts were definitely made in London to access the sons of Edward IV who were then still living in the Tower. There is no conclusive evidence to show whether these attempts were intended to rescue the boys or to kill them, and previous writers have tended to make the latter assumption. However, there are no real grounds for reaching that conclusion, and the most likely explanation seems to be that someone wished to extract the boys *alive* in order to have control over their future – and the future of the country. It is also far from clear whether the attempts succeeded or failed. But despite the fact that the surviving evidence is somewhat meagre, there is no doubt whatever that such attempts took place. Moreover, the additional fact that subsequently the whereabouts of the two sons of Edward IV and Elizabeth Woodville seems to have been a mystery – even to the government – strongly suggests that the two boys had indeed been abducted.

It is highly significant, therefore, that the initial aim of Buckingham's Rebellion was to restore the crown to Edward V. It is also very interesting to note that some Continental sources tell us that it was none other than the Duke of Buckingham who was responsible for the disappearance of the two so-called 'princes in the Tower'. For example, Philippe de Commines suggests that Buckingham actually killed the two boys.[9] Also, according to the private secretary of the late Portuguese King Alfonso V (died 1481), 'after the passing away of king Edward in the year of '83, another one of his brothers, the Duke of Gloucester, had in his power the Prince of Wales and the Duke of York, the young sons of the said king his brother, and turned them to the Duke of Buckingham, under whose custody the said Princes were starved to death'.[10] In his role of Constable of England, Buckingham potentially had sufficient authority to access the Tower of London. It is a distinct possibility, therefore, that, taking advantage of Richard III's absence on his royal tour, Buckingham sent men into the Tower in July 1483, in order to rescue the sons of Edward IV.

Buckingham presumably wished to have the boys in his own hands and under his control. Almost certainly his plan was to use them in some way for his own advantage. His first move (had his rebellion succeeded) would presumably have been to get rid of Richard III, and restore Edward V as king – no doubt with himself as the new protector. Subsequently, of course, his wider ambitions may have included the thought that he himself might one day wear the crown. We have already seen that Buckingham seems to have had his own axe to grind throughout. Almost certainly it was Buckingham's involvement in the mysterious disappearance of the two sons of Edward IV that subsequently caused Richard III to describe his cousin as 'the most untrue creature living'.

A small beam of light – though it is still a very murky light – is shed upon what had taken place in London by Richard III's decision to send John Howard, Duke of Norfolk (the Earl Marshall of England), back to London, on or just before Wednesday 23 July 1483. Thus Howard only accompanied the royal party as far as Reading and the shrine of Our Lady of Caversham. The king then asked Howard to return to the capital on an important mission, which seems to have been connected with men who had been arrested, and who were detained at Crosby's Place in Bishopsgate (Richard III's former London home as Duke of Gloucester).

A warrant which Richard III subsequently issued on Tuesday 29

July at Minster Lovell was almost certainly linked with Howard's mission. It refers to prisoners detained for their recent involvement in some 'enterprise'. No details of the alleged crime are specified in the warrant. However, we know from other sources that there had been unauthorised attempts to secure the persons of Edward IV's children, by extracting his daughters from sanctuary at Westminster and removing his sons from the Tower of London. A plot by a number of Londoners in favour of the sons of Edward IV was reported by the Frenchman Thomas Basin, who probably wrote down his account early in 1484. Later, the sixteenth-century chronicler, John Stow, also speaks of a plot to abduct Edward V and his brother from the Tower after setting off diversionary fires.

It seems probable that, upon receipt of the king's instructions from Minster Lovell, the Chancellor, Bishop Russell, and the royal council deferred to the Duke of Norfolk, whom the king had apparently sent to sit in judgement upon those prisoners who had plotted to secure some or all of Edward IV's children. It appears that the trial of at least some of these individuals took place at Crosby's Place, during the following month. References to the expenses incurred in preparing Crosby's Place for the trial are to be found in John Howard's accounts for the beginning of August.[11]

It is impossible to know for certain whether Buckingham had succeeded in securing the persons of Edward V and his brother the Duke of York. However, the event known as 'Buckingham's Rebellion' began in the south and south-west of England and, as we have seen, its initial and openly declared aim was to restore Edward V to the throne. The supporters of this movement were a mixed bunch. Some were men who had been loyal to Edward IV, but who had now been dismissed and replaced with his own loyal servants by the new king, Richard III. Others were members of the Woodville family and its supporters. Presumably both these groups felt either a genuine loyalty to, or a self-interest in, Edward IV's son. Probably they also either did not understand the complex reasoning behind his illegitimacy, or they did not care about it.

At the same time, other people involved in 'Buckingham's Rebellion' had a very different political background. Some of them were former Lancastrians. These men presumably had a totally different idea of who should now be king of England. Indeed, they were probably behind the subsequent change in the focus of the rebellion – from support for the cause of Edward V, to support for the cause of the Beaufort descendant, Henry 'Tudor'. One thing which is certain is that this Lancastrian group was then behind the spreading of a rumour that Edward V was dead. Of course, this was a story which was potentially very much in their interests, since it would hopefully persuade the former supporters of Edward V to transfer their allegiance to Henry 'Tudor'.

However, it is quite possible that the story was true. During his residence at the Tower of London during the summer of 1483, Edward V had been receiving regular visits from his physician, Dr John Argentine. The young lad was reported to be melancholy and low – unlike his younger brother, Richard, who was described in a contemporary letter as 'merry'.[12] It is therefore possible that, like his sister, Mary, and other children of Edward IV and Elizabeth Woodville, Edward V was suffering from serious ill health. The present writer has previously published documentary evidence showing that Edward V was considered to be dead by the town clerk of Colchester in September 1483,[13] and there is evidence to show that a requiem mass was offered for the repose of his soul in the Sistine Chapel in Rome in that same month.[14] However, there is no evidence of the death of the younger 'prince', Richard of Shrewsbury, Duke of York. On the contrary it is clear that he was widely believed to be still living in the 1490s, when 'Richard of England' ('Perkin Warbeck') claimed the English throne under his identity (see below, chapter 12).

As for the Duke of Buckingham himself, his role and his ambitions are unclear. As we have seen, possibly initially he was hoping to make himself protector, with one of Edward IV's young sons on the throne as king. It is also conceivable that, since Edward V had formally been declared illegitimate and ousted as king by Parliament, Buckingham may have considered it better to dispose of the elder boy, while retaining Edward IV's younger son, Richard Duke of York, as a living potential claimant to the throne. In either case, Buckingham's longer-term aim might well have been to claim the throne for himself.

However, later 'Tudor' accounts tell us that Buckingham was then won over by Margaret Beaufort, Countess of Richmond and Derby, to give his support to her son Henry 'Tudor'. Certainly Buckingham wrote to Henry 'Tudor' on 28 September. By this time the sons of Edward IV seem to have somehow disappeared from the picture, and the plan – reshaped by such cunning Lancastrians as Dr John Morton, Bishop of Ely – was now to enthrone Henry 'Tudor' and to marry him to Edward IV's eldest daughter.

It was not until Saturday 11 October that Richard III discovered that Buckingham had betrayed him. On Wednesday 15 October the king formally proclaimed that Buckingham was a rebel and traitor. It was on Saturday 18 October that Buckingham openly unfurled his rebellious banners. In addition to trying the men who had freed (or attempted to free) the 'princes in the Tower', John Howard, Duke of Norfolk, also played an important part in suppressing 'Buckingham's Rebellion'. He defended London, and then isolated and defeated the rebels in Kent and Surrey. Based on the news he received from John Howard, Richard III decided there was no need for him to defend London in person. Instead, the king focussed his attention on the rebels in the south-west.

On Friday 24 October Richard led his army to Coventry. Meanwhile Buckingham's banners had not attracted any great support. Bishop John Morton abandoned Buckingham, fleeing first to the fenlands around his cathedral at Ely, and then taking ship to the Low Countries. Buckingham, now in despair, disguised himself in peasant's clothing and tried to hide himself in Shropshire. By the end of October he had been captured and was brought to Richard III at Salisbury. The panic-stricken Buckingham begged the king to see him, but Richard absolutely refused. Whether, if Richard had agreed, Buckingham would have been able to reveal to the king the hiding place of Edward IV's sons – or perhaps the burial place of the elder son and the hiding place of the younger – we shall now never know. On Sunday 2 November 1483 Henry, Duke of Buckingham was beheaded in Salisbury Market.

PART 3

THE RED ROSE OF BEAUFORT

10

THE RED ROSE WINS

On the evening of 7 August 1485, Henry 'Tudor' and his small
invasion force crossed the Channel from France in seven ships, and
landed in Wales, at Mill Bay, at the mouth of the Milford Haven
waterway.

Why did Henry choose Mill Bay? Familiarity was one reason. Henry
was born in Pembroke Castle, on the opposite side of the Milford
Haven waterway. His uncle, Jasper Tudor, was nominally Earl of
Pembroke and had maintained contact with people in the area while
bringing up his nephew in France.

Another reason for choosing Mill Bay was to avoid detection
by the king's observers at Dale Castle, some 3km further north.
Inevitably, news of Henry's landing travelled quickly – the king knew
about it by 11 August. Crucially, however, the decision to land in this
secluded bay allowed the fledgling army to come ashore unopposed.

It was also imperative for Henry to start his march to Bosworth in a
sympathetic region, because the army would quickly need provisions
from supportive locals as well as extra soldiers from gentry who

would rally to his cause. His strategy paid off, and he received a hearty welcome in Haverfordwest, the first major town on his route.

His chief supporter in Wales was Rhys ap Thomas, whose homes included Carew Castle, near Pembroke. He marched across Wales via a different route to gather more soldiers for the battle. The story was later romanticised to portray Rhys standing at Mill Bay to welcome Henry.[1]

Henry was twenty-eight years old and had lived most of his life in exile in Brittany and France. In France he had advanced a blatantly lying claim to be a real, and very senior, Lancastrian prince, for he had stated that he was 'the son of the late King Henry [VI] of England'![2] By this and other means, he had managed to attract the support of the French government, 'which wanted Henry in order to keep its island neighbour at bay'.[3] His success in this regard was in spite of the fact that intelligent French political observers such as Philippe de Commynes (who had met Henry) correctly considered his claim to the English throne non-existent.

With Henry, when he set sail for England in August 1485, were about 2,000 French mercenary soldiers, funded for him by his second cousin, Charles VIII, King of France (reigned 1483–1498).

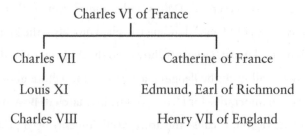

Family Tree 9: The relationship of Henry VII and Charles VIII.

After landing at Milford Haven, Henry and his small army climbed up to the little castle which commanded the bay, but which they found deserted. From there they made their way through Wales to Shrewsbury.

Of course, Richard III was well aware of the French-backed 'Tudor' / 'Lancastrian' plot against him. However, the knowledge does not seem to have given rise to any great anxiety on his part. Indeed, the king was taking a hunting holiday in Sherwood Forest at the time when his enemy crossed the Channel. After all, Richard's own forces had already successfully crushed 'Buckingham's Rebellion', in which Henry 'Tudor' had played a part. Therefore, the king seems to have had every hope that the new attempt against him would simply prove to be another vain attempt, and that once it had been defeated he would be able to reign in peace.

It was on about 14 August – the vigil of the Feast of the Assumption – that Richard's great supporter, John Howard, Duke of Norfolk, received his royal summons to the king's array. At that time Howard was probably at Sudbury, in Suffolk. He had a devotion to the shrines in the eastern counties, particularly the local shrines of the Virgin Mary. This is shown by the itinerary of his journey through the region in the summer of 1483, in celebration of his elevation to the dukedom of Norfolk.[4] The town of Sudbury was not far from Howard's ancestral manor house at Stoke-by-Nayland, and it housed a pilgrimage centre in honour of the Blessed Virgin. The Feast of the Assumption was observed with special solemnity at the shrine of Our Lady of Sudbury. Once he had received the royal summons, John Howard ordered his men to assemble at the nearby town of Bury St Edmunds.

It was on the Feast of the Assumption itself (Monday 15

August) that Richard III's summons reached the city of York. The city's response was somewhat laid-back. Initially the city council dispatched no military force. Instead the mayor simply sent to ask the king for further information. Eventually, however, York sent a force of eighty men to Richard III's support.

It was also on the religious feast day that Richard III – then still at the hunting lodge in Sherwood Forest – received a message from Lord Stanley, regretting that he would be unable to obey the royal summons (which he had also obviously received). He explained to the king that, sadly, he was suffering from the sweating sickness. More will be said about this disease shortly. But whether or not he was really ill, Lord Stanley had apparently now decided to start (or resume) sitting on the fence. In spite of this, the king responded in a very gentle manner, by simply asking Stanley to send his son and heir, George, in his place. Lord Stanley complied with this request.

On Friday 19 August Richard III, who had meanwhile returned from his hunting lodge to the royal castle at Nottingham, set off for Leicester. Two years earlier, on his only recorded previous over-night visit to Leicester, Richard had stayed at Leicester Castle, and probably he did so again in 1485. Although a widespread popular myth asserts that the king stayed at an inn called the Blue (or White) Boar in Leicester, there is no surviving evidence that he did so – or even that such an inn existed in Leicester in 1485.[5]

The 'inn' legend also claims that Richard brought his own bed with him to Leicester, and that he left it at the inn when he rode on. However, the surviving bed said to be Richard's, and now preserved at Donington-le-Heath Manor House, appears to be a piece of sixteenth-century furniture. It was probably created long after Richard III was killed, and is therefore unlikely ever to have been used by the king.

On the day after Richard's departure from Nottingham to Leicester – Saturday 20 August – the Earl of Northumberland and his men joined the royal host. Although some writers have sought to suggest that Northumberland was not truly committed to Richard's support, there is no real evidence for that contention. As we shall see, the earl's subsequent lack of active participation in the Battle of Bosworth can probably be explained simply by the position assigned to him and his men by the king, and by the unpredictable action taken by Richard III himself.

In this context it is, perhaps, also worth noting that some writers sought, after the battle, to make the ludicrous suggestion that the Duke of Norfolk had been half-hearted in his backing for the king. In reality, of course, Norfolk was fully committed to Richard, as he had always been, and he backed that commitment to the extent of losing his own life.

The Duke of Norfolk, together with his East Anglian troops, had reached Leicester before the Earl of Northumberland. Thus, by Sunday 21 August, with the exception of the Stanley contingent, the royal army was at full strength. It was a very large force – reportedly twice as big as the opposing army of rebels. The royal army was assembled outside Leicester. There, on Sunday 21 August, accompanied by the Duke of Norfolk and the Earl of Northumberland, it is said that Richard III conducted a crown-wearing ceremony before his men, prior to leading them westwards to prevent Henry 'Tudor' and his rebel forces from following the Roman road of Watling street towards London. Richard is also said by later sources to have ridden a grey Arab stallion called 'White Syrie'. Once again, the evidence for that story is by no means certain. However, the name of the horse sounds plausible, so the story may possibly be true.[6]

When Richard III rode out of Leicester he must have crossed the River Soar over Bow Bridge, which in those days was a small, stone-built structure with a humped back. The legends report that, as the king rode across the narrow bridge, his heel struck the stone parapet, whereupon an elderly woman prophesied that where his spur struck, his head would later be broken. However, that story sounds like a later invention, made with the benefit of hindsight. Leicester's medieval Bow Bridge was quite a narrow stone construction, and Richard III was riding across it accompanied by his huge army. It is therefore somewhat difficult to imagine how a beggar woman could have been sitting on or by the bridge on that occasion.

The royal army camped for the night of 21/22 August by the little village of Sutton Cheney, not far from Market Bosworth. Richard III may well have made a will on the night before the coming battle – for that was quite a normal practice before a fight. If he did, the contents of the will could potentially have been fascinating – but unfortunately no such document has survived.

It is reported that the king suffered a sleepless night. If true, that could perhaps have been partly due to the scoliosis from which he suffered. However, another possible explanation for Richard's reportedly disturbed night could be that he was ill. Maybe the king had caught the sweating sickness which was then inflicting England. In 1485 when this disease was spreading in this country for the first time, there were 'contemporary impressions of strong age, class, and sex predispositions of the victims of the sweating sickness to young, rich males'.[7] Such a victim description would obviously fit King Richard. It was certainly the case that most of the victims of sweating sickness who lived in London in July 1485 were male. Another interesting point is the fact that this disease only proved fatal in a relatively small number of cases.

Modern research also indicates 'that the causative agent of the sweating sickness was spread by human-to-human contact as well as initially through a zoonosis or an environmental vector. ... Furthermore, Dyer sees the spread of the epidemic at a national level as following lines of communication and human contact; "The national epidemic displays a disease capable of very rapid movement at certain times, consistent with distribution by travellers"'.[8]

These findings would be consistent with the fact that in the summer of 1485, Lord Stanley claimed that he was suffering from sweating sickness, and that, while reportedly fighting this infection, Stanley had sent a messenger to the king, bearing the news of his illness. If Lord Stanley was telling the truth it is obviously conceivable that the messenger whom he dispatched to Richard at Nottingham Castle might have borne to the king not only the message which his lord had asked him to convey, but also the germs of the infection from which his lord was suffering.

Interestingly, a fever such as sweating sickness could account for the fact that Richard III's night of sleep was disturbed on 21-22 August. However, it could also pontentially explain why the king was reportedly thirsty during the early stages of the battle on the following morning. Moreover, such a fever might also explain the king's subsequent rather impetuous and ill-considered conduct during the battle itself.

As for Henry 'Tudor', he spent the night of 21 August at Merevale Abbey, just over the county boundary in Warwickshire. And it seems that Henry also had a sleepless night. Before dawn, he rode some miles across country to the Stanley camp. There, he engaged in a secret conference with Sir William Stanley – a conference which William's brother (and Henry's stepfather), Thomas, Lord Stanley, may also have attended – though he later denied it. Henry was trying hard to convince the Stanleys that they should commit their force to his cause in the coming battle. But the Stanleys were obviously afraid that Richard III's much larger army would win the battle, and did not wish to do anything which would be seen as treason by the victorious king. Therefore they refused to commit themselves on Henry's side, and remained sitting on the fence, waiting to see what would happen.

Whether he slept well or badly during the night of 21-22 August 1485, Richard III probably woke in the small hours of the following morning. He reportedly rose at dawn. The date was 22 August, according to the fifteenth-century Julian calendar. This would correspond to 31 August in terms of the modern, Gregorian calendar. Therefore the hour of sunrise would have been at about 06.12 BST (or 05.12 GMT). It was quite normal for fighters to arise early on the morning of a battle, for the fighting itself often started at an early hour, before which personal preparations and military dispositions all had to be dealt with.

A comparatively recent story which was added to the Bosworth legend in the 1920s tells us that on the morning of the battle Richard III walked up to the parish church at Sutton Cheney to attend mass there. Once again, there is no contemporary record to support this story, which appears, for a number of reasons, to be an unlikely modern invention. A church building was (and is) not essential for the celebration of mass. Normally, in a medieval military camp, mass would simply have been said in the royal tent. It is absolutely clear that Richard III had his own chaplains with him in his camp on the morning of 22 August, and all Catholic priests were (and are) required to celebrate mass daily.

The contemporary documentary evidence for the presence of the royal chaplains is quite specific and comes from the Crowland Chronicle (see below). There is also a piece of material evidence of the presence of clergy, in the form of the fifteenth-century Bosworth processional crucifix, which was found in the vicinity of the battlefield site in the late eighteenth century.[9]

The Crowland chronicler reports that 'at dawn on Monday morning the chaplains were not ready to celebrate mass for King Richard'.[10] Although the chronicler is unlikely to have been present in person in the royal camp on that morning, his statement may, nevertheless, be literally correct, because there is also other surviving evidence which suggests that some confusion may have surrounded the preparations for the royal mass on the morning of 22 August. The prime sources for these accounts seem to have been the surviving members of Richard III's own immediate entourage.

In his later *Account of Miracles Performed by the Holy Eucharist*, which Henry Parker, Lord Morley presented to Queen Mary I in 1554, Morley – himself the son of a Yorkist who fought for Richard III at Bosworth – ascribed this information specifically to one particular servant of Richard's called Bygoff (now usually identified as Sir Ralph Bigod). As reported by Lord Morley, this man 'sayd that Kyng Richard callyd in the morning for to have had mass sayd before hym, but when his chapeleyne had one thing ready, evermore & they wanted another, when they had wyne they lacked breade, And ever one thing was myssing'.[11]

But of course, actually the necessary preparations for celebrating a low mass were and are quite basic (and would have been very familiar to the royal chaplains). Any experienced priest would easily have been able to get everything ready in less than half an hour. Therefore, even though his chaplains may not have had everything ready for the celebration of mass at the moment when the king got up on the morning of 22 August, they would presumably have begun their preparations as soon as they became aware of the fact that the king had arisen. As for the celebration of the mass itself, that would also have been comparatively short (lasting probably about thirty minutes).

It is also reported by the continuator of the Crowland Chronicle that breakfast was not ready when the king first got up. This point, together with the information that the royal chaplains did not have everything ready to celebrate his mass when the king arose, certainly appears to indicate that either that the king had arisen rather earlier than anticipated, or that his various servants had overslept somewhat. However, this would not have caused any real problem. After all, a medieval breakfast was usually a very simple meal. Probably the royal breakfast on this occasion would simply have comprised more bread and wine. This could have been prepared very quickly, while the king was taking part in his morning mass. If he was taking Holy Communion (as he presumably was on this occasion), Richard would not have been able to break his fast until after the mass had been celebrated.

Various names have been assigned at different times to the last battle of King Richard III. But while it is true that the fighting did not take place in close proximity to the town of Market Bosworth, twenty-six years later, in 1511, Henry VII referred to the battle under the name of 'Bosworth Field'. Therefore the name 'Bosworth' is probably the most widely know appellation, and it has been consistently employed here. There have also been a number of different accounts of precisely where the fighting took place, and what exactly happened. Even so, there is general agreement that Richard III's army considerably outnumbered the opposing rebel forces. It also seems that Richard's army was all English, unlike Richard's opponents, who were mostly French or Welsh (making this a questionable 'civil war' battle). The king's army is understood to have been well disposed strategically, upon higher ground. The sum of this information appears to suggest that logically Richard III should have had the advantage. His ultimate defeat is therefore somewhat intriguing.

To summarise the early morning events, as we have seen, Richard III had arisen by about ten minutes past six (BST) on the morning of Monday 22 August. He may have slightly surprised his staff, and there were perhaps slight delays in their preparations for his morning mass and his breakfast as a result. However, there is no reason to suppose that there would have been any serious problems.

Probably the celebration of mass in the royal tent would have begun at about six forty. By about ten past seven, Richard III was probably consuming his modest breakfast. Shortly afterwards, the king's esquires will have started to buckle their sovereign into his royal armour. Finally the king will have donned his helmet surmounted by an open crown of gilded base metal. At around seven thirty, Richard III must have left the royal tent to address his army. His chaplains probably accompanied the king to bless the men of his army, bearing the Bosworth Crucifix, mounted as a processional cross. Incidentally, it appears to have been a bright and sunny morning.

Spies probably advised the king that the forces of the enemy had spent the night about five miles away at Merevale, which is located on Watling Street – a direct route to London. When Richard left his camp he therefore marched his men in a westerly direction, with the intention of preventing Henry 'Tudor' from continuing in the direction of London. However, the banner of the Stanleys was already to the south-west of Dadlington, near Stoke Golding. Since the precise intention of the Stanleys remained unclear, the king and his army did not go quite as far as Watling Street. Richard therefore took the cautious approach at this stage, positioning himself to the north-west of Stoke Golding's Crown Hill, as it would later be called – though for obvious reasons, Richard III would never have heard that name.

Probably shortly before eight o'clock, the royal host will have taken up its position on a low ridge. The king disposed his army on the higher ground in an extended line. The Duke of Norfolk was in command of the north-western contingent, while the Earl of Northumberland's men were on the south-eastern side. King Richard himself commanded the centre. At this point the Crowland Chronicle reports that Richard ordered the execution of George Stanley, Lord Strange. However, this appears to be an invented story, since we know for certain that George Stanley was not executed.

The ground below the ridge was somewhat marshy. Beyond the marshy area, the much smaller force of Henry 'Tudor' was assembled. At about eight o'clock BST the rebels began a slow advance towards the royal army, skirting the boggy ground. At first the king took no action, but eventually, seeing that the rebel forces were clearing the marshland, he gave orders to oppose their further advance.

When John de Vere (*soi-disant* 'Earl of Oxford', and one of Henry 'Tudor''s most experienced commanders) saw that the royal forces were moving into a position to oppose himself and his men, he swiftly ordered his own troops to hold back and maintain close contact with their standard bearers. Although this slowed down the rebel advance, Henry 'Tudor''s men thereby effectively prevented any serious incursion into their ranks by maintaining a fairly tight formation. In total, this slow manoeuvring and counter manoeuvring may have taken about an hour.

At that point something odd and unexpected appears to have happened. Perhaps Richard glimpsed his second cousin, Henry 'Tudor' – or at least, Henry's pretentious royal standard – among the rebel forces. Either out of bravado, or possibly from a sense of *noblesse oblige* – and either in response to his fury at seeing 'Tudor' displaying the undifferenced royal arms, or perhaps because he himself was feeling ill (suffering from a fever) – Richard unpredictably summoned his cavalry and led them at the gallop, to settle Henry's fate once and for all. This was a hasty, and in some ways ill-considered move. It appears to suggest that perhaps Richard was not thinking very clearly. Indeed, in some ways the king's action on this occasion recalls his father's ill-advised *sortie* from Sandal Castle. That had resulted in the Duke of York's death in December 1460. But at the battle of Wakefield his father had been in a somewhat weak position. On the other hand, Richard III was in command of a large army, and should logically have had a good prospect of winning the Battle of Bosworth.

In spite of the possible dangers, the king's sudden and dramatic charge came very close to succeeding. Richard's cavalry cut through the 'Tudor' lines, and Richard himself engaged his rival's standard bearer, William Brandon, whom he swiftly cut down, felling the 'Tudor' standard. Only Sir John Cheney now stood between the king and his enemy, and he must have had every hope of victory at this point.

But at that point something unexpected happened once again. The foreign mercenaries of Henry 'Tudor' rapidly deployed themselves in a defensive manoeuvre hitherto unseen in England. They fell back, enclosing Henry in a square formation of pikemen. The mounted warriors of the king's army found themselves unable to penetrate this defensive alignment. Thus the leadership of Richard's cavalry charge was stalled, and the men in his rear found themselves riding into their halted leaders. Many must have been unhorsed as a result.

When he saw that the royal charge had been broken by the wall of pikemen, the treacherous leader of the Stanley contingent (whichever Stanley brother he was) finally decided to commit his forces on the 'Tudor' side. His army cut more or less unopposed through the muddled melee of the royal cavalry, and in a matter of minutes the balance of the field was reversed. The king's horse had now either been killed beneath him, or Richard III had been unhorsed. In falling to the ground, he lost his crowned helmet. He rose to find himself surrounded by a small force of the enemy, one of whom struck the king from behind, wounding the top of his skull and probably stunning him and bringing him down to his knees. As he struggled to rise, one of Richard's own men offered the king his horse, crying to him to flee, so that he could regroup and fight again. However, the king refused to do this. Meanwhile a further heavy blow was aimed at the back of his bare head, and proved fatal. The king's defeat and death clearly lay at Stanley's door. Thus, the report that his last words were 'Treason – treason' may well be true.

The king had died some six weeks short of his thirty-third birthday. Polydore Vergil's account of his death recorded simply that 'king Richerd, alone, was killyd fyghting manfully in the thickkest presse of his enemyes'.[12] Although this account was written by and for Richard's enemies, it is a fitting tribute. Interestingly, it is also one which, in the final analysis, acknowledges without question the one key point which Richard himself was defending, namely his kingship.

Meanwhile the rest of the vast royal army, most of whom had as yet done no fighting whatever, must have watched aghast as their sovereign fell. The quick-thinking John de Vere now seized the initiative. Taking rapid advantage of the new situation he hurled himself and his men at the position defended by his cousin, the Duke of Norfolk (who was in command of the royal archers). As de Vere grappled with his cousin the latter unluckily lost his helmet. It was in that instant that an arrow, loosed at a venture, pierced the duke of Norfolk's skull and he too fell dead.[13]

Now, in effect, the royal army had become a leaderless rabble. As the great host began to disintegrate, and its individual men-at-arms started to flee in the direction of Dadlington, the men of the smaller 'Tudor' army began to pursue them and cut them down. The premise that the final stages of the combat were located in the vicinity of Dadlington is based upon the known fact that Henry VIII later established a perpetual chantry at Dadlington parish church for the souls of those who had been killed in the battle.

By about ten o'clock in the morning the fighting was over. It was only from this point onwards that Henry 'Tudor' would have had the leisure to detail a search for Richard III's body, because obviously at the moment when the king had been killed, Henry's army still had the greater part of Richard III's force still to deal with, so they simply had to carry on fighting. Thus the royal corpse had simply been left lying where it fell, somewhere near Henry's position at the outset of the battle.

A small group of Henry's soldiers now found Richard's body. He was still lying where he had fallen. But the body – which must still have been enclosed in the royal suit of armour when the king was killed, because he suffered only fatal head injuries – was now found lying naked. No doubt it had been stripped of its valuable clothes and armour by looters. Indeed, it seems possible that one of them had pulled the gilded crown off the royal helmet and had tried to conceal it in a hawthorn bush. Maybe he planned to come back and collect it later, after nightfall. If so, unfortunately for the looter, Henry's soldiers discovered the crown first. They collected it and took it to the new king at Stoke Golding. There, on what subsequently became known as 'Crown Hill', the commander of the Stanley forces placed Richard's crown on the rebel leader's head and proclaimed him King Henry VII.

Incidentally, the Battle of Bosworth seems to have been the first conflict for the throne of England in which the white rose badge of the house of York was clearly opposed by a red rose badge – the emblem of Henry VII, and of his mother, Margaret Beaufort. Although the white *rose-en-soleil* had been used by Edward IV, and the white rose also appears to have been one of the several badges used by his father, there is no clear evidence that red and white rose badges had ever both been used previously in any of the armed conflicts for the throne. But it is certain that, once he became king, Henry VII used the red rose as his badge, and it seems probable that, while the chief badge of Richard III was a white boar, he did also use the white rose emblem which had been employed by both his father and his elder brother, Edward IV.

At all events, following his seizure of the crown, Henry VII definitely attributed the white rose badge to his wife, Edward IV's daughter, Elizabeth of York. Henry then depicted their marriage as a reunion of the two rival families, and he did this specifically by the symbolic use of the two roses. For example, at his reception in the City of York in 1486, when a pageant was presented, this depicted a garden of flowers which included 'a rioall rich red rose ... unto which rose shall appeyre another rich white rose',[14] after which all the other flowers in the garden had to bow to the pair of roses.

It is therefore arguable that the Battle of Bosworth, which has often been (erroneously) called the last battle of the Wars of the Roses, was actually, in one sense, the *first* battle of the Wars of the Roses. For from this point onwards, the English dynastic conflict was definitely represented by all those involved in the struggle, for approximately the next forty years, as a conflict between two rival houses symbolised by a red rose and a white rose. This explicit use of opposing red and white rose emblems seems to have come to an end, as we shall see, in 1524/5, with the death of Richard III's nephew and namesake, Richard de la Pole 'Duke of Suffolk' – known specifically as the last 'White Rose'.

11

RICHARD III'S HEIR, 'KING EDWARD VI'

Henry's battlefield 'coronation' was insufficient, of course. He had to make his way to London and arrange for a proper coronation ceremony at Westminster Abbey. He also had to summon a parliament, officially open it as the reigning king, and then persuade it to accept him as the new monarch. 'He took great care not to address the baronage, or summon Parliament, until after his coronation, which took place in Westminster Abbey on 30 October 1485.'[1] As we have already seen, in the 1480s it was not thought acceptable for an *uncrowned* king to open Parliament.

Nevertheless, the legality of the whole process undertaken by Henry VII in 1485 is, of course, open to question. It also offers an interesting contrast to what had occurred in the summer of 1483. On that occasion, when the occupancy of the throne had been in dispute, Richard, Duke of Gloucester, had not been crowned as King Richard III of England until *after* he had been formally requested to mount the throne by an unopened 'parliament' – the three estates of the realm.

When Henry VII's first parliament was opened, it is well known that he stated before that assembly that the basis of his claim to the throne was twofold — by right of conquest and by right of blood. The Crowland Chronicle continuator, who sometimes puts things in a rather misleading way (he was obviously a politician!) stated that

> in this Parliament the king's royal authority was confirmed as due him not by one but by many titles so that he may be considered to rule rightfully over the English people not only by right of blood but of victory in battle and of conquest.[2]

But as we can see, in spite of his reference to 'many titles', the justifications for Henry's accession which the chronicler adduces are in fact only two in number: inheritance and victory.

The Act of Parliament which formally vested the royal power in the person of Henry VII was actually very short and extremely vague – unlike the detailed act of 1484, which had set out in specific terms the reasons why Richard III should be king. Henry VII's Parliament, having no good case to put, simply said, 'By auctoritee of thys present Parliament ... the Inheretance of the Crounes of the Roialmes of England and France ... be, rest, remaine and abide in the most Royall persone of our now Soveraigne Lord King Henry the VIIth, and in the heires of hys body lawfully comen, perpetuelly with the grace of God so to endure, and in noon other.'[3]

Meanwhile, following the king's instructions, Henry's Parliament also annulled the act of *Titulus Regius* of Richard III's Parliament, thereby setting aside the late king's claim to the throne. The 1484 Act was repealed without being quoted. This was an unprecedented action, but absolutely essential in the eyes of the new king because he wished to airbrush out of history and public memory all mention of Edward IV's marriage to Eleanor Talbot, and the consequent illegality of that king's subsequent union with Elizabeth Woodville. As he himself explicitly stated, the object of the repeal without a quoted text of the 1484 Act was to ensure that the contents of that Act of 1484 'maie be for ever out of remembraunce and allso forgot'.[4]

In 1486 the new king then married Elizabeth, eldest daughter of Edward IV and Elizabeth Woodville, whom he now had represented to the nation as a legitimate English princess and the Yorkist royal heiress. In actual fact, of course, by his repeal of the act of *Titulus Regius*, Henry had effectively also restored the claims to the throne of Elizabeth of York's two brothers, Edward V and Richard of Shrewsbury, Duke of York. Following the repeal of the 1484 act, the claims of Edward IV's two sons would once again have been superior to the claim of their sister. But Henry was obviously hoping that Edward IV's two sons by Elizabeth Woodville were now out of the picture in some way, since otherwise he would have had no grounds for claiming that Elizabeth of York was her family's heiress.

Following his seizure of power in August 1485, Henry VII would, of course, have had access to the Tower of London. However, no sons of Edward IV, either living or dead, were found there, and Henry VII had no knowledge of their whereabouts, since no statement on the subject had ever been published by Richard III or his government. Consequently, nothing specific was (or could be) said by the new government, regarding what had become of the two sons of Edward IV. Indeed, Henry VII's subsequent actions clearly suggest that at the beginning of his reign the fate of the so-called 'princes in the Tower' was one of his many points of uncertainty.

Nevertheless, there is no doubt that Henry VII was concerned about potential Yorkist rival claimants for the crown which he himself had just seized in battle. Most of the young members of the house of York had been housed and educated by Richard III at Sheriff Hutton Castle, just outside the city of York. Henry VII now rounded them up and had them brought to London, where he took charge of them.

He was most particularly interested in the young Edward of Clarence, Earl of Warwick, whom he now placed under the guardianship of his own mother, Margaret Beaufort.[5] If it had not been for the act of attainder passed by Edward IV against this boy's father, George, Duke of Clarence, the young Earl of Warwick would have had a strong claim to be the Yorkist heir to the throne of the late king, Richard III. What is more, as we saw earlier, Henry VI had also decreed in 1470 that the Duke of Clarence was the *Lancastrian* heir to the throne after himself and Edward of Westminster. Therefore, since Clarence had been executed – arguably illegally, from a Lancastrian point of view – by the usurping Yorkist king, Edward IV – in actual fact the legal Lancastrian heir to the throne in 1485 was not the usurping and effectively non-royal Henry VII, but Clarence's surviving son, Edward, Earl of Warwick.

It is easy to be misled by hindsight. Many historians have treated the victory at Bosworth, in August 1485, as a clear 'final outcome'. But it would not have been seen in that way at the time. In spite of his subsequent marriage to Edward IV's daughter, in 1486, Henry VII was by no means universally accepted as the new king of England. Indeed, he was opposed by leading members of the royal house of York. These included two of the late king's closest relatives: his sister, Margaret, Duchess of Burgundy, and his eldest surviving nephew, John de la Pole, Earl of Lincoln. The two of them now focussed their opposition to Henry around a boy whom they claimed – and almost certainly truly believed – was Edward of Clarence, Earl of Warwick, the son and heir of George Duke of Clarence. In the summer of 1486, Henry VII became aware that the boy in question was staying at Margaret of York's palace in Mechelen. There he had been received and acknowledged as her late brother's son by the dowager Duchess of Burgundy.

This situation in Mechelen was a potentially dire one from Henry VII's point of view. His response to it was to publicly parade *his* young Earl of Warwick, whom he had brought to London in 1485 from Sheriff Hutton Castle, through the streets of London to St Paul's Cathedral. Of course, it was Henry's aim and intention that Londoners and his courtiers should thereby recognise that he had under his control the real Earl of Warwick – and that the boy at the palace in Mechelen must therefore be an imposter. Unfortunately, however, it is only too obvious that Henry VII would not himself have been in any position to recognise and identify the boy brought to him from Sheriff Hutton in 1485, since he would never have seen him before. It is also doubtful how many (if any) citizens of London or courtiers would have been in a position to identify this boy as the true Earl of Warwick.

Indeed, the problem is actually much greater than that. The boy in the hands of Henry VII was presumably identical with the one who had been accepted by Richard III and Edward IV as the Earl of Warwick. He But he had been delivered into the hands of Edward IV from the Clarence nursery at Warwick Castle in the spring of 1477/8. This had followed the execution of his father, the Duke of Clarence, which had left the little boy as an orphan. The little boy who was handed over to the care of Edward IV in 1477/8 had then been three years old. However, there is no clear evidence that Edward IV had ever seen the child before. If he had, it would have been at the boy's baptism, when the baby was only a few days old.

It is known for certain that Edward IV had been one of the little boy's godfathers. But of course, the king might have had that role fulfilled for him vicariously, without actually having been present in person at the christening. At best, therefore, Edward IV was presented in 1478 with a three year-old-boy whom he had last seen when the child was just a few days old. The worst scenario was that the king was presented with a child whom he could never claim to have seen before. In either case, there would probably have been no way in which Edward IV would actually have been able to personally recognise and identify the child presented to him in 1478. It is therefore clear that, on that occasion, the king must simply have accepted the statement of his late brother's household servants regarding the identity of the little boy who was handed over to him.

Normally, of course, there would be no problem with that. However, the unique feature of this particular situation is the extraordinary role which had been played by the Duke of Clarence himself. As we saw earlier, in 1477 the Duke of Clarence – who was then possibly in a somewhat mentally disturbed state, and who feared for the life of his son and heir – had invented a definite project to smuggle the little Earl of Warwick out of the country, either to Ireland or to Flanders. This was coupled with a plan for the introduction of a substitute boy into the Clarence nursery at Warwick Castle. There the substitute child would assume the identity of the Earl of Warwick. What is not certain, however, is to what extent this plan had been carried to fruition.

In 1477/8 Edward IV's government had obviously interrogated the Abbott of Tewkesbury, together with John Tapton and Roger Harewell. These were three men who were accused of having agreed to produce a substitute child, who would then take on thje identity of the Earl of Warwick, for the Duke of Clarence. In answer to the questions put to them by the officials of Edward IV, these three men denied that they had in fact introduced a substitute child into the Clarence nursery. But of course they might simply have made that statement because they were afraid to admit carrying out such a substitution. Moreover, there is no way of proving that the Duke of Clarence might not have put in place more than one set of substitution plans.

Even more significant is the fact that Clarence's servant John Taylour does not seem to have been interrogated at all by the government officials of Edward IV. Yet Taylour was a key figure in the substitution plot. He is named in the act of attainder against the Duke of Clarence as the man dispatched by the Duke to collect the real Earl of Warwick from the Clarence nursery and transport him out of England. And one possible reason for the lack of government questioning in the case of Taylour might well have been that Taylour really had taken the young Earl of Warwick abroad somewhere – with the result that he himself was still out of the country and inaccessible for questioning at the time of the official investigation.

In other words, it is absolutely certain that the Duke of Clarence had *planned* to substitute an impostor for his real son and heir. However, it remains uncertain to what extent this plan had actually been carried out. Nevertheless, it does appear that a child may subsequently have been brought up in Ireland under the name of the Earl of Warwick, probably under the care of Clarence's deputy as Lieutenant of Ireland, the Earl of Kildare. Although, by itself, this does not prove that the boy in question really was the true Earl of Warwick, it appears that at some stage after 1478 Margaret, Duchess of Burgundy became aware of the child's existence. She then sent for the boy in question. This was the 'son of Clarence' who was received at her palace in Mechelen in 1486. But whether that boy, or the boy in the hands of Henry VII, in London, was the real Earl of Warwick remains unclear.

After living for a time in Mechelen, with Margaret of York, the alternative 'son of Clarence' was shipped, with the Earl of Lincoln; with Richard III's close friend, Francis, Viscount Lovell, and with an army recruited for them by the dowager Duchess of Burgundy, back to Ireland – which was probably the place where the young boy had been brought up. There, in Christ Church Cathedral, Dublin, this 'son of Clarence' was then proclaimed and crowned as King of England with the royal name and title of Edward VI.[6]

After the boy-king's coronation in Dublin, the Earl of Kildare, who had been appointed lieutenant's deputy by the new monarch's putative late father, George, Duke of Clarence, remained the effective head of the government in Ireland. But he and the Earl of Lincoln recruited Irish men-at-arms to augment the mercenary troops sent to Ireland by Margaret of York, with the aim of taking the newly crowned 'King Edward VI' across the Irish Sea to England, to contest the tenure of the usurper, King Henry VII.

At Whitsun 1487 King Henry VII was at Kenilworth when he received news from York of people conspiring against him who had been apprehended and questioned. Henry later sent copies of papal bulls in his favour to Yorkshire to be publicly proclaimed, in the hope of making support for the rival king, 'Edward VI', appear potentially sinful.

Meanwhile, in Dublin, the key supporters of 'King Edward VI' were making the final preparations to transport their German mercenaries and Irish foot soldiers to invade England. News had also been received in England of the coronation of 'Edward VI' in Dublin. This extraordinary information provoked some amazement and unrest. The small group of ships bearing the mixed race men-at-arms from Dublin landed on Foulney Island on 4 June 1487. This island was a rather unpromising place in itself. However, it gave the rebels access to potentially strong Ricardian loyalist territory in Yorkshire.

A key figure who now emerged to back the claim to the throne of 'King Edward VI' was Sir Thomas Broughton, a former retainer of King Richard III, who had received Lord Lovell at his home of Broughton Tower the previous year (1486). Sir Thomas now greeted the men from Dublin when they landed, and helped them secure supplies from the nearby Cistercian Abbey of Furness.

Tradition tells us that the army of 'Edward VI' spent the night of 4 June – its first night in England – at Ulverston. Four days later 'King Edward' and his putative cousin, Lincoln, had reached Masham. Meanwhile, by this time King Henry VII had left Kenilworth and was marching to meet them at the head of his forces. He made first for Leicester – a place which must have been rather full of recent memories for him. But since he had been victorious at Bosworth Field, possibly the memories were encouraging ones. On the advice of Archbishop Morton, Henry VII had declared a kind of martial law. Meanwhile in another echo of the events of August 1485, the Stanley family once again appeared to be hedging its bets between the two contesting kings of England.

The city of York was also divided. In spite of popular mythology on this subject, York was not actually completely committed in its support for the royal house which bore its name. Some men from York had fought earlier for Henry VI. The city had declined to allow Edward IV to enter as king in 1471, and in 1485, when Richard III sent to York for troops, the city's response had by no means been instantaneous. Now some men of York – most particularly the civic authorities – were apparently inclined to support Henry VII. They preferred the usurper who had been crowned at Westminster over the young king crowned in Dublin – probably because his men appeared to hold the effective power in England.

'King Edward VI' (or those acting for him) wrote to the mayor of York from Masham, requesting entry and support, and a copy of this letter is preserved in the city archives. However, at that point the request was refused. Meanwhile Lord Clifford and the Earl of Northumberland had reached York with their forces, in support of Henry VII. Indeed, it was Lord Clifford who made the first armed contact with the army of 'Edward VI'. This proved something of a disaster, because Clifford was defeated, and forced to retreat to York. Following this initial victory of the forces of the boy-king crowned in Ireland, the two Lords Scrope then attacked York in the name of 'King Edward'. Like the earlier initiative of their opponent, Lord Clifford, their attack also failed. However, it prevented the Earl of Northumberland from joining Henry VII. Indeed, when he left York, instead of attempting to join Henry, Northumberland just retreated northwards with his men, lying low and sitting on the fence.

This proves that at this stage in the conflict, opinion in England was by no means convinced that Henry VII would prove to be the victor.

Indeed, the army of 'King Edward' had now enjoyed a second victory, this time against Henry VII's cavalry, in Sherwood Forest. The fact that 'Edward VI' had now scored two victories and seemed to be the up-and-coming power finally caused the city of York to alter its stance. Although hitherto York had accepted the sovereignty of Henry VII, and had declined to allow 'Edward VI' to enter, the city now about-turned and publicly declared its support for 'King Edward'. Meanwhile, false rumours began to spread that Henry VII was in flight. To counteract these, Henry VII appeared to his army on 14 June (the Feast of Corpus Christi) and tried to restore their confidence. Henry then assembled his now quite impressive forces close to Nottingham, and began to move along the south bank of the river Trent.

Young 'King Edward', together with the Earl of Lincoln and their army, was on the northern side of the same river. Curiously, however, overall Edward had attracted less armed support in England than had been hoped for. Nevertheless, on 15 June Lincoln, who was in practical command of his putative young cousin's army, crossed the river Trent and set up camp in the village of East Stoke.

On the following day 'there was a soore batell, in the which th'erl of Lincolne and many othre, as well Ynglisshmen as Irissh, to the nombre of vM^I [5,000] were slayne and murdred ; the Lord Lovell was discomfotid and fled, with Sir Thomas Broghton and many othre, and the child which they callid ther King was takyn and broght unto the Kinges grace'.[7]

According to the standard 'Tudor' accounts, the boy king from

Dublin subsequently became first a kitchen boy in Henry VII's palace, and later a falconer in the royal household. Curiously, however, the person in question was apparently not spontaneously recognised by Irish peers who visited Henry VII in 1489, even though Henry VII seems to have been eager to have the young man identified by them.[8] What is more, Henry VII's kitchen servant was subsequently reported to have been older than the boy who had been crowned in Dublin. For example, Polydore Vergil employed the Latin word *puer* (boy) to describe this person in the 1534 published version of his text. However, he modified this to the word *adolescens* (youth) in his later published version of 1546. This raises a question as to whether the person captured by Henry VII – or at least, the person later employed in his kitchens – really was his rival, 'King Edward VI'.[9]

In the context of this question, it is intriguing to discover that, one Continental source recounts that although 'Edward VI' was indeed captured at Stoke, he did not subsequently remain in the hands of Henry VII, and certainly never served in the royal kitchens. According to this version of the story,

> the Earl of Lincoln and Martin Zwarte [commander of the forces provided by Margaret, Duchess of Burgundy] fell with about five thousand men. But the king [Henry VII], who acted in a kindly way towards foreigners, commanded that all the prisoners from Ireland should be strangled. The young Duke of Clarence [*sic* 'King Edward VI'] was also captured, whom the Earl of Suffolk carefully delivered, and he fell back with him to Guisnes.[10]

At first sight, the identity of the 'Earl of Suffolk' seems somewhat mysterious in 1487. At that time the Earl of Lincoln's father was still alive and held the title 'Duke of Suffolk'. However, later, when Adrien De But was writing his Chronicle, the Suffolk title had passed to the Earl of Lincoln's younger brother, Edmund de la Pole, and the family title had indeed been demoted to an earldom. Edmund de la Pole was certainly very well known as a Yorkist prince in the Low Countries (see below). Therefore it seems probable that De But is referring to Edmund.

Of course, there is no solid proof that Edmund managed to get 'Edward VI' away from England and back to the Low Countries. Curiously, however, there has been a more recent suggestion of the existence of a supposed Yorkist prince who lived secretly in the Low Countries in the late fifteenth century. In 1978 Jack Leslau published a complex interpretation of a 'Holbein' painting of the family of Sir Thomas More.[11] The present writer by no means agrees with Leslau's conclusions. However, some of his arguments are interesting. He included the suggestion that the man depicted as standing in the doorway, who is labelled in a kind of Latin as *Johanes heresius* is 'John, the rightful heir' (interpreting the word *heresius* as two words: *heres ius* – though the grammar of this Latin is arguably somewhat odd). Leslau therefore concluded that the 'John' in the doorway was, in reality, a Yorkist prince. In Leslau's view, he was one of the 'princes in the Tower'.

Based on his interpretation of the More family painting, Leslau went on to claim that the 'John' in question was actually the person usually known as Dr John Clements (a son-in-law of Sir Thomas More). Moreover, he argued that this person was identical with the John Clements, who had been inscribed as a student at the University of Louvain (Leuven) on 13 February 1489.[12] On the basis of the evidence from the University of Leuven, Leslau also deduced that in 1489 John Clements had been aged about sixteen, implying a birth date of 1473. However, in actual fact the age for entry to university in England in the fifteenth century was generally about fifteen. Therefore the John Clements in question could perhaps have been born a little later than 1473 – perhaps in 1474, or even in 1475.

The chronology of a single individual bearing the name 'John Clements', as produced by Leslau, was obviously very complex, and rather hard to believe. It is certain that a John Clements (married to one of Thomas More's daughters) later worked in Italy, lived on the European mainland for religious reasons in the reign of the second ('Tudor') King Edward VI, subsequently served as physician to Queen Mary and was eventually buried (with his wife) at St Rumboldt's Cathedral in Mechelen in 1572. Yet it seems that this person can hardly have been identical with the John Clements who studied at the University of Leuven in the late 1480s and who was probably born in England (or at least, of English parents) in about 1474. However, there is the possibility of a family connection between the two Johns. Perhaps Sir Thomas More's son-in-law was a son of the elder John Clements who had been a student at the University of Leuven in 1489. This suggestion was first put forward by Alwyn Allen in 1979,[13] – though Leslau did not agree with it.[14]

At all events, in the context of the Dublin-crowned Yorkist 'King Edward VI', the earlier John Clements (student at Leuven) revealed by Leslau, and claimed by him to have been a Yorkist prince, is an interesting figure, and his first name is possibly significant. This is because the surviving text of the *Heralds' Memoir 1486–1490* reports that after the battle of Stoke, the boy-king 'Edward VI' was captured by a man called Robert Bellingham. It then goes on to state that the boy's real name was subsequently revealed to be John [–]. The text in question runs as follows:

> On the morne, whiche was Satirday [16 June 1487, Henry VII] erly arros and harde ij masses, wherof the lorde John [*sic* for Richard] Fox, bishop of Excester, sange the ton. And the king had v good and true men of the village of Ratecliff, whiche shewde his grace the beste way for to conduyt his hoost to Newark, ... of whiche guides the king yave ij to therle of Oxinforde to conduit the forwarde [vanguard], and the remenant reteynede at his pleasur. And so in good order and array before ix of the clok, beside a village called Stook, a large myle oute of Newarke, his forwarde [vanguard] recountrede his enemyes and rebelles, wher by the helpe of Almyghty God he hade the victorye. And ther was taken the lade that his rebelles called King Edwarde (whoos name was in dede John) – by a vaylent and a gentil esquire of the kings howse called Robert Bellingham.[15]

When taken together with Adrien De But's account that the young 'King Edward VI', who was captured after the battle of Stoke, was then aided by Edmund de la Pole (later Earl of Suffolk), and was smuggled by him to the Low Countries, this raises the question of whether this boy then went on to become a student at the University of Leuven under the name of John Clements, and whether he may subsequently have produced a son bearing the same name who then went on to marry one of the daughters of Sir Thomas More. In this context it is perhaps a pity that Leslau's attempts to have the body of the Dr John Clements who was buried in Mechelen Cathedral exhumed and genetically examined were not, in the end, successful.

Meanwhile, in England, following the defeat at Stoke, the Yorkist cause appeared to be lost, and the 'Wars of the Roses' seemed over. However, both points proved not to be the case, as we shall see.

12

EDWARD IV'S HEIR, 'KING RICHARD IV'

Despite the defeat of the Yorkist 'King Edward VI' at the battle of Stoke, and the birth of 'Tudor' heirs to the throne, the Yorkist cause was by no means at an end. A few years after the Yorkist defeat at the battle of Stoke, a young man surfaced in Ireland, in Scotland and on the mainland of Europe who called himself 'Richard of England'. In some ways he seems to have been a relatively modest individual, for initially he made no claim to be king. However, he did say that he was the younger of the two sons of Edward IV and Elizabeth Woodville.

It is just as difficult to tell the story of 'Richard of England' as it is to tell the story of the Dublin-crowned Yorkist King 'Edward VI' – and for the same reason. Incidentally, in this present study, the boy who was crowned in Dublin is generally referred to under the royal name and number which he used, as Edward VI – but in inverted commas to distinguish him from the 'Tudor' monarch who subsequently adopted the same name and number. On the other hand, 'Richard of England' will not generally be referred to as 'Richard IV', since he was never crowned as King of England,

and there is no surviving evidence of his use of the royal numeral 'IV'.

In both cases it is very hard (indeed, arguably impossible) to ascertain what is the real story. According to the official Tudor government account, 'Richard of England' was born in about 1474, the son of Jehan de Werbecque and Nicaise Farou (or John Osbek and Kataryn de Faro), a prosperous couple from the town of Tournai. This information was based upon an alleged confession of the claimant, following his capture by the English government in 1497. However, the value of the confession is doubtful, since it was almost certainly extracted under duress. Incidentally, if this account is true, Richard's native language would presumably have been French, though it is also claimed in this version of the story that he had later learned Dutch (Flemish).

Despite the fact that the basic information about the Werbecque family and their associates given in the confession appears to be accurate, not all historians have accepted this as proof that the wider information provided on the subject of their alleged connection with 'Richard of England' is the truth. Some have suggested that 'Richard of England' deliberately lied in his confession about how he came to put forward his claim, partly in order to conceal the truth about his background, and partly in the hope that he would thereby escape the death penalty (as, apparently, his predecessor, 'Lambert Simnel', had done).

Moreover, although the young man stated in his confession that he was a member of the Osbek / Werbecque family of Tournai, he himself had also stated earlier that he was Richard of Shrewsbury, Duke of York, the younger son of Edward IV and Elizabeth Woodville, born on 17 August 1473. He claimed that he had been delivered from the Tower of London by an English Lord in the late summer of 1483, and smuggled to safety in the Low Countries. If this story were correct, obviously his native language would have been not French, but English, though as an English royal prince he would probably also have been given some training in French and Latin. In England and elsewhere there was (and is) uncertainty regarding the fate of Edward IV's sons by Elizabeth Woodville – and most particularly, the fate of the younger of the two sons (who was known as Richard of Shrewsbury, because that was where he was born).

A third possibility for the origin of 'Richard of England' is the one which we began to explore earlier in chapter 8 (above). For Edward IV and Richard Duke of Gloucester had been in exile in the Low Countries from October 1470 until the end of February 1470/1. During these five months either of them could potentially have taken a local mistress and engendered a bastard son in the Low Countries. Given what is known about their characters at this period, Edward IV would probably have been more likely to do this than his brother Richard. Thus it is possible that 'Richard of England' was an illegitimate son of Edward IV. If so, he would have been born, probably, in The Hague, in about August or September 1471. In that case his first language might possibly have been neither English nor French, but Dutch (Flemish) – though of course this may have depended upon the native language of his unknown mother, and upon where precisely in the Low Countries (or elsewhere) he was actually brought up as a child (see below – Bernard André). Perhaps he was initially fostered to the Osbek / Werbecque family in Tournai. Possibly, through his mother, he was even related somehow to the Osbek / Werbecque family. Incidentally, one intriguing point related to this third hypothesis regarding the origin of 'Richard of England' is the fact that some early accounts do actually suggest that he was an illegitimate son of Richard III (Richard, Duke of Gloucester).[1]

Bernard André (Henry VII's historian, and the tutor of his son, Arthur, Prince of Wales) stated that 'they feigned that a certain Pierre of Tournai, brought up by a certain Jew named Edward and subsequently sponsored as a godfather by King Edward and reared in this nation, was the younger son of King Edward IV and pretended that he had grown up in various nations'.[2] This could potentially be consistent with the notion that 'Richard of England' was a bastard son of Edward IV, born in the Low Countries in about September 1471. In this case the boy must subsequently have been shipped to England by Edward Brampton and patronised (if not specifically recognised) by his royal father. However, that was certainly not the overall view of 'Richard of England' which Bernard André intended to convey.

Depending on which of the three origin hypotheses is correct, there could have been a difference of a maximum of two years between the age of 'Richard of England' and the age of Richard of Shrewsbury. During childhood such an age difference could potentially have been significant and noticeable. But by the time he reached his teens such a discrepancy would have begun to vanish, particularly since 'Richard of England' was an unusually tall lad. By 1490 (when 'Richard of England''s identity claim was first voiced), Richard of Shrewsbury would have been seventeen years old. A royal bastard conceived in 1470-71 would have been nineteen. As for the putative son of Osbek / Werbecque, he would have been about sixteen.

As we have seen, the various possible accounts of the origin of 'Richard of England' would imply different native languages and a different range of acquired foreign languages. Unfortunately, however, we have no clear information as to which language was the mother tongue of 'Richard of England'. Nor do we know how he spoke English, or whether he had any kind of accent when he did so. For obvious reasons, no recordings exist of his voice. Therefore it is not possible now to ascertain precisely how he spoke. However, he was evidently able to speak English, and no contemporary source ever implies that he had a strong or noticeable foreign accent when he did so. This may suggest that he had been at least partly brought up in an English-speaking environment. That would appear to contradict one version of the Osbek / Werbecque story, which suggests that he only learnt English in his teens, from a merchant in Middleburg called John Strewe. As we have already seen, though, another version of the Osbek / Werbecque story appears to suggest that he had been brought up in England, in the household of the converted Portuguese Jew, Edward Brampton.[3] It seems possible that 'Richard of England' was able to write Latin (since he wrote to Queen Isabel of Castile in that language). The surviving accounts of his royal career from about 1490 onwards also seem to imply that he was familiar with French, for he is said to have served for a time with a merchant from Brittany, and was later received by the French King, Charles VIII.[4] As we have already noted, his confession would appear to imply that French would have been his mother tongue, but that he later learned Dutch (Flemish).[5]

Accounts suggest that, whoever he was, between the years 1485 and 1487 'Richard of England' had lived in Flanders, just north of Mechelen (the home of Margaret of York, dowager Duchess of Burgundy), in the city of Antwerp, in Bergen op Zoom, and in Middelburg (see map). However, in the spring of 1487 Richard

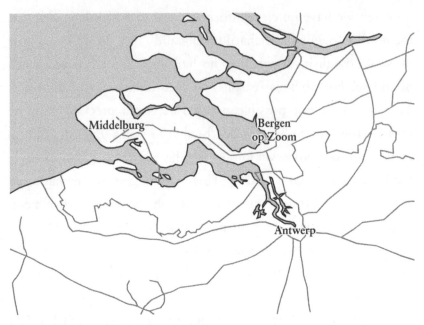

The Low Countries, showing where the young 'Richard of England' reputedly lived.

left the Low Countries, and accompanied Sir Edward and Lady Brampton (D. Margarida Bemonde), to the Portuguese court.

As we have seen, Sir Edward Brampton (or Brandon), KG, (Duarte Brandão) was a Portuguese Jew who had fled to England in 1468 to escape a possible accusation of crime. Since Jews were not then allowed to reside in England, Duarte converted to Christianity under the patronage of Edward IV, who stood as his godfather at his Christian baptism. Brampton may well have accompanied Edward IV and Richard, Duke of Gloucester to the Low Countries in the winter of 1470-71. Later, following his return to England, he had been knighted by Richard III. But in 1485, when that king was killed at Bosworth, for reasons which are not precisely documented, but which were presumably related to the change in English royal dynasty, Sir Edward left England.

It is not known for certain how, when or where Brampton had become acquainted with 'Richard of England', though one seventeenth-century account actually goes so far as to suggest that Brampton was 'Richard"s father![6] If the second of the possible stories of the boy's origin is correct and the young lad really was Richard of Shrewsbury, Brampton may have been personally responsible for his transportation to the Low Countries, following his delivery from the Tower of London by an unnamed English Lord. Possibly the lord in question was the Duke of Buckingham – and in that context it is, perhaps, significant (given Brampton's Portuguese origin and connections) that a contemporary Portuguese source states that Buckingham was responsible for the fate of the so-called 'princes in the Tower'. In any case, if Brampton had transported Richard of Shrewsbury to the Low Countries, he would obviously have been aware of 'Richard' and his royal origin throughout, and would have assumed some kind of responsibility for this twelve-year-old prince from August 1483.

Similarly, if the third hypothesis for the origin of 'Richard of England' is correct, Brampton may have acted as the boy's guardian in England, after the shipping of the young royal bastard to his father's homeland. Alternatively, he may have been acquainted with the boy's mother in the winter of 1470-71, when she became the mistress of Edward IV (or possibly of Richard, Duke of Gloucester) in The Hague. He may also have been aware that, when the royal party returned to England, in March 1470/1, this girl was left behind in the Low Countries in a state of pregnancy. Since she was possibly a member of the Gruuthuse household, and since Brampton's base in the Low Countries, when he settled there again after August 1485, was Brugge (the home of Gruuthuse), he may have heard from Gruuthuse shortly after his arrival at Brugge, in August 1485, the story of the 1471 birth of a Yorkist royal bastard son. Indeed, he would probably have met the boy (who would have been about fourteen years old), at about that time – assuming, of course that he had not known all about him long before and been involved in shipping him to England.

On the other hand, if the story of the Osbek/Werbecque origin of 'Richard of England' is the true one, this leaves us with absolutely no idea of how Brampton came to meet the boy. Nevertheless, however they met, Brampton must always have been aware of the notable physical resemblance between this boy and his own late patron, King Edward IV.

Whatever the truth about his origin, in 1491, 'Richard of England' sailed from Portugal to Ireland – where, as we have already seen, his predecessor and putative cousin, 'King Edward VI' had recently enjoyed support and had even been given the honour of a coronation. However, the significant difference between the claims of 'Edward VI' and 'Richard of England' was that the former boy had probably already been very well known to the Earl of Kildare and other members of the Anglo-Irish aristocracy for almost all his life.[7] On the other hand, 'Richard of England' had been completely unknown in Ireland prior to 1491. Moreover, there is also the significant fact that, in the end, Irish support for 'Edward VI' had failed to bring that boy's claim to the English throne to a successful conclusion.

At all events, 'Richard' won little support in Ireland, so he returned to the mainland of Europe, where he was initially honourably received by King Charles VIII of France. Unfortunately, the following year a treaty between the governments of Charles VIII and Henry VII ensured that 'Richard' was then expelled from French territory. Meanwhile, 'Richard' had now been formally recognised as her nephew by Margaret of York, the dowager Duchess of Burgundy. Some historians have suggested that Margaret knew 'Richard' to be an impostor, and that she was simply using him to oppose the usurper, Henry VII. However, this suggestion appears incredible. If Margaret's aim was to further the interests of her own dynasty – the royal house of York – what would have been the advantage of ousting Henry VII (who was married to Margaret's niece, and whose children were therefore Margaret's great nephews and nieces) in favour of a fraudulent claimant to whom she was unrelated? Logic suggests that, whatever the truth of the situation, Margaret of York must have managed to convince herself that 'Richard of England' was the son of her elder brother, the late king Edward IV. This might still allow for the possibility that she may have been aware that 'Richard' was actually an illegitimate son of Edward IV, with a Flemish or Burgundian mother.

Although the English government complained to Margaret's step-grandson, Philip of Habsburg, and ultimately imposed a trade embargo on the Low Countries in an attempt to have 'Richard of England' thrown out of that territory, the Habsburg / Burgundian court continued to support his claim, and he was also acknowledged by other heads of state. In 1493, when he attended the funeral of the Emperor Frederick III, he was formally recognised as King Richard of England, and it is usually asserted that this was under the title of 'Richard IV'. Actually there appears to be no surviving explicit evidence for his use of the royal numeral 'IV', though that would arguably have been logical.

In the summer of 1495, an expedition backed financially by Margaret of York shipped 'King Richard' to Kent. However, no local support was forthcoming and 'King Richard' never even set foot on the English soil. Instead he returned to Ireland, where this time he attracted the support of the Earl of Kildare's cousin, the Earl of Desmond. Once again, however, he enjoyed no military success and he finally fled to Scotland.

King James IV saw personal advantages in the presence in Scotland of this English throne claimant, and agreed to the marriage of 'King Richard' to his relative, Lady Catherine Gordon, daughter of the second Earl of Huntly. Catherine's mother was either Huntly's first (second) wife, Annabella of Scotland, the youngest daughter of King James I, or Huntly's second (third) wife, Elizabeth Hay, the descendant in two lines of the founder of the Stuart (Stewart) dynasty, King Robert II. Thus, whoever her mother was (and the records are not clear on this point), Catherine Gordon was undoubtedly a relative of the Scottish king in some degree.[8]

Once his Scottish royal marriage had been celebrated in Edinburgh, 'Richard of England' joined forces with his new relative-by-marriage, King James IV and an invasion of England was prepared which took place in September 1496. A suitable royal banner and suit of armour were prepared for Richard, and prayers were offered for the success of the enterprise at Holyrood Abbey. Meanwhile, Henry VII's spies were well aware of the forthcoming invasion. However, they advised the king that it would probably peter out in less than a week, because of a lack of supplies.

These predictions proved more or less correct. The Scottish forces crossed into England on 21 September and destroyed some small defences, but they only penetrated a few miles into English territory. No notable English support materialised for 'Richard of England' – possibly because he formed part of a Scottish invasion. Moreover the Scottish forces themselves withdrew after only four days, when they found themselves confronted by an English army under the command of Lord Neville. Richard's Scottish alliance had proved of little real value. Moreover, James IV now wished to rid himself of 'Richard of England', and hired a ship called the *Cuckoo* to ferry him across the sea, back to Ireland. Thus, in July 1497, 'Richard' found himself in Waterford with little or no support. While James IV made peace with Henry VII, 'Richard' tried to besiege Waterford but after just over a week he was driven off and forced to flee from Ireland.

'Richard of England' now landed in Cornwall, where he hoped to benefit from Cornish resentment of English dominance. Initially he enjoyed some success. Cornishmen rose in his support and proclaimed him king of England. With a new Cornish army, Richard took Exeter and advanced on Taunton. However, it now becomes clear that 'Richard' was not a very confident claimant. When he heard that scouts of Henry VII were approaching, he fled from his own Cornish army, leaving them with no leader. As a result, they had little choice but to surrender to Henry VII. As for 'Richard' himself, he sought refuge at Beaulieu Abbey, but when Henry VII's men found him there, he surrendered to them. Initially imprisoned at Taunton, 'Richard' was then taken to London and incarcerated in the Tower (from which he claimed to have escaped almost exactly fourteen years earlier). On the way, he was paraded through the streets of London, where he was greeted with derision.

In the Tower of London, 'Richard of England' came to know his putative cousin, Henry VII's Earl of Warwick (see above). Possibly their encounters and the subsequent events were engineered by Henry VII's men. For the two Yorkist princely claimants eventually plotted (or at least, were alleged to have plotted) an escape, which, naturally, failed, and this was then used as a pretext by Henry VII's government for the execution of both of them. The official Earl of Warwick was executed royally, by being beheaded. However, 'Richard of England' was dragged on a hurdle from the Tower to Tyburn, where he read a confession and was hanged.

Incidentally, the physical resemblance of 'Richard' to Edward IV is well documented and caused Henry VII to have him beaten up before his execution, in an attempt to prevent this resemblance from being noticed. This has led to speculation that, even if he was not the genuine Richard of Shrewsbury, Duke of York, 'Perkin Warbeck' (as Henry VII's government now officially called him) may perhaps have been somehow connected with the royal house of York. As we have seen, he might possibly have been a royal bastard.

As we have also seen, one of the possible techniques employed by the government of Henry VII in order to bring about the final destruction of both Henry VII's Earl of Warwick and 'Richard of England' seems to have been to allow them to fraternise in the Tower. Another method may well have been the staging of yet another royal imposture – one which no-one could really have taken seriously. This occurred shortly before the trials and executions of the two 1490s 'princes in the Tower'.

Little is known about the 1498/9 pretender, except his name, which is recorded as Ralph Wilford. However, Ralph's appearance on the scene could well have been one of the key factors which led to the executions, not only of himself, but also of 'Richard of England', and of the official Earl of Warwick. Indeed, that may have been the reason why he was encouraged to put himself forward as a Yorkist pretender.

Polydore Vergil failed to record Ralph's name, but recounted the story of the young man's imposture as follows:

There was [a] certain Augustinian monk [*sic* for friar or canon] named Patrick, who, I suppose, *for the purpose of making the earl [of Warwick] unpopular*, began to suborn a disciple of his (whose name, as far as I know, is not recorded) and drum into his ears that he could easily gain the throne, if he would agree to follow his advice. The student not only did not refuse, but asked [*sic*] again and again asked him to be quick in putting his design in to practice. For what man is there who fears the law or danger to the extent that he refuses to do or suffer anything in the world for the sake of gaining a crown? Therefore the monk shared his plan and both of them went boldly to Kent, a county on other occasions not deaf to innovations. There the young man first revealed to some the secret that he was Edward of Warwick, lately escaped from the Tower of London by Patrick's help and art. Then he openly proclaimed this and begged all men's help. But the sedition lost its leadership before they could bring it to fruition, when teacher and pupil were both enchained, the latter put to death, and the former consigned to eternal darkness of prison because he was a monk. For among the English the clergy are held in such respect that a priest condemned of treason, like ordained priests guilty of other crimes, is spared his life.[9]

About a century after the events, Francis Bacon, wrote that this new pretender's name was Ralph Wilford, and stated that he was the son of a cordwainer.[10] The latter fact had been recorded much earlier, in the *Great Chronicle of London* (written in the late fifteenth century or early in the sixteenth century). The *Great Chronicle* also states precisely that Ralph Wilford had put forward his claim between 8 and 24 February of the fourteenth year of the reign of Henry VII (1498-99).

In this passing of tyme In the bordurs of Norffolk and Suffolk was a newe maumet [*puppet*] arerid which namyd hym sylf to be the fforenamid earle of warwyk, The which by sly & coverty meanys essayed to wyn to hym soom adherentis, But all In vayn, In conclusion he was browgth before therle of Oxynfford, To whom at length he confessed that he was born In london, and that he was sone unto a Cordyner dwelling at the blak Bulle In Bysshoppsgate street, afftir which confession he was sent up the the kyng & ffrom hym to prison, and upon that areygnyd & convict of treason, and ffynally upon shrove tuysday [12 February 1498/9] hangid at Seynt Thomas watering[11] In his shirt, where he soo hyng styll tyll the Satyrday ffoluyng [16 February], and then ffor noyaunce of the way passers he was takyn doun & buried, being of the age of xix yeris or xx^{ti}.[12]

So how does the unfortunate Ralph Wilford fit into the wider story of post-1485 Yorkist claimants to the English throne? He appears simply to have been a false Earl of Warwick, but it is difficult to understand what he could have hoped to achieve. Unlike 'Edward VI' and 'Richard of England', Ralph Wilford enjoyed no key Yorkist backing for his cause. For example, he did not enjoy the support of Margaret of York, who appears never to have heard of him. Thus he had little or no real chance of ever acquiring the crown.

The likeliest explanation for Ralph's claim therefore appears to be that those who wished to bring about the deaths of Henry VII's Earl of Warwick and of 'Richard of England' thought that by producing a third (and obviously false) Yorkist pretender they could first further undermine the claim of 'Richard', and second, bring about the executions of all three Yorkist claimants. It is therefore possible that the inspiration for the claim of Ralph Wilford secretly came from the 'Tudor' government, which was at that point rather eager to assure the Spanish monarchs that all Yorkist claimants had been dealt with, and that the projected marriage between Arthur, Prince of Wales, and the Infanta Catherine of Aragon could now safely take place.

In this context it is worth noting that, following the executions of Henry VII's Earl of Warwick and 'Richard of England', the Spanish ambassador, de Puebla, reported that although there had been pretenders to the English crown, these two executions had ensured that not 'a drop of doubtful Royal blood' now remained.[13] This shows that, while the Spanish, in the context of their proposed royal alliance with the heir of Henry VII, were definitely concerned about the situation in England, their ambassador in London may have somewhat overestimated the effect of the executions he mentioned. As for the Infanta herself, many years later, when her second royal marriage in England (to King Henry VIII) was falling apart, she is reported to have seen the break-up of her marriage as a kind of Divine judgement upon her, due to the fact that her initial English alliance had been brought about specifically by shedding the innocent blood of Yorkist claimants.

However, Henry VII had various plans for ensuring, not only that the proposed Spanish royal marriage of his son and heir should take place, but also that there would be no further Yorkist attempts to dethrone him. He hoped that his executions of Ralph Wilford, of 'Richard of England' and of his officially imprisoned Earl of Warwick would move both aims forward. Subsequently, and with the same aims in mind, his government went on to sponsor the allegation that Sir James Tyrell, 'who was executed on

May 6 1502, for his involvement in the conspiracy of Edmund de la Pole against Henry VII',[14] had made a secret confession, stating that he had murdered the two 'princes in the Tower' on the orders of Richard III.

Tyrell's alleged confession was later reported by Sir Thomas More in the following words:

> Very truth is it and well known that at such time as Sir James Tyrell was in the Tower for treason committed against the most famous prince, King Henry the Seventh, both Dighton and he were examined and confessed the murder [of the "princes in the Tower"] in the manner above written, but whither the bodies were removed they could nothing tell.[15]

The assertive wording of More's account was, of course, purposely composed, in order to conceal the true facts: first, that no such confession actually exists (or ever existed), and second, that the story was a deliberate (and rather late) invention of the 'Tudor' government, designed to prevent any future claimant from putting himself forward as a living 'prince in the Tower'. Likewise, the story that the dead bodies had been moved after the alleged murder – so that the alleged murderers were unable to reveal where they now lay – also appears to have been deliberate, in order to account for the lack of any known tomb of the 'princes in the Tower'. Of course one (unforeseen) result is, however, that this part of More's story strongly tends to undermine the alleged identity of the remains found at the Tower of London in 1674, and subsequently royally interred by Charles II at Westminster Abbey!

One point which is clearly demonstrated by Sir James Tyrell's genuine involvement in the latest Yorkist movement, in favour of

Edmund de la Pole, Earl of Suffolk, is that fact that at the start of the sixteenth century, Henry VII was still perceived as a kind of Lancastrian claimant to the English throne, in a context in which some regret was felt at the passing from power of the royal house of York (see below). Thus, even if the story of the Tyrell confession succeeded in making it more difficult for anyone to claim to be a living son of Edward IV, this did not by any means solve the Yorkist problem completely. There remained a number of surviving members of the rival royal house of York – including Edmund de la Pole – who might yet choose to assert their legitimate claims to the English throne.

13

DE LA POLES, POLES AND COURTENAYS

Tyrell's real crime in terms of Henry VII's government had been, not his murder of the 'princes in the Tower' (who were potential dangerous rivals of Henry VII, as shown by the case of 'Richard of England') but his support for another key Yorkist contender for the crown of England. This was Edmund de la Pole, Earl of Suffolk, the Earl of Lincoln's younger brother. Born in about 1473, Edmund was the eldest surviving son of Elizabeth of York senior, Duchess of Suffolk – the middle sister of Edward IV and

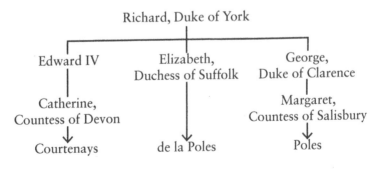

Family Tree 10: Heirs of the House of York

Richard III – and was therefore a very strong potential Yorkist claimant.

In spite of the role played by his elder brother, the Earl of Lincoln, in the Yorkist campaign of 1486–1487, initially Edmund appears to have shown no overt opposition to Henry VII. He was only about fourteen years old when his brother was killed, and his mother and he seem to have maintained a good relationship with Henry's consort, Elizabeth of York junior, who was Edmund's first cousin. Even so, according to the account of Adrien De But (see above), Edmund seems reputed to have been sufficiently Yorkist in 1487 to have rescued the defeated Yorkist King 'Edward VI' and helped him escape to Flanders.

Later, Henry had treated Edmund somewhat oddly. When his father, John, Duke of Suffolk, died, in October 1492, Henry allowed Edmund – then aged about nineteen – to inherit the *earldom* of Suffolk, but not the *dukedom*. This was done on the grounds that Edmund had insufficient financial means to support the high ducal rank. However, in that same year the king awarded Edmund the Order of the Garter. Two years later, in November 1494, Edmund played a ceremonial role at a Westminster tournament which was held to celebrate the significant investiture of Henry VII's second son (later King Henry VIII) as the new Duke of York. And the following year the king paid Edmund a royal visit at the young earl's home at Ewelme in Oxfordshire.

Like his elder brother, the Earl of Lincoln, Edmund de la Pole appears to have had no personal desire for the crown of England while senior Yorkist claimants existed. The potential senior Yorkist claimants in question were the Dublin-crowned 'King Edward VI', Henry VII's official Earl of Warwick prisoner, and 'Richard of England' – the alleged sons of George, Duke of Clarence, and of

Edward IV, two of whom had been publicly acknowledged and backed by the senior independent Yorkist princess, Margaret, Duchess of Burgundy.

It is known that Edmund de la Pole believed that 'Richard of England' truly was a son of Edward IV. As for 'King Edward VI', his major Yorkist male sponsor had been Edmund's elder brother, the Earl of Lincoln, and we have seen that according to a Flemish account, Edmund himself was supposed to have rescued 'Edward VI' from the hands of Henry VII after the battle of Stoke. Later Edmund may well have tried to save 'Richard of England' and Henry VII's official Earl of Warwick from the Tower of London.

However, once such claimants were about to be exterminated by Henry VII, Edmund realised that he himself was now on the verge of becoming the senior surviving Yorkist male heir. Thus he apparently began to have a rather different perception of his position. Edmund, now in his mid-twenties, seems to have become a rather hot-headed young man. In 1499, following his involvement in the death of a man called Thomas Crue, and a subsequent court hearing, he left England. Henry VII's historian, Polydore Vergil recorded the following version of this story.

> Edmund de la Pole, Earl of Suffolk, the son of Duke John of Suffolk and King Edward's sister Elizabeth, a bold fellow, brave, headstrong in his counsels, was guilty of homicide because he killed a lowborn man in a quarrel, and, although the king spared him, he took it amiss that he was called required to stand his trial as an accused man (for this is a mark of disgrace). A little later he went to his maternal aunt Margaret in Flanders, without obtaining royal leave. But immediately thereafter he so excused his deed to Henry that he seemed to be free of guilt, and therefore came home with immunity.[1]

As Vergil reports, Edmund's flight abroad coincided chronologically with him finding himself in a most denigrated position in relation to the government of Henry VII. It was in the summer of 1499 that Edmund – the senior surviving, free Yorkist prince of the blood – was obliged to defend himself before an ordinary law court for killing a man. Feeling insulted at not being treated according to his royal rank, Edmund left the country on 1 July. This was four months after the execution of the pretender Ralph Wliford, and at a time when the executions of Henry VII's Earl of Warwick and of 'Richard of England' were approaching. Possibly another part of Edmund's motivation was his desire to try to forestall or prevent these two executions.

Although Henry VII (and Polydore Vergil) assumed that the Earl of Suffolk was on his way to his aunt's palace in Mechelen, actually, Edmund went, not to his aunt Margaret, but to the Castle of Guisnes, just outside Calais. This may have been a place he knew, for he was earlier reported to have smuggled the Dublin-crowned 'King Edward VI' to Guines after the battle of Stoke. At Guisnes Edmund was received by the governor of the castle, Sir James Tyrell, whose earlier loyal support for the house of York was well-remembered. As we have seen, Tyrell was subsequently executed for involvement in the schemes of Edmund de la Pole.

Guisnes formed part of Henry VII's realm, so that in effect, initially Edmund had not gone 'abroad'. Subsequently, however, he sought refuge just across the border in Artois. At that point, Henry VII appealed to the Archduke Philip of Austria (Margaret of York's step-grandson), reinforcing his appeal with a threat of a trade war. As a result, Philip's government then persuaded Edmund de la Pole to return to England. They assured him that if he did so, Henry VII would forgive him. However, when

Edmund did return to England he found himself heavily fined by Henry VII – a point which Vergil neglected to mention in his account.

Vergil continued the story as follows:

While the marriage of Arthur [Prince of Wales] and [the Infanta] Catherine was being celebrated at London and all the people were given over to pleasure, and while Henry in particular was relishing his happiness, [Edmund] went back to Flanders with his brother Richard, either because he was oppressed by debt (he had contracted a lot for that marriage), or was solicited by his aunt, or again because he was provoked by envy, not being able to stand the sight of Henry, a man of the opposing faction, reigning for so many years.[2]

In actual fact, however, this time the impetus for the flight abroad of Edmund de la Pole and his brother, Richard, had come directly from Archduke Philip's father, the Emperor Maximilian.

In 1501, Lord Curzon, who was also a baron of the Holy Roman Empire, travelled to Turkey. On the way he mentioned the Earl of Suffolk's problems with Henry VII to Margaret of York's step-son-in-law, the Emperor Maximilian. The response he received from Maximilian was 'that if his majestie mighte have oon of king Edwardis blode in his handis, he wold helpe him to recover the coroune of England and bee revenged upon H[enry VII]'.[3] Maximilian's mother, the Empress Eleanor, had been the daughter of King Edward (Duarte) of Portugal, and was therefore the granddaughter of Henry IV's sister, Philippa of Lancaster. Thus Maximilian was a distant Lancastrian cousin of the Earl of Suffolk.

Thanks to receiving Maximilian's message of potential support,

Edmund de la Pole now began a definite campaign against Henry VII, and in favour of his own interests

the said duke of Suff[olk][4] was by the lord Corson acerteyned, and soo departed out of the reame of England. And at the said ducis commyng to Seyntjone [St Johann in the Tyrol?], he sent to the kings [*sic* – Emperor's] majestie his lackey with his lettres declaring to the king the cause of his commyng, and to knowe his plaisure for his commyng to his presence.

Upon this the said duc came to the kings presence at Ympst, declaring playnely to his grace the murders doon by H[enry VII], and that H[enry] also entended to have murdred him and his brodre, with the wronges H[enry] had doon to him. Wherupon the said duc besought the kings majestie, insomuche as he was emprower, of his ayde, according to justice to helpe the said duc to his right.

The kings majestie welcomed the said duc, taking him as his kynnesman, and desired him to goo to his logging. And sent to him to his logging his counsaillors doctor Newdek, chaunceller of Austriche, and the queens chaunceller. Whiche on the kings behalves hewed to the said duc, that by means of the pais bytwix H[enry] and my lord archduc, and insomuche also that the la[kkey] of my lord archduc the kings majestie had sent to him his seal for tract of pais bytwix his grace and H[enry], his grace mighte not ayde the said duc. Neverthalas, the kings majestie by his said counsaillors offered to the said duc his saufconduit [safe-conduct] to abyde within the empier and al other countreys belonging to the kings patrimony and inheritance.[5]

Meanwhile, in England, Henry VII had found that others were

also involved in the de la Pole plot against him, including Suffolk's other brother, William de la Pole. Henry VII therefore ordered the arrest of all concerned. Since William de la Pole was still in England, he was therefore arrested and imprisoned in the Tower of London. He remained there for thirty-eight years, and, as a result of his imprisonment, he died without producing any children. Henry VII also arrested and subsequently executed Sir James Tyrell for his involvement in Edmund's schemes.

As for Edmund de la Pole, he remained in Maximilian's territories for more than ten years. In 1502 Maximilian planned with him an invasion of England. This was to take place in Danish ships provided by John, King of Denmark, Norway and Sweden. The funding for this expedition was to be made available to Edmund on St George's Day (23 April) 1502. But in the end the initial, hopeful-sounding agreement between Edmund and the Emperor 'toke noon effect'.[6]

Looking at what took place retrospectively, it appears that to some extent the emperor was using the Earl of Suffolk as a kind of lever to try to manipulate Henry VII and his government. However, even if the Emperor was well-intentioned in respect of Edmund, there was also the practical problem that, in spite of his lofty-sounding and numerous titles, in actual fact Maximilian did not have the necessary funding to back an attempt by Edmund upon the throne of England. Nevertheless, his support for Edmund de la Pole had caused a panic in the government of Henry VII, and the English king had Edmund publicly excommunicated in an attempt to undermine his plausibility as a possible Yorkist King of England.

According to one source, the excommunication of Edmund de la Pole was carried out in the seventeenth year of Henry's reign (1502), the second sonday of lent after [20 February – but see footnote][7] was sir Edmonde de la Poole was pronuncyd acursed opynly wyth boke, belle, and candell, at Powlles crose at the sermonde before none. And in Ester weke nexte after dyscecyd the prince Arture at Ludlow, and burryd at Worceter. ... And sir James Tyrryll and sir John Wyndham be-hedyd [6 May 1502].[8] Thys yere the qwene Elizabeth dyde [11 February 1502/3] at the towre, and burryd at Westmyster.[9]

The demise of Elizabeth of York, which actually occurred about a year after the excommunication of her cousin, Edmund, was greeted with great regret in England. Thomas More penned a poem of 'Lamentation' for the deceased royal consort, which included the lines,

> Was I not born of old worthy lineage
> Was not my mother queen, my father king?[10]

More's assertion of Elizabeth Woodville's queenship was presumably a firm part of the 'Tudor' political correctness under which he had been brought up. However, his insistence on the fact that Elizabeth of York's father had been king, and upon her 'worthy lineage', may have raised some significant questions (if the questions were not already there) in the mind of More's hearers and readers, in respect of the comparative lineage of her husband, the reigning (but actually usurping) quasi-Lancastrian king, Henry VII.

Probably the questions were already there, for the 'Tudor' claim to the throne had always been seen as somewhat odd, and not truly Lancastrian. It was for that reason that Henry VII and his propaganda machine had tried to put forward various other picturesque and inventive claims about Henry's right to the throne. These included reference to his possible descent from King Arthur (hence the name given to his son and heir). They also included reference to the even more bizarre story of Henry's alleged descent from ancient Trojan royalty.

> In Dark-Age Wales, as related by Nennius, it was told that the founder of Britain was one Brutus, who was descended from 'Ilius' who 'first founded Ilium, that is Troy'. This story was popularised by Geoffrey of Monmouth in his famous story of Brutus' founding of London as Troynovant, or New Troy. Though dismissed by the historian Polydore Vergil, this story was accepted by most Elizabethan poets as part of the Tudor myth, and it became a commonplace of Elizabethan thought. The Tudors, it was argued, were of Welsh or ancient British descent, and therefore, when they ascended the throne of England after the Battle of Bosworth in 1485, so ran the myth, the ancient Trojan-British race of monarchs once more assumed imperial power and would usher in the Golden Age.[11]

In this context, could it perhaps be significant that one surviving late fifteenth-century depiction of the Trojan arch-enemy, the Mycenaean (Greek) king, Agamemnon, in the dramatic process of sacrificing his own daughter, Iphigenia, prior to the Greek attack on Troy, bears a rather stunning resemblance to the features of the ousted and slaughtered Yorkist English king, Richard III?[12]

Two years after the death of Queen Elizabeth of York, a winter storm in England and the English Channel produced various effects.

xxj°. A°. [1505/6] Thys yere the xv. day of January [Sunday] at twelve of cloke at none rose soche a tempest of wynde tyll it was twelve at mydnyth, that it blew downe tres and tyles of howsys, and that same nyght it blewe downe the weddercoke of Powlles stepulle the lengthe of the ende of Powlles church unto the syne of the blacke egylle; at that tyme was lowe howses of bokebynderes wher nowe is the scole of Powles. And that same nyght was the duke of Burgone that was callyd Phyllype with hys lady and many shepes of hys, the wyche intendyd to a gone into Spayne to a bene crownyd kynge, but by tempest ware drevyne to Porchemoth havyne, and soo the kynge send many of the nobyll lordes and states of the realme both sperituall and temporall to reseve hym and all hys pepull, and soo browte them to London; and there the kynge nobylly reseved them and made them grete chere and soo departyd them home agayne. And that same yere at that tyme was soch a sore snowe and a frost that men myght goo with carttes over the Temse and horse, and it lastyd tylle after candelmas. And then it was agreed betwene the kynge and the duke of Burgone that Edmond de la Poole shulde be send home agayne, and so he was.[13]

Even so, in the end it was only in 1513, as a result of treaties between Henry VIII and Maximilian, that Edmund de la Pole was finally extradited and brought back to England. The death of Henry VII in 1509 and the accession of Henry VIII had meanwhile potentially somewhat altered the picture. While Henry VII had been seen – both in England and abroad – as a Lancastrian claimant to the English throne (albeit a rather weak and disputable Lancastrian claimant), Henry VIII was now perceived principally as a Yorkist claimant (through the blood of his late mother). This was very strongly backed by the young Henry's notable physical resemblance to his maternal grandfather, King Edward IV. Specific evidence to show that the new 'Tudor' king of England was perceived as more Yorkist than Lancastrian will be offered in the next chapter.

Thus the role of the de la Pole 'White Roses' in respect of the English throne was now unclear, and in the eyes of Emperor Maximilian and his family the situation in respect of claims for the English crown had perhaps changed – and was still changing – significantly. Thus, Edmund de la Pole was now a kind of irrelevancy in terms of Habsburg policy. Shipped back to his homeland, Edmund was tried and executed for treason. He left no sons to inherit his claim, for his marriage to Margaret Scrope had produced only one child, a daughter, who later chose to become a nun. Edmund's heir was therefore his younger brother, Richard de la Pole.

When Edmund was extradited back to England, his younger brother, Richard, remained abroad, as he was not in the hands of the Habsburgs, but was living in the kingdom of France. There, indeed, Richard de la Pole was now recognised as the rightful king of England. And there, he served King Louis XII and later King Francis I. On two occasions Richard formulated plans to invade England via Scotland in an attempt to seize the crown to which he arguably had a better claim than the new king, Henry VIII. However, these plans came to nothing. In the end, Richard de la Pole – known as 'the White Rose' – was killed fighting at the battle of Pavia in 1525. Like all his brothers, John, William and Edmund; Richard left no legitimate issue. Thus the once large family of Elizabeth of York, Duchess of Suffolk, the middle sister of Edward IV and Richard III, finally petered out.

Of course, there were other living descendants of the house of

York in the sixteenth century. These included Edward Courtenay, Earl of Devon (?1527–1556). Edward was a great grandson of King Edward IV, the grandson of Edward IV's younger daughter, Catherine of York. Because of his royal descent Edward Courtenay was at various times considered as a potential spouse for one of Henry VIII's daughters. But nothing ever materialised. Until 1538, Edward's life was comparatively uneventful, but then he and his parents suddenly found themselves imprisoned by Henry VIII and accused of conspiracy with their cousin, Cardinal Reginald Pole, grandson of George, Duke of Clarence (see below). Edward's father, Henry Courtenay, Marquis of Exeter, was executed, and Edward was imprisoned in the Tower of London, with his great grandmother's cousin, Margaret of Clarence, Countess of Salisbury and her grandson. Edward then remained in prison in the Tower of London until the death of Edward VI in 1553.

However, the immediate cause of these arrests was not so much the Yorkist descent of Edward and his father, but rather the religious contentions which had now become an important part of the English scene. Edward's family had enjoyed a close relationship with Catherine of Aragon, and Edward was well-regarded by Catherine's daughter, Mary. Since Edward Courtenay – together with his Pole cousins – retained his faith in Catholicism and papal supremacy, he (and they) were now potential enemies of Henry VIII. Subsequently Edward Courtenay continued in the same position in relation to Henry's son and successor. But after the death of the protestant 'Tudor' King Edward VI, when Edward's older half-sister, Mary, overthrew the usurpation of her cousin, Jane Grey, Edward Courtenay was at last released from the Tower.

He was then briefly a favourite of his cousin, Queen Mary. She created him Earl of Devonshire, and Edward played a prominent role at Mary's coronation. At first he hoped that he would become Mary's husband, but when she decided to marry her other cousin, Philip II of Spain, he turned his eyes to Mary's younger half-sister, Elizabeth. As a result, he then came to be seen by Queen Mary's government as potentially implicated in Wyatt's Protestant rebellion. As a result, both Edward Courtenay and Elizabeth were arrested. Their trials, however, were unable to produce any proof that either Edward or Elizabeth had actually taken any part in Wyatt's Rebellion. Edward was finally released in 1555, but was then sent into exile on the European mainland. He settled in the Republic of Venice where he died childless the following year. It has been suggested that he may have been poisoned, but there is no proof of this.

An alternative group of potential Yorkist contenders for the English crown comprised the family of Margaret of Clarence, Countess of Salisbury. Margaret was the daughter of George Duke of Clarence and his wife, Isabel Neville. Margaret had been under the guardianship of Edward IV and Richard III following her father's execution. In the reign of Richard III she dwelt with her young Yorkist royal cousins at Sheriff Hutton Castle near York.

After the accession of the new king, Henry VII, and the failure of the Yorkist uprising in the name of her putative brother, 'King Edward VI', the fourteen-year-old Margaret was given in marriage to Henry VII's cousin, Sir Richard Pole. This marriage probably took place in about November 1487. Pole's mother was the half-sister of Lady Margaret Beaufort. Henry VII's intention in arranging this marriage was probably to ensure that it would be difficult for any of his enemies to use Margaret as a focus for their plotting. Sir Richard Pole held a variety of offices in Henry VII's government, the highest being Chamberlain for Arthur, Prince of

Wales, the king's son and heir. When Arthur married the Infanta Catherine of Aragon, Margaret Pole became one of Catherine's ladies-in-waiting, but she lost that post when young Arthur died in 1502.

Margaret bore her husband five surviving children: Henry, Arthur, Ursula, Reginald and Geoffrey. And she has a very large number of descendants living today. On the accession of her cousin, Henry VIII, she was again appointed a member of Queen Catherine's household, and also granted in her own right the Earldom of Salisbury. She was one of only two women in sixteenth-century England to be a peeress in her own right,[14] and she enjoyed a close relationship with Queen Catherine.

Like her father, George, Duke of Clarence, and her grandfather, Richard Neville, Earl of Warwick, Margaret possessed a strong and sometimes rather challenging character. In 1518 she became involved in a dispute with her cousin, the king, over parts of her Earldom of Salisbury, which Henry VIII was attempting to reclaim for himself. Subsequently, her relations with the king were further damaged by her devotion and loyalty to Catherine of Aragon. Margaret had been governess to Catherine's daughter, the future Queen Mary, and tried as far as possible to protect Mary from her father and her new step-mother, Anne Boleyn. However, Margaret's offer to continue to serve Mary without pay in 1533 was rejected by the king.

Following the fall of Anne Boleyn, Margaret returned to court briefly. As in the case of the Courtenay family, however, (see above) the focus of problems between her and Henry VIII was now largely religious. Margaret was imprisoned in the Tower of London for two and a half years. She was confined with her grandson Henry Pole (who was fated to spend the rest of his short life in the Tower) and their cousin, Edward Courtenay. Despite their imprisonment in the Tower, the three of them did enjoy the benefit of some financial support from the king. This included the provision of servants, and a grant of clothing.

In 1540, Margaret's enemy, Thomas Cromwell was attainted and executed. However, this did not rectify the situation from Margaret's point of view. Although she consistently denied that she was in any way a traitor, she was finally – and rather brutally – executed by Henry VIII, in 1541. The religious (rather than Yorkist) nature of her conflict with her cousin the king is underlined by the fact that Pope Leo XIII subsequently beatified Margaret as a Catholic martyr on 29 December 1886 ('Blessed Margaret Pole'), and also by the subsequent appointment of her son, Cardinal Reginald Pole, as the last Catholic Archbishop of Canterbury, following the accession of Queen Mary I.

As we have seen, following the seizure of the English throne by Henry VII, a number of genuine Yorkist descendants remained in existence. Some of these known descendants did advance claims to the throne – although the strongest Yorkist movements against Henry VII were centred not upon any of the publicly acknowledged Yorkist royal descendants, but upon individuals whom the king and his government denounced as impostors.

One reason for this is possibly the irony of the situation, following Henry VII's repeal of the act of *Titulus Regius* of 1484 and the new king's subsequent marriage with Elizabeth of York. The effect of these actions was that Yorkist claimants to the throne such as the de la Poles, the Poles and the Courtenays were all logically inferior, in terms of their position in the Yorkist hierarchy, to the royal 'Tudor' descendants of Henry VII himself: the heirs borne to Henry by his royal consort, Elizabeth of York.

Given that the Act of Parliament of 1484, which had declared the children of Edward IV and Elizabeth Woodville bastards, had been repealed, Elizabeth was arguably the rightful Yorkist heiress to the throne. Only her brothers, the so-called 'princes in the Tower', would have clearly outranked her – if they were still alive.

As we are about to see, the ironic result of Elizabeth of York's status was that, following the death of her husband, the usurper, Henry VII, in 1509, the subsequent generations of the 'Tudor' royal family were actually perceived not as *Lancastrian* claimants to the English throne, but as *Yorkists*. By chance, this view of things was also strongly promoted by the serendipity of the very strong physical resemblance which the new young English sovereign, Henry VIII, bore to his late grandfather, King Edward IV.

And the consequence of this was that the chief opponents of Henry VIII and of the later 'Tudors' were to be, not the junior lines of surviving Yorkist princes, such as Poles and Courtenays, but the legitimate royal descendants of the royal house of Lancaster. For, according to the Parliamentary legislation which was in force from 1485, all the surviving Yorkist heirs now ranked lower in the English order of succession than the descendants of Edward IV's eldest daughter. However, the Lancastrian heirs were very high ranking indeed, for they were European reigning sovereigns – the heads of the royal houses of Spain and Portugal and the Holy Roman Emperor.

PART 4

'TUDOR' = YORK; HABSBURG = LANCASTER

14

THE LAST LANCASTRIAN CLAIMANTS

By the end of the story of the Wars of the Roses, the direct male lines of both the Lancaster and the Mortimer royal families were extinct. The Beaufort *name* had also more or less died out, but the effective Beaufort descendants and heirs were the so-called 'Tudors'. Thus, the fighting in what are often regarded as the final battles of the Wars of the Roses (the battles of Bosworth and of Stoke) had focused on the contest between the York family and the 'Tudor' family.

In the person of King Henry VII, the 'Tudors', as Beaufort descendants, had claimed to be the only surviving heirs of the Lancaster royal family, to whom they were distantly related. But that claim was always a blatant lie. The Lancastrian princesses Philippa and Catherine (a sister and a half-sister of King Henry IV) had married kings of Portugal and of Castile (Spain) respectively. Thus the descendants of those two princesses comprised the real surviving Lancastrian bloodline claimants to the English throne. Initially, of these two lines of descent, the family of the full-blood sister of Henry IV – Philippa of

Lancaster, Queen of Portugal – had the senior claim. In the end, though, this question of seniority became unimportant, because, through diplomatic marriages, the two lines of Lancastrian descent combined into one, namely the Spanish royal family (see below: Family Tree 11).

Charles V & I, Holy Roman Emperor and King of Spain, and his son Philip II of Spain were both the senior living heirs of Philippa of Lancaster. But, through Charles' mother, Joanna the Mad, Queen of Castile, they were also the heirs of Philippa's younger half-sister, Catherine of Lancaster. In the end this descent of the Spanish rulers from the house of Lancaster was one of several factors which led to the sixteenth-century Habsburg interest in the English succession. Thus the great Spanish Armada of 1588 was the last attempt by the true living heir of the royal house of Lancaster to reclaim the English crown.

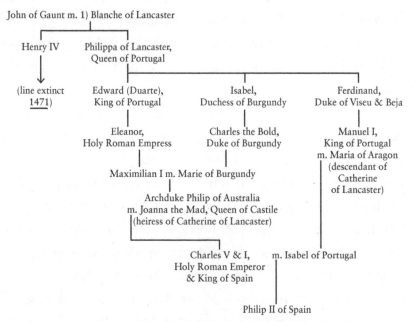

Family Tree 11: The Lancastrian Blood Line of Descent

But the assertion of his inherited claim to the crown of England was by no means initiated by Philip II. In the 1530s his father, the Emperor Charles V, had been encouraged to take seriously the case for his rightful Lancastrian claim to the English throne by his ambassador at the court of Henry VIII, a man named Eustace Chapuys.

The Emperor Charles was the nephew of Catherine of Aragon, whose marriage to Henry VIII was then a matter of dispute. Ambassador Chapuys' initial interest had been to defend Queen Catherine, in the face of Henry VIII's annulment of his marriage to her. But in a very interesting and illuminating letter written to the emperor on 16 December 1533, Chapuys, a well-informed diplomat, referred obliquely to the fact of Edward IV's first secret marriage, to Eleanor Talbot. Chapuys began his letter with implied criticism of Henry VIII, praising the virtues of Margaret, Countess of Salisbury (the daughter of George, Duke of Clarence) for her conspicuous loyalty to Catherine of Aragon's daughter, Mary, whom the king had now set aside as a bastard. He then told his emperor,

> You cannot imagine the grief of all the people at this abominable government. They are so transported with indignation at what passes, that they complain that your Majesty takes no steps in it, and I am told by many respectable people that they would be glad to see a fleet come hither in your name ... [for] they say you have a better title than the present King, who only claims by his mother, who was declared by sentence of the bishop of Bath [Stillington] a bastard, because Edward had espoused another wife before the mother of Elizabeth of York.[1]

As we can see, Chapuys was putting to his sovereign two points. The first was that Henry VIII's only possible claim to the throne was through his maternal line of descent from the royal house of York. However, the ambassador's second point highlighted the fact that such a claim was questionable because, based on Bishop Stillington's evidence, Elizabeth Woodville's marriage to Edward IV had been declared invalid, making all the couple's children – including Elizabeth of York – illegitimate.

About a year later, on 3 November 1534, Chapuys brought these points to the emperor's attention once again, this time referring specifically to the act of Parliament of 1484. In that act,

> Richard III declared by definitive sentence of the bishop of Bath that the daughters of king Edward, of whom the king's mother was the eldest, were bastards, by reason of a precontract [previous marriage] made by Edward with another lady before he married their mother.[2]

Chapuys' motive for bringing up this sixty-year-old piece of history was obviously to disparage the 'Tudor' claim to the English throne. As he observed, Edward IV's first marriage to Eleanor had made all of the children born as a result of his later 'marriage' to Elizabeth Woodville bastards, incapable of inheriting or transmitting rights to the throne. This blanket illegitimacy of the Woodville children applied not only to Edward IV's sons but also to his daughters – including Henry VIII's mother, Elizabeth of York. The point Chapuys was making was that the illegitimacy of his mother completely invalidated the claim of Henry VIII to the English crown.

It is therefore obvious that, by the 1530s, no-one took seriously the *Lancastrian* claim to the throne which had been advanced by

Henry VII. As perceived by a high ranking European diplomat, Henry VIII's only possible right to be King of England was thought to depend upon his maternal-line descent from the house of York. In other words, after the demise of the usurper, Henry VII, the claim to the throne of the 'Tudor' dynasty as personified by the son (and later the grandchildren) of Henry VII's consort, Elizabeth of York, was clearly understood to be a *Yorkist* claim.

That is why it was Henry VIII's maternal (and only valid) Yorkist inheritance upon which Chapuys was casting doubt. In his letters he did not even bother to go into any detail regarding Henry VII's supposed Lancastrian claim. He merely (but explicitly) dismissed the late king's Lancastrian pretence by simply asserting that Henry VIII's claim to the throne was only through his mother. However, he then went on to insist that the Lancastrian claim to the English throne of the Emperor Charles V was far superior – which indeed it was.

Chapuys' views in respect of the Lancastrian claim were, of course, nothing new. We have already seen that one of Charles V's Lancastrian royal ancestors, his great grandmother, Isabel of Portugal, Duchess of Burgundy, had explicitly submitted her own claim as a candidate for the English throne to the English Parliament as early as 1471, as soon as she had received news of the death of her cousin, King Henry VI. However, the Emperor Charles V never actually attempted to make good his claim to the English throne by force. Thus the fleet which Chapuys had proposed to him in 1533 never set out for England at that time, or in Charles' name. It was left to his son, King Philip II of Spain, to take up the cause in a practical manner.

Philip II was the cousin once removed of Henry VIII's daughter, Queen Mary I, and he subsequently became her husband. Indeed, as a result of his marriage to Mary, Philip had, for a while, enjoyed the rank of king consort of England. But it was in 1588, long after Mary had died, and at a time when England had passed into the hands of her half-sister of dubious legitimacy, Queen Elizabeth I, that Philip launched his great Armada against England, seeking to make good his claim to the English throne. Maybe he was still hoping to receive the welcome from the English people which Chapuys had promised to his father fifty-five years previously. If so, however, he was destined to be disappointed.

Some previous writers on the subject have suggested that King Philip's claim to the throne of England was advanced purely on the basis of his earlier marriage to Mary Tudor. However, on the basis of the evidence we have seen regarding the claims of his father and earlier ancestors, this is clearly a false conclusion. Philip also believed that Mary, Queen of Scots, who had finally been executed by Elizabeth I in 1587, had formally acknowledged him as the rightful heir to the English crown. That fact, coupled with his own legitimate and direct multiple-line descent from the House of Lancaster, gave Philip good cause to see himself as the legitimate Lancastrian heir to the English crown. Thus, the defeat of the Spanish Armada can, in truth, be seen as the last battle of the 'Wars of the Roses'. This was a contest in which Philip's Habsburg dynasty now represented its ancestors of the house of Lancaster, while – rather bizarrely – the 'Tudor' Queen Elizabeth I was now perceived as personifying her ancestors of the house of York.

Of course, there were also much more recent causes for the sending of the Spanish Armada. These included the bastardy of Elizabeth I, the religious issues provoked by the Reformation, and Elizabeth I's support for Protestant rebels in the Spanish Netherlands. There was also the illicit action of English pirates against Spanish shipping in the Atlantic and Pacific Oceans. The Spanish Armada of 1588 comprised the largest episode of an ongoing conflict between Spain and England which had begun in 1585, and which then continued until 1604. Although no formal declaration of war between England and Spain ever took place, the fighting was fairly continuous. For example, in the year following the Spanish Armada, England launched an equally unsuccessful Counter Armada against Spain, which is often referred to as the Drake-Norris Expedition.

Because of the religious issue which had arisen in the sixteenth century, the Spanish campaign of 1588 was supported by the Papacy. Pope Sixtus V viewed Philip II's Armada as a kind of crusade against protestant England. For this reason he promised King Philip II that, once the Spanish forces had succeeded in landing in England, Rome would accept a duty to back the expedition in terms of financial support. As we shall see shortly, the Pope's focus on the landing of a military force in England was by no means his own invention. This was also the key aim of Philip's intended campaign, which is often misinterpreted as a naval war. In the meanwhile, as an initial piece of practical support for the venture, Pope Sixtus gave King Philip permission to levy a special 'crusade tax', in order to help finance the expedition. There were also other forms of papal support for the campaign. The formal blessing of the Armada's banner on 25 April 1588 was very similar to a ceremony which had been employed in 1571, prior to the crusading battle of Lepanto against the Turks. In addition, a papal indulgence was granted to the men serving on Philip II's vessels, thereby releasing their souls from purgatory, should they happen to be killed at any stage in the fighting.

Originally, the intended commander of the Spanish fleet was

to have been Álvaro de Bazán, Marquis of Santa Cruz. He was a very skilful and experienced naval officer. But the Marquis died in February 1587/8. As a result, the command was then transferred into the hands of the Duke of Medina Sidonia. Although the latter was a man of exalted birth, unfortunately he had little or no naval experience. But perhaps that was not an obviously significant issue as perceived by King Philip when he made the appointment. After all, in the longer term the king did not envisage a naval war.

Initially, the Armada comprised 130 vessels. Interestingly, however, only twenty-two of these were naval warships. The remainder were merchant ships. The latter had been adapted for naval warfare, just in case they needed at any stage to protect themselves against English vessels. However, the key point in all this is that it was never intended or envisaged that the Armada itself would carry out the main fighting in Philip II's campaign for England.

The original intention was simply for the fleet to sail eastwards along the English Channel towards the coast of Flanders. On the way the Spanish vessels would of course defend themselves if necessary. But with luck, fighting at sea would not happen very much, because it was not ships which were intended to fight Philip II's main battles.

Once the Spanish vessels arrived safely off the coast of the Spanish Netherlands, they would simply anchor there, and await the arrival from the Spanish territory in the Low Countries of the Duke of Parma and his army. These men were to form the real invasion force for the conquest of England. The Armada would then fulfil its intended role by simply acting as transport for the army, thus conveying Parma's men across the Channel to south-eastern England. There the soldiers were to be landed at a suitable location, as close as possible to the English capital – the city of London. In other words, the ships were basically seen simply as a method of transport for an invading army. It was the invasionary force (not the ships) which were meant to carry out the conquest of England. Parma's men would fight on land. They would defeat and oust the Yorkist bastard usurper, who called herself Queen Elizabeth, and would thus restore the English crown to the royal Lancastrian heir – and faithful Catholic – King Philip II.

It is clear that the proposed nature of the coming conflict was also very well understood at the time in England. Although the navy was seen as England's first potential line of defence, detailed provisions were also made to defend the land itself against possible invading forces.

Sir John Norris, appointed on April 6th to supervise the defences of the maritime counties from Norfolk to Dorset, took up his headquarters at Weymouth to organise the defences of what prevailing opinion took to be the most threatened area. The famous system of fire-beacons was arranged to direct the militiamen to their assembly points and give them their line of march. Trained pioneers hurried in with spade and pick-axe to construct forts and trenches, artillerymen to rear their gun platforms. At Warham Bridge a barrier was prepared in the event of a retreat, when the roads were to be cut and the water let in, while special companies of petronels – horsemen armed with pistols – drove off the cattle and burned everything that could not readily be carried away. By June, when the Armada was expected to sail, 27,000 infantry, 200 light and 500 heavy cavalry waited in the south to resist a landing or, if it succeeded, to oppose the enemy's progress inland.

They formed part of an available total of over 130,000 – according to the returns made by the Lord Lieutenants of the counties in answer to a circular issued by the Privy Council on April 2nd – the largest host ever mustered in the island and one far exceeding the Crown's ability or the willingness of their native shires and boroughs to maintain on a war footing. Nevertheless by June, after frequent exchanges between ministers and local authorities of letters of abuse and appeal, three further armies had been assembled. One, of fourteen regiments each 2000 strong under the earl of Huntingdon, waited in East Anglia and did not much enter into the picture. Another, under the Earl of Leicester, of 20,000 foot and 2000 horse, covered the mouth of the Thames and the approaches to London. A third, of 34,000, under Lord Hunsdon, lay to the west of London to act as a mobile striking force when the actual site of the invasion was known, and in addition to guard the person of the Queen and put down internal insurrection – a very real danger if the widespread fear of a Catholic rising once the Spaniards had gained a foothold was realised.[3]

Thus, the picture is very clear. The English government deeply feared both a successful invasion by the Spanish forces from the Netherlands, and also the possibility of support for the invading army from within England itself.

Actually, King Philip was not a warlike or ambitious man. But he saw himself as having a divinely appointed role to accomplish. This role had a number of parts to it. For example, Philip had claimed the Portuguese throne in 1581, following the childless deaths, first, of his nephew, King Sebastian, and then of Sebastian's great uncle, the Cardinal-King Henry I. Thus, on 28 May 1588 it was from the Portuguese capital of Lisbon that the Spanish

Armada set sail – since Portugal now comprised one of Philip's Iberian kingdoms.

Philip had been the king consort of England in respect of his marriage to his cousin, Queen Mary. He also saw himself (as his father the Emperor Charles had done before him) as the legitimate Lancastrian heir to the English throne. Thus, he would not have perceived his intended invasion of England as a foreign conquest. He was simply repossessing part of his rightful realm. As the legitimate Lancastrian heir it was his duty to do so. Moreover, that duty was strongly reinforced by the fact that the Yorkist bastard usurper, Elizabeth, had turned England away from the true, Catholic faith to which it had hitherto belonged. In addition, Elizabeth had also acted outrageously in another way, by putting to death her rival, the true, legitimate and faithful Catholic Yorkist heiress, Mary Queen of Scots.

Initially Philip II's ships headed northwards along the Portuguese and Spanish (Galician) west coast towards the English Channel. That same day, the English ambassador in the Netherlands was trying hard to engage representatives of the Duke of Parma in peace negotiations. The Spanish fleet had now slightly increased in size, and comprised 151 ships. There were twenty-eight purpose-built warships, twenty galleons, four galleys and four Neapolitan galleasses. There were also armed carracks and hulks, and thirty-four light vessels.

Even before they reached the Flemish coast, the ships themselves were manned by 8,000 sailors and 18,000 soldiers. A further 30,000 soldiers waited to join them in the Spanish Netherlands. The total would have been a huge army for the period. The ships carried a total of 2,500 guns, 1,500 of them made of brass and 1,000 made of iron. It took two days to get all the vessels out of the port of Lisbon. Some English vessels were waiting for the Armada. They tried to engage it in the Bay of Biscay, in order to prevent the Spanish ships from progressing into the Channel, but without success. The rest of the English naval force was awaiting news of the Spanish vessels at Plymouth. The English ships outnumbered the Spanish, but were somewhat ill-provisioned. They also had fewer guns than the Spanish Armada.

Inevitably, perhaps, meteorological conditions proved a significant factor. The Spanish fleet was somewhat delayed by bad weather. As a result, five of its vessels were lost. On 19 July the Spanish vessels were sighted from the Lizard in Cornwall and this news was conveyed to London by a network of beacons which had been prepared all along the south coast. Ideally the English fleet would have sailed out of Plymouth to try to block the Spanish Armada before it could progress any further. But unfortunately the tide was against the English vessels, and they were unable to do so. As the Spanish fleet approached Plymouth, some of its captains proposed that they should take advantage of the situation immediately, and use the tide to sail in to Plymouth and attack the English fleet. However, obedient to the instructions he had received, Medina Sidonia refused to do this. His aim was very clear to him. It was not to engage in a naval war, but to get to the Low Countries and act as transport for the army of the Duke of Parma. *That* was the force which would then carry out the conquest of England.

Thus, Medina Sidonia ordered his ships to sail onwards towards the Isle of Wight. But, when the tide turned, his fleet was pursued by some English ships, commanded by Lord Howard of Effingham and Sir Francis Drake. The English vessels attacked the Spanish fleet at dawn on 21 July. As they approached the Spanish ships from the western side, the latter moved themselves into a crescent-shaped defensive formation, with its open curve facing towards the oncoming enemy. The strongest Spanish vessels were positioned at the centre of the curve and at its points, in an attempt to protect the weaker vessels.

Unlike the Spanish, the English to some extent did (and often still do) see the Armada as a naval campaign. Thus they tried to make use of the greater speed and manoeuvrability of their ships to keep out of range of the Spanish guns, while they themselves fired on the Spanish vessels. Perhaps not surprisingly, this did not work very well. If they stayed out of the range of the Spanish guns, then the enemy were equally out of the range of the English guns. Neither side lost a single ship as a result of enemy fire – though unfortunately two more of the Spanish ships were lost because they collided with one another.

But the English also made mistakes. That night, when Francis Drake tried to loot some of the Spanish ships, seeking to capture gunpowder and money, he succeeded in scattering the entire English fleet. When day broke the English ships were all over the place, and it took them a whole day to get themselves together again and set off again in pursuit of the Spanish. Ultimately, however, the greater speed of the English vessels did then allow them to catch up with the enemy again after about a day.

On 23 July the two sides engaged once more, off Portland. This time the Spanish sought to attack the English vessels but were outmanoeuvred. When Lord Howard sought to make a counter-attack that also proved unsuccessful. In short, little was achieved by either side.

However, the Solent was not a useful place for the Spanish vessels to linger in and wait for news of Parma and his army. They had to anchor in a position where there would be some hope of direct contact with the Duke of Parma and his men. Therefore Medina Sidonia decided to make for Calais. His ships anchored not far from Dunkirk on 27 July and waited there for Parma's men to join them. But then they heard that the port of Dunkirk was encircled by an enemy fleet of Dutch vessels. That meant that it would be impossible for Parma to transport his army to the Spanish fleet from Dunkirk, even if he had boats to transport them – which he did not.

On the following night the English, who had once again caught up with the Spanish vessels, sacrificed eight of their own ships as fireships, which they sent downwind towards the Spanish fleet. Although Medina Sidonia succeeded in averting two of the English fireships, the others could not be turned aside, and they caused a major panic. As a result, many of the Spanish ships scattered, leaving the planned crescent formation of the Armada in ruins.

Medina Sidonia then tried to reassemble his fleet at the port of Gravelines. At this point the English ships began their attack. As a result of their earlier engagements – and the capture of one damaged Spanish vessel, the *Rosario* – the English had now learnt something of Spanish fighting techniques. Although the Spanish ships possessed far heavier gun power than the English fleet, the Spaniards had been trained not to concentrate on using their naval firepower. Instead they had been encouraged to see the whole campaign as a kind of army action – even while they were on their ships. Thus their on-board soldiers tried to act as marines, climbing aloft in their own rigging and then attempting to board the English ships. This technique had proved very successful earlier, at the battles of Lepanto and Ponta Delgada (1582). However, it did not work well against the English, who now foresaw what the

Spanish were trying to do, and who therefore sought to keep their ships at a distance. The lighter weight and the manoeuvrability of the English vessels made this English plan work rather well. Thus it proved extremely difficult for the Spanish soldiers to board them.

At the same time, despite the fact that their vessels enjoyed less firepower, the English gunfire did prove very effective. However, the chief problem for the English was their lack of ammunition. In the end, because of this, their ships were forced to pull back at about 4 o'clock in the afternoon, but by that time several Spanish ships had been lost. Even more significant for the Spanish Armada was the fact that Medina Sidonia had now realised that there was no way in which he could achieve his planned aim of uniting his fleet with the army of the Duke of Parma.

In spite of this, the Spanish ships themselves remained a serious threat to the English. However, Medina Sidonia was not able to wait indefinitely off the coast of the Low Countries. The Spanish commander therefore decided that the aim of the Armada had failed, and that his fleet should return to Spain. Unfortunately he aimed to achieve this by sailing round the northern coast of Scotland and then down the western side, past Ireland. Thus he began to sail northwards, along the east coast of England. Not surprisingly, he found himself pursued by the English vessels. And unfortunately, he had made no allowance for the adverse weather conditions which his ships encountered. Medina Sidonia had been in command of just over 150 vessels, but fifty of these never returned to their homeland. More than twenty-four of them were wrecked on the western coastline of Ireland.

By September 1588 the Spanish Armada had sailed around Scotland and Ireland into the North Atlantic. By this time some of the ships were showing wear from the long voyage, and had to have their hulls wrapped around with cables to hold them together. In addition there was now a very short supply of both food and water, since of course such a long voyage had not been planned for. Indeed, the unfortunate cavalry horses were thrown into the sea. Also the Spanish had no knowledge of the effect of the Gulf Stream, which forced them northwards and eastwards as they tried to move in a southerly and westerly direction. Many of their ships were driven onto the rocks. Thus more Spanish ships and sailors were lost as a result of weather conditions than had been lost in conflict with English vessels. Philip II reportedly protested, when he heard this news, that he had sent the Armada against men, not against God's winds and waves.

In effect, therefore, the last intended battle of the English dynastic conflict never really took place. What Philip II had envisaged had been a campaign by his soldiers in England, which would restore this Lancastrian heir to the English throne. But the Spanish forces had never succeeded in landing in England. Indeed, Parma's army had never even embarked upon the ships of the Spanish fleet which was meant to pick them up in the Spanish Netherlands. The only fighting which had taken place had been at sea, and that was not at all what Philip II had intended and planned.

Meanwhile, fate was about to bring about another result. The final Lancastrian attempt upon the English crown had failed. Indeed, arguably, it had never really been embarked upon. But at the same time the demise without heirs of the last 'Tudor' / Yorkist tenant of the English throne was now fast approaching. Soon after the dawn of the seventeenth century a new dynasty donned the English crown. This was a royal dynasty only remotely descended from the 'Tudor' family, and one of the reasons for the succession of James VI of Scotland as James I of England was the fact that it had now become rather hard to find valid claimants to the English throne.

Curiously, however, after 1688, when the house of Stuart itself had become split in two, the Jacobite side of this new divided ruling dynasty adopted the white rose as one of its emblems. It is doubtful whether the Jacobite princes saw themselves as really connected in a significant way with any of the contesting sides of the so-called 'Wars of the Roses'. But possibly the Catholicism of the de la Pole, Pole and Courtenay 'Last White Roses' who, from the mainland of Europe, had tried to stand up against their anti-papist cousin, King Henry VIII, was distantly recalled. At all events, the Jacobite 'White Rose Day' is now 10 June. It commemorates the birthday of King James III and VIII, who is usually known as 'the Old Pretender' in the realm to whose crown he (like some of the earlier pretenders we have met) ultimately failed to succeed.

15

CONCLUSIONS

Although he had predecessors in the Greek world (who had written earlier accounts of what had happened in the past, but whose work does not survive), the 'Father of History' is generally said to be the Greek writer Herodotos of Halicarnassus, who lived in the fifth century BC. However, one noticeable feature of the *History* written by Herodotos was his tendency to accept myths. This was a practice theoretically questioned and opposed by Thukydides and subsequent historians. Nevertheless, the tendency to accept mythology has unfortunately persisted. Thus, earlier published accounts of the so-called 'Wars of the Roses' undoubtedly contain elements of mythology. The most obvious of these are the assumed significance of white and red roses, and the categorisation of the dynastic conflict as 'York versus Lancaster'. These are certainly something which the present work attempts to highlight and look behind.

Later, in 1377, the Tunisian historian, Ibn Khaldun, in his important historical work entitled *Muqaddimah (Introduction)*, focused attention upon the fact that historians tend to make a number of mistakes in their attempts to record what happened in the past. Two of the most significant problems which Ibn Khaldun highlighted were a tendency to be partisan, and a desire to gain favour of those in positions of power by slanting the historical account in support of them. Once again, the present work has tried hard to get behind the partisan nature of the history of England's dynastic conflict as it was recorded by the writers of the 'Tudor' regime. The great problem is the extent to which the partisan 'Tudor' accounts of writers such as Polydore Vergil and Thomas More have subsequently been recycled, often uncritically, by later historians.

Ibn Khaldun also highlighted another problem: the difficulty of placing an event in its true context. In the Introduction we saw that the sequence of events popularly known as the Wars of the Roses is generally perceived as a kind of civil war, but it was by no means the first potential 'English civil war'. Moreover, on some occasions foreign military forces played a significant role in these contests for the English throne. Examples include France and Scotland fighting against the Lancastrian usurpation of Henry IV in the early fifteenth century; Scottish forces fighting on the Lancastrian side in 1461 and 1464; Burgundian support for Edward IV in 1469 and French support for the Lancastrians in 1470; French troops on the side of Henry VII at the Battle of Bosworth in 1485, German mercenaries employed by the dowager Duchess of Burgundy backing 'King Edward VI' in 1487; Scottish and other foreign forces giving support to 'Richard of England' in the 1490s; Habsburg and French support for the de la Pole 'White Roses' in the early decades of the sixteenth century; and the Spanish involvement in the conflict of 1588.

Fighting for the throne has taken place in England at various periods, but this particular struggle – which began in the reign of Richard II and was only finally brought to an end when the Scottish king, James VI and I ascended the English throne – included a mixture of armed conflicts, quite widely separated at times by long periods of peace. In respect of its overall dates, this conflict between rival families for the right to wear the crown of England arguably began in the 1390s and lasted for almost two centuries. Also, while it certainly included the fighting of a number of significant battles, the conflict sometimes took other forms. At times there were also prolonged periods of what seemed to be peace. Moreover, some of the fighting which took place in England during these two centuries was unconnected with the main objective, but comprised private battles, which had nothing whatever to do with who should be sitting on the English throne.

As for the royal rivals, we have seen that the traditional picture of York versus Lancaster is a gross oversimplification. To begin with, the contest for recognition as the heirs of Richard II took place between the house of Lancaster and the Mortimers. Later the Beaufort family was disputing with the house of York who should be regarded as the heir presumptive of Henry VI. Although the house of York appeared to win both this contest and the throne itself, ultimately it then found itself defeated by the so-called 'Tudor' descendants of the Beauforts. Initially, in the person of Henry VII, the 'Tudors' were then seen (or presented themselves) as quasi-Lancastrians. But after the death of Henry VII their so-called Lancastrian claim was largely discounted, and ironically the later 'Tudors' were then perceived, both in England and abroad, as heirs of the house of York. Thus the final attempt upon the English crown was staged against Henry VIII's last surviving child by the key living descendant of the house of Lancaster.

As for the name 'Wars of the Roses', that is in many ways inappropriate. There is no sign that either the English kings of the house of Lancaster, or their legitimate (Spanish and Portuguese) heirs, ever used a red rose badge. According to the received account, that badge was selected at some point prior to the 1450s, by the Beaufort family, but there is no solid proof of precisely when, why or by whom it was chosen. Later, however, the red rose was definitely used by the Beaufort descendants, Margaret, Countess of Richmond and Derby, and her son, Henry VII. Thus the contest between red and white roses can only be proved to have been a relevant part of the rivalry for the throne between approximately the 1480s and the 1520s. This by no means corresponds with the dates traditionally assigned by historians to the so-called 'Wars of the Roses'.

The conflict of rose badges seems to have died out by the middle of the sixteenth century, and there is no more evidence that red and white roses were in conflict in 1588, than that they had been in conflict in the first three quarters of the fifteenth century. Ironically, however, the white rose emblem was subsequently revived, or re-invented, by the Jacobites, towards the end of the seventeenth century. This is intriguing, given that 'England is usually represented by a red rose'.[1] Unfortunately, the origin of the red rose as a symbol of England seems not to have been fully documented, but it would be interesting if any evidence could be found to suggest that the use of this red flower as the national emblem was an eighteenth-century Hanoverian response to the Jacobite revival of the white rose.

One important point which has emerged very clearly from this review of the Wars of the Roses is the extent to which Henry VII – like many more recent dictators who seized power illegally and militarily – went on to conducted a campaign of political propaganda and the rewriting of history. Hopefully the extent to which Henry VII's editing has subsequently, and rather naïvely, tended to be generally accepted has been exposed here. But the main points of the 'Tudor' rewriting of history will now be briefly summarised once again as part of the conclusion.

There are a number of key points to underline in this respect. The first of them is Henry VII's faked 'Lancastrian' claim to the throne. Clear evidence has been presented to show that in 1460 the female-line nature of the genuine Lancastrian claim (which focused upon Henry IV's descent from Edmund Crouchback) was very well understood and remembered. In respect of that genealogy it is obvious that in the 1480s the rightful lineal descendants of the house of Lancaster were the Portuguese royal family. An alternative Lancastrian point of view could have chosen to focus instead upon the legislation of the last Lancastrian king, Henry VI. He had formally acknowledged as his ultimate heir George, Duke of Clarence – whose living heir in the 1480s was his son, the Earl of Warwick. Against these two very strong cases, there was no possible legal validity for any Lancastrian claim on the part of Henry VII. And indeed, Henry VII himself, when making a blood claim to the throne in Parliament, in 1485, actually avoided any specific use of the word 'Lancastrian'.

The second key point about Henry VII's rewriting is his airbrushing out of history of Eleanor Talbot and her relationship with Edward IV. The precise conduct of Henry VII in this instance very strongly suggests that he and his government could produce absolutely no evidence to disprove the decision (made initially by the three estates of the realm in 1483, and then confirmed by Parliament in 1484) to the effect that Eleanor had been Edward

IV's legal wife, and that consequently Elizabeth Woodville never had a valid claim to be Edward's queen consort.

Henry VII's subsequent claim that Elizabeth of York was the Yorkist 'heiress' was the logical sequence of his deliberate removal from history of Eleanor Talbot. Thereafter his claims regarding the identity of the real Earl of Warwick, his government's invention of the ill-documented and unprovable 'Lambert Simnel' story, the claims made about the identity of 'Richard of England' and finally the story invented (almost twenty years after the alleged event) in respect of Sir James Tyrell's supposed 'confession of the murder of the princes in the Tower' at the instigation of Richard III comprise the other key points of the 'Tudor' distortion of history. Every single one of these was clearly aimed at securing to the maximum extent Henry VII's dubious tenure of the English throne.

It is also interesting to note that, while Henry VII's rewriting of history may have succeeded in England (where his government was in power), elsewhere he was not so successful. Some continental writers may have picked up Henry's colourful mythology about Richard III's murder of the 'princes'. However, serious diplomats remembered clearly the evidence about Edward IV's Talbot marriage – evidence which Henry had suppressed in England. Also foreign writers were obviously not convinced by Henry VII's story about 'Lambert Simnel'.

Partly thanks to Henry VII and his government, and partly thanks to the simplistic way in which many later writers have simply gone along with the story as it had been handed down to them, the picture of the Wars of the Roses has hitherto contained many errors of interpretation. Hopefully, however, the true picture has now been presented rather more clearly.

Appendix 1

TEXT OF THE 'REMARRIAGE OF WIDOWED QUEENS' STATUTE OF 1427.[1]

Original in French.

Item, it is ordered and established by the authority of this parliament for the preservation of the honour of the most noble estate of queens of England that no man of whatever estate or condition make contract of betrothal or matrimony to marry himself to the queen of England without the special licence and assent of the king, when the latter is of the age of discretion, and he who acts to the contrary and is duly convicted will forfeit for his whole life all his lands and tenements, even those which are or which will be in his own hands as well as those which are or which will be in the hands of others to his use, and also all his goods and chattels in whosoever's hands they are, considering that by the disparagement of the queen the estate and honour of the king will be most greatly damaged, and it will give the greatest comfort and example to other ladies of rank who are of the blood royal that they might not be so lightly disparaged.

NOTES

Introduction
What were 'The Wars of the Roses'?

1. He also bore the title 'King of France'. Usually this meant little or nothing – though for part of the reign of Henry VI it had real meaning.
2. The starting date is disputed, but the fighting began in either July or September 1939 and ended in September 1945.
3. The name comes from the Latin *planta genista* (broom plant), because the broom seed-pod was the original family badge.
4. Henry II's father, Geoffrey of Anjou, had undoubtedly employed the surname 'Plantagenet'.
5. http://en.wikipedia.org/wiki/Wars_of_the_Roses (consulted December 2014).
6. J. Ashdown-Hill, 'The Red Rose of Lancaster?', *Ricardian*, vol. 10, June 1996, pp. 406–420 (pp. 408–09).

Part 1: Multicoloured Plantagenets

1. How the Trouble Started

1. A. R. Myers, ed., *English Historical Documents* vol. 4, London 1969, p. 180.
2. 'Lord Edmund, the king's younger son'. J.O. Halliwell, ed., *The Chronicle of William de Rishanger*, London 1840, p. 118. William de Rishanger (1250–1322) was a Benedictine monk of St Alban's Abbey and historiographer to King Henry III, so he was well-placed to know the facts. The correct dates of birth of both Edmund and his brother, Edward I, are given in Family Tree 1.
3. C. W. C. Oman, *England and the Hundred Years' War*, London 1898, p. 96.
4. L. Stephen and S. Lee, eds, *Dictionary of National Biography*, London 1891, vol. 26, p. 35.
5. *Rotuli Parliamentorum*, vol. 3, 1377–1411, pp. 422–423.
6. J. S. Davies, ed., *An English Chronicle of the Reigns of Richard II, Henry IV, Henry V and Henry VI*, London (Camden Society) 1856, p. 18.
7. Oman, *England and the Hundred Years' War*, p. 96.
8. This traditional appellation may be a misreading of the medieval French 'de Verwik' (= 'of York'). http://en.wikipedia.org/wiki/Edward_of_Norwich,_2nd_Duke_of_York (consulted December 2014).
9. http://en.wikipedia.org/wiki/Edward_of_Norwich,_2nd_Duke_of_York (consulted December 2014).
10. Oman, *The Hundred Years' War*, p. 98.

2. The Ambitions of the Beauforts

1. The eldest of Henry V's younger brothers, Thomas, Duke of Clarence, had died in 1421, leaving no legitimate children.

2. Some historians claim that Catherine died on 3 January 1437.

3. Edmund had been Count of Mortain in Normandy since 1427: *ODNB*, C. Richmond, 'Beaufort, Edmund, first Duke of Somerset' (consulted March 2015).

4. *In proximo anno, secundo die Januarii, obiit Katerina regina et mater Henrici sexti, quae habuit tres filios, licet in occulto, eo quod domini de regis concilio noluerunt consentire, in tempore iuventutis regis, ipsam esse alicui desponsandam, quia voluit habuisse dominum Edmundum Bewforde comitem de Morten; sed dux Glocestriae et quamplures alii domini renuerunt, statuentes, contra apostoli consilium, ut qui eam desponsare praesumeret, in forisfactionem omnium bonorum et in mortis supplicium, tanquam regis proditor, puniretur. Quae ipsa, non valens passiones carnales penitus refraenare, accepit Owinum armigerum, parum in bonis possidentem, unde valeat forisfacere, et in occulto, ut non ejus vitam titulo rationis vindicarent.* J. A. Giles, ed., *Incerti scriptoris chronicon Angliae de regnis trium regum Lancastriensium Henrici IV, Henrici V et Henrici VI*, London, 1848, Part Four, p. 17. I am grateful to Marie Barnfield for checking my translation of this text.

5. http://www.nature.com/ncomms/2014/141202/ncomms6631/full/ncomms6631.html (consulted December 2014).

6. He was given his first title, Count of Mortain in Normandy, in 1427. *ODNB*, C. Richmond, 'Beaufort, Edmund, first Duke of Somerset' (consulted April 2015).

7. G. L. Harriss, *Cardinal Beaufort: a study of Lancastrian ascendancy and decline*, Clarendon, Oxford 1988, p. 144.
8. Giles, ed., *Incerti scriptoris Chronicon Angliae de regnis trium regum Lancastriensium*, Part Four, p. 17.
9. Harriss, *Cardinal Beaufort*, p. 159.
10. Harriss, *Cardinal Beaufort*, p. 178, citing J. Amundesham, *Annales Monasterii S. Albani, Rerum Britannicarum Mediaevi Scriptores*, vol. 1, 1857, p. 28. 'King's Lynn' was at this time known as 'Bishop's Lynn'.
11. Harriss, *Cardinal Beaufort*, p. 178, n. 34.
12. The 'Parliament of Bats' met at Leicester. Its first session was from 18 February to 20 March 1425/6 and its second session from 29 April to 1 June 1426. http://www.historyofparliamentonline.org/volume/1422–1504/parliament/1426 (consulted February 2015).
13. Harriss, *Cardinal Beaufort*, p. 144.
14. Harriss, *Cardinal Beaufort*, p. 178, n. 34; C. Richmond, 'Edmund Beaufort, 1st Duke of Somerset', ODNB (consulted online January 2015).
15. See J. Ashdown-Hill, *Royal Marriage Secrets*, Stroud 2013, plates 5-8.

3. Beaufort versus York

1. '1400-50s: late Middle English *Jakken-apes*, literally jack (i.e., man) of the ape, nickname of William de la Pole 1396–1450), Duke of Suffolk, whose badge was an ape's clog and chain.' http://dictionary.reference.com/browse/jackanapes (consulted April 2015).

2. A heavy block of wood attached to a chain, to hinder the movement of the ape. This was the badge of William de la Pole.

3. The *Nicholas of the Tower* was the ship which intercepted him.

4. F. Madden, 'Political Poems of the Reigns of Henry VI and Edward IV', *Archaeologia*, vol. 29 (1842), pp. 318-347 (p. 320). *Placebo* and Dirige respectively are the old names for the offices of Vespers of the Dead and Matins of the Dead.

5. H. T. Riley, ed., *Ingulph's Chronicle of the Abbey of Croyland*, London 1908, p. 411.

6. Riley, ed., *Ingulph's Chronicle of the Abbey of Croyland*, p. 418.

7. *quum opus exigit, aut necessitas compellat, vestrum auxillium invocabimus*. Giles, ed., *Incerti scriptoris chronicon Angliae de regnis trium regum Lancastriensium*, Part Four, p. 42.

8. B. Wolffe, *Henry VI*, London 1981, p. 273.

9. J. Gairdner, ed., *The Paston Letters*, vol. 1, London 1907, pp 259–61.

10. Gairdner, ed., *The Paston Letters*, vol. 1, pp. 263–64.

11. See J. Ashdown-Hill, 'The Red Rose of Lancaster?', *Ricardian*, 10 June 1996, pp. 406-20.

12. F. Madden, 'Political Poems of the Reigns of Henry VI and Edward IV', *Archaeologia*, vol. 29 (1842), pp. 318–347 (p. 332), citing MS Trinity College, Dublin, D.4,18.

13. Madden, 'Political Poems of the Reigns of Henry VI and Edward IV', pp. 334–35.

14. Madden, 'Political Poems of the Reigns of Henry VI and Edward IV', p. 341, note a.

15. Ashdown-Hill, 'The Red Rose of Lancaster?', pp. 407–09.

16. Madden, 'Political Poems of the Reigns of Henry VI and Edward IV', p. 340.

17. J. Ashdown-Hill, 'Roses with Thorns: The Dangers of Restoration and Interpretation', *Ricardian*, vol. 11, no. 141, June 1998, pp. 297–301 (p. 300).

4. Queen Margaret of Anjou versus York

1. J. Gairdner, ed., *The historical collections of a citizen of London in the fifteenth century*, London (Camden Society, new ser., 17) 1876, [hereinafter Gairdner / Gregory's Chronicle] p. 198.

2. *ibid.*

3. Wolffe, *Henry VI*, p. 294.

4. Wolffe, *Henry VI*, p. 297.

5. H. Morley, ed., John Stow, *A Survay of London* (1598), London 1893, p. 93.

6. *Gregory's Chronicle*, pp. 203-04, as cited in Wolffe, *Henry VI*, p. 312.

7. H.T. Riley, ed., John Whethamstede, *Registrum Quorundum Abbatum Monasterii Sancti Albani*, two vols., R.S. 1872 and 1873, vol. 1, pp. 337–38.

8. 'considering the enemies of everyside approaching us' TNA, E.28/88/49, as cited by Wolffe, *Henry VI*, p. 317.

9. Gairdner / Gregory's Chronicle, p. 205.

10. *ibid.*

11. Gairdner / Gregory's Chronicle, p. 206; p. 207.

12. Davies, ed., *An English Chronicle of the Reigns of Richard II*,

Henry IV, Henry V and Henry VI, pp. 99 & 100, and Rotuli Parliamentorum vol. 5, 1439–1467/8, p. 375.

13. Madden, 'Political Poems of the Reigns of Henry VI and Edward IV', p. 341.

14. Gairdner / Gregory's Chronicle, p. 210.

15. Davies, ed., *An English Chronicle of the Reigns of Richard II, Henry IV, Henry V and Henry VI*, pp. 106-07.

Part 2: The White Rose of York

5. The White Rose Wins

1. *CPR 1452–1461*, London (HMSO) 1971, p. 659.

2. Gairdner / Gregory's Chronicle, p. 211.

3. *ibid.*

4. Gairdner / Gregory's Chronicle, pp. 211–12.

5. Gairdner / Gregory's Chronicle, p. 212.

6. Gairdner / Gregory's Chronicle, p. 214.

7. *ibid.*

8. Erroneously repeated in the MS.

9. Gairdner / Gregory's Chronicle, p. 215.

10. Morley / Stow, *A Survay of London*, p. 93.

11. *ibid.*

12. Gairdner / Gregory's Chronicle, p. 215.

13. Madden, 'Political Poems of the Reigns of Henry VI and Edward IV', pp. 343–44.

14. Morley / Stow, *A Survay of London*, p. 93.

15. Madden, 'Political Poems of the Reigns of Henry VI and Edward IV', p. 343, citing MS Trinity College, Dublin, D.4, 18.

16. *ibid.*

17. *ibid.*

18. Gairdner / Gregory's Chronicle, p. 216.

19. *ibid.*

20. Gregory's Chronicle lists him as Earl of Devon*shire* though most accounts of the English peerage claim that title was a much later invention.

21. Gairdner / Gregory's Chronicle, p. 218. Gregory's account ends in 1469.

22. J. Ashdown-Hill, *Eleanor the Secret Queen*, Stroud 2009, chapters 14 and 15.

23. J. Ashdown-Hill, 'Norfolk Requiem: the Passing of the House of Mowbray', *Ricardian*, vol. 12, March 2001, pp. 198–217.

24. For the evidence on these points see J. Ashdown-Hill, *Royal Marriage Secrets*, Stroud 2013, pp.83–84, citing *CPR* 1461–1467, pp. 72, 191, and J. Ashdown-Hill, 'Lady Eleanor Talbot: New Evidence; New Answers; New Questions', *Ricardian*, vol. 16, 2006, pp. 113–32, citing Warwickshire County Record Office, L 1/85 in respect of Eleanor's tenure of property in Wiltshire, for which no writ of *diem clausit extremum* was issued by the king when she died.

25. Obviously this is not solid evidence and it depends on how one interprets it. Nevertheless, the reference to a wife is intriguing – though mention of a fair daughter is somewhat mysterious.

26. Madden, 'Political Poems of the Reigns of Henry VI and Edward IV', p. 347.

27. N. Davis, *Paston Letters and Papers of the fifteenth century*, vol. 1, Oxford 1971, p. 279

6. Warwick versus the Woodvilles

1. There is, however, some debate about this issue. For the arguments behind the proposed chronology of Edward IV's relationship with Elizabeth Wayte (Lucy), see M. St Clare Byrne, ed., *The Lisle Letters*, 6 vols, Chicago 1981, and J. Ashdown-Hill, 'The Elusive Mistress: Elizabeth Lucy and her Family', *Ricardian* 11 June 1999, 490–505.

2. Riley, ed., *Ingulph's Chronicle of the Abbey of Croyland*, pp. 439–40.

3. R. S. Sylvester, ed., St Thomas More, *The History of King Richard III*, London 1976, p. 62.

4. Riley, ed., *Ingulph's Chronicle of the Abbey of Croyland*, p. 440.

5. Riley, ed., *Ingulph's Chronicle of the Abbey of Croyland*, p. 445.

6. J. Gairdner, ed., *Letters and Papers illustrative of the Reigns of Richard III and Henry VII*, 2 vols., vol. 1, London 1861, pp. 73–74.

7. *ibid.*

8. For a detailed account of the evidence relating to the execution of Desmond and the possible involvement of Elizabeth Woodville, see J. Ashdown-Hill & A. Carson, 'The Execution of the Earl of Desmond', *Ricardian* 15 2005, pp. 70–93.

9. The present author's research suggests that the true original of 'Robin Hood' may have been a manorial lord from Yorkshire.

10. A.R. Myers, ed., *English Historical Documents, 1327–1485*, London 1969, p. 300; Scoffield, *Edward the Fourth*, vol. 1, p. 495.

11. Henry VI's half-brother, Jasper, also claimed the earldom of Pembroke – as the Lancastrian contender for that title.

12. *Le roy en eut les nouvelles dont il fut moult desplaisant, si dist quil estoit trahy, et fist habillier tous ses gens pour aller audevant de son frere le duc de Clarence et son cousin de Warewic lesquelz venoient audevant de luy et estoient desja entre Warewic et Coventry ou ilz furent advertis que le roy venoit a lencontre deulz. si nestoit pas a croire que son frère de Clarence ne son cousin de Warewic voulissent penser trahison a lencontre de sa personne; pourquoy le roy se traist en ung village prez et se loga illec atout ses gens non gueres loingz du lieu ou estoit logie le comte de Warewic. Environ heure de myenuit vint devers le roy larchevesque d'Yorc, grandement adcompaignie de gens de guerre, si buscha tout hault au logis du roy, dissant a ceulz qui gardoient son corpz quil luy estoit necessaire de parler au roy, auquel ilz le nuncherent; mais le roy luy fist dire quil reposoit et quil venist au matin de lors il le orroit voullentiers. De laquele responce larchevesque ne fut pas content, si renvoia les messages de rechief dire au roy que force estoit quil parlast a luy, comme ilz le firent, et alors le roy leur commanda quilz le laissassent entrer pour oyr quil diroit, car de luy en riens ne se doubtoit. Quant larchevesque fut entre en la chambre, ou il trouva le roy couchie il luy dist prestement : 'Sire levez vous', de quoy le roy se voult excuser, disant que il navoit ancores comme riens repose ; mais larchevesque comme faulz et desloyal quil estoit, luy dist la seconde fois : 'Il vous fault lever et venir devers mon frere de Warewic, car a ce ne povez vous contrester' Et lors le roy doubtant que pis ne luy en advenist se vesty et larchevesque lemmena*

sans faire grand bruit au lieu ou estoient ledit comte et le duc de Clarence entre Warewic et Coventry. W. & L.C.P Hardy, eds, Jehan de Wavrin, *Recueil des Chroniques et Anchiennes Istoires de la Grant Bretaigne, a present nommé Engleterre*, vol. 5, London 1891, reprinted Cambridge 2012, pp. 584–86.

7. Private Wars

1. N. Davis, *Paston Letters and Papers of the fifteenth century*, two volumes, Oxford 1971, 1976, vol. 2, pp. 234–35.

2. Davis, *Paston Letters and Papers of the fifteenth century*, vol. 1, pp. 199, 392.

3. Davis, *Paston Letters and Papers of the fifteenth century*, vol. 1, pp. 270, 274, 282.

4. Gairdner, *The Paston Letters*, vol. 4, pp. 204–05.

5. J. Strachey, ed., *Rotuli Parliamentorum; ut et Petitiones, et Placita in Parliamento*, vol. 6, (*ab Anno Duodecimo R. Edwardi IV. ad Finem eiusdem Regni*), London 1777, p. 232; CPR, 1467–77, p. 190.

6. J. Maclean, ed., J Smyth, *The Berkeley Manuscripts*, 3 volumes, Gloucester 1883–85, vol. 2, 1883, p. 66.

7. Maclean, ed., J Smyth, *The Berkeley Manuscripts*, vol 2, pp. 109–110. Thomas reached the age of twenty-one, apparently, in summer 1469, and was 'under the age of twenty-two years' when he was killed in March 1469/70. The inquisition *post mortem* of his aunt, Eleanor, Lady Boteler, identified him in August 1468 as her nearest heir, and gave his age then as twenty, which it defined as being of

full age. TNA, C 140 / 29: '*Thomas Talbot miles, dominus Lisle, est heres eius propinquior, ... et est etatis viginti annos et amplius*'.

8. 'Kingmaking'

1. M. Jones, ed., Philippe de Commynes, *Memoirs*, Harmondsworth, 1972, p. 183
2. *ibid.*
3. Jones,/ Commynes, *Memoirs*, p. 185.
4. Jones,/ Commynes, *Memoirs*, p. 186.
5. Morley / Stow, *A Survay of London*, p. 86.
6. Jones,/ Commynes, *Memoirs*, p. 186.
7. *ibid.*
8. Jones,/ Commynes, *Memoirs*, p. 187.
9. *ibid.*
10. Jones,/ Commynes, *Memoirs*, pp. 188–89.
11. M. Clive, *This Sun of York*, London 1973, p. 155.
12. In recent discussions relating to the reburial of Richard III, David Monteith, Dean of Leicester, and other representatives of Leicester Cathedral, argued that the term 'Church of England' would never have been used in the Yorkist period. This quotation proves that the term was used – albeit with a different meaning from the one which it acquired in the sixteenth century.
13. J. Bruce, ed., *Historie of the Arrivall of Edward IV. in England and the Final Recouerye of his Kingdomes from Henry VI. A.D. M.CCCC.LXXI*, London 1838, pp. 1–2.
14. Bruce, *Arrivall*, p. 2.

15. Bruce, *Arrivall*, p. 10,
16. Bruce, *Arrivall*, pp. 11–12.
17. Bruce, *Arrivall*, p. 13.
18. Bruce, *Arrivall*, p. 14.
19. *ibid.*
20. Bruce, *Arrivall*, pp. 15–16.
21. Bruce, *Arrivall*, p. 17.
22. Bruce, *Arrivall*, p. 21.
23. Bruce, *Arrivall*, p. 31.
24. Bruce, *Arrivall*, p. 30.
25. Bruce, *Arrivall*, p. 38.
26. Anon., *Prince Henry the Navigator and Portuguese Maritime Enterprise* (British Museum catalogue, October 1960), London 1960, p. 2, citing B.M. Add. Charter 8043.

9. New Succession Problems

1. Strachey, ed., *Rotuli Parliamentorum; ut et Petitiones, et Placita in Parliamento*, vol. 6, pp. 193–95, 'from the original in the Tower of London'.
2. *Regina memor contumeliarum in genus suum et criminum in seipsam obiectorum, quod scilicet more maiorum legitima regis uxor non esset.* C. A. J. Armstrong, ed., D. Mancini, *The Usurpation* [sic] *of Richard the Third*, Gloucester 1989, p. 63.
3. See J. Ashdown-Hill, *The Third Plantagenet*, Stroud 2014, chapter 12.
4. *erat quaedam prophetia, quod post E. id est, post Edwardum quartum, G regnaret, sub hoc ambiguo Georgius dux*

Clarentiae, medus amborum fratrum Edwardi et Ricardi regum, dux ob hoc Georgius peremptus est. T. Hearne, ed., *Joannis Rossi Antiquarii Warwicensis Historia Regum Angliae*, London 1716, p. 215.

5. The suggestion that the prophecy referred to Richard, Duke of Gloucester, was a later invention, based on the fact that Gloucester (not George) actually succeeded to the throne in 1483.

6. A.B. Emden, *Biographical Register of the University of Oxford*, 3 volumes, Oxford 1957–59, vol. 3, p. 1778.

7. For fuller details, see Ashdown-Hill, *The Third Plantagenet*, chapter 14.

8. Morley / Stow, *A Survey of London*, p. 94.

9. Jones / Commines, *Memoirs*, p. 397.

10. Alvaro Lopes de Chaves, *Livro de Apontamentos (1438–1489)*, (Codice 443 da Coleccao Pombalina da B. N. L.), Imprensa Nacional – Casa da Moeda, Lisboa, 1983.

11. See J Ashdown-Hill, *Richard III's 'Beloved Cousyn', John Howard and the House of York*, Stroud 2009, p. 98 et seq.

12. Letter written by Simon Stallworth to Sir William Stonor on the 21 June, 1483. C. L. Kingsford, ed., *The Stonor Letters and papers*, vol. 2, Camden third series, XXX, London 1919, p. 161.

13. J. Ashdown-Hill, *The Dublin King*, Stroud 2015, p. 48.

14. C. S. L. Davies, 'A Requiem for King Edward', *Ricardian*, vol. 11, no. 114, September 1991, pp 102–05.

Part 3: The Red Rose of Beaufort

10. The Red Rose Wins

1. http://historypoints.org/index.php?page=henry-tudor-s-landing-site (consulted May 2015).

2. *fils du feu roy Henry d'Angleterre*. M. Jones, *Bosworth 1485: Psychology of a Battle*, Stroud 2002, pp. 124-25.

3. T. Penn, *Winter King*, London 2011, p. 4.

4. Ashdown-Hill, *Richard III's 'Beloved Cousyn'*, pp. 105-06.

5. The earliest surviving reference to the Boar Inn dates only from the 1570s. The story that Richard III stayed at the 'Boar Inn' was first recorded in writing by John Speede in about 1611. The story of the treasure found in a bed at the inn – a bed which was sunsequently presumed to have belonged to Richard – was first written down in Sir Roger Twysden's 'Commonplace Book' in about 1650. Incidentally, John Speede is also the earliest documentary source for the 'body in the river' myth, which claimed that Richard III's body was dug up in 1538 and reburied under Bow Bridge – or in later versions of the story, thrown into the River Soar. This second story was discredited by the present writer in 2004-05, leading to the erection of a small corrective plaque near Bow Bridge in 2005, and ultimately to the rediscovery of Richard III's lost remains on the Greyfriars' site in 2012.

6. On 'White Syrie', see J. Jowett, ed., *The Tragedy of King Richard III*, Oxford 2000, p. 336 and n. 43, also N. de Somogyi, ed., *The Shakespeare Folios: Richard III*, London 2002, p. 267, n. 90. For the list of Richard III's horses, see

Harl. 433, vol. 1, pp. 4-5. The list of Richard III's horses includes twenty named mounts which were either grey (*liard*, *lyard* or *gray*) or white (*whit*). Among these was 'the gret gray … being at Harmet at Nottingham'. There is no horse specifically named 'White Syrie', but not all the horses are named, nor are all described in terms of their colour.

7. http://www.ncbi.nlm.nih.gov/pmc/articles/PMC1043971/pdf/medhistoo024-0104.pdf (consulted May 2015).

8. http://www.ncbi.nlm.nih.gov/pmc/articles/PMC1043971/pdf/medhistoo024-0104.pdf (consulted May 2015), citing A. Dyer, 'The English sweating sickness of 1551: an epidemic anatomized', *Medical History*, 1997, 41:362-84 (pp. 376, 382).

9. One nineteenth-century source questioned the story that this crucifix had genuinely been found on the Bosworth battlefield site, and suggested that it might actually have come from Husbands Bosworth. However, this proposal was researched by the present writer, who concluded that the nineteenth-century suggestion is without foundation. J. Ashdown-Hill, 'The Bosworth Crucifix', *Transactions of the Leicestershire Archaeological & Historical Society*, vol. 78 (2004), pp. 83–96.

10. N. Pronay & J. Cox, eds., *The Crowland Chronicle Continuations: 1459–1486*, London 1986, pp. 180-81.

11. BL, Add. MS 12060, ff. 19–20, as quoted in Foss, *The Field of Redemore*, p. 54. See also R.M. Warnicke, 'Sir Ralph Bigod: a loyal servant to King Richard III', *Ric*. 6 (1982–84), pp. 299–303. It should be noted that Morley was an old man in 1554, while Sir Ralph Bigod had died in 1515. It is also worth

noting that similar tales exist relating to the losers of other battles, including Agincourt and Coutrai (see, for example, J. W. Verkaik, 'King Richard's Last Sacrament', *Ricardian*, vol. 9, [1991–93], pp. 359–360).

12. H. Ellis, ed., *Three Books of Polydore Vergil's English History*, London 1844, p. 224.

13. During a nineteenth-century investigation of Howard burials at Framlingham Church in Suffolk a male body was found, 'wrapped in sheet lead. On cutting through the lead near the place where there were three folds of lead, the skull of an older person presented itself – if we may judge from the state of the teeth. There was a large hole in the front of this skull, as if the head must have had some severe blow at some time or other. ... [This might be] the body of the Duke of Norfolk slain at Bosworth, when an arrow pierced his brain'. J. Ashdown-Hill, *Richard III's 'Beloved Cousyn', John Howard and the House of York*, Stroud 2009, p. 129, citing the account of the Revd J. W. Darby, who was present at the opening of the tombs.

14. S. Angelo, *Spectacle, Pageantry and Early Tudor Policy*, Oxford 1969, p. 24, citing York Civic Records vol. 1, p. 156.

11. Richard III's Heir, 'King Edward VI'

1. http://en.wikipedia.org/wiki/Henry_VII_of_England (consulted May 2015).

2. *In hoc Parliamento confirmatum est Regnum domino Regi, tanquam sibi debitum non ex uno sed ex multis titulis, ut non tam sanguinis quam victoriae bellicae conquaestusque jure*

rectissime populo Anglicano praesidere credatur. N. Pronay and J. Cox, eds, The Crowland Chronicle Continuations: 1459–1486, London 1986, pp. 194–195.

3. *Rotuli Parliamentorum*, vol. 6, p. 270.

4. *Rotuli Parliamentorum*, vol. 6, p. 289.

5. 'Forasmoche as oure moste dere moder, at our singuler plesure and request of late hadde the keping and guiding of the ladies, doughters of King Edward the iiij[th], and also of the yong lordes, the duc of Buk, [Buckingham] therles of Warwik and of Westmerland, to her grate charges': SB no. 166, published in W. Campbell, ed., *Materials for a History of the Reign of Henry VII*, vol. 1, London 1873, p. 311.

6. See Ashdown-Hill, *The Dublin King*, p. 43, citing the contemporary copy of a letter from 'King Edward VI' to the mayor of York (York City Archives, York House Book 6, f. 97r).

7. A. Raine, ed., *York Civic Records*, vol. 2, Yorkshire Archaeological Society 1941, pp. 23–24.

8. W. Bullen & J. S. Brewer, eds, *Calendar of the Carew Manuscripts preserved in the Archiepiscopal Library at Lambeth: The Book of Howth*, London 1871, p. 190.

9. For fuller details of the evidence in this respect, see Ashdown-Hill, *The Dublin King*.

10. *Cecedit comes Lincolniensis et Martinus Zwarte cum fere v[m] hominum, sed rex, pie cum extraneis agens, omnes de Yrlandia captives strangulari mandavit; captus quoque fuit juvenis dux Clarentiae [sic], quem suptiliter comes de Suffolc liberans transfretavit cum eo et apud Guizam se recepit.* Baron Kervyn de Lettenhove, ed., *Chroniques relatives à*

l'histoire de la Belgique sous la domination des Ducs de Bourgogne, vol. 1 (Adrien de But, Chroniques), Bruxelles 1870, pp. 674–75.

11. J. Leslau, 'Did the Sons of Edward IV Outlive Henry VII', *Ricardian*, vol. 4, no. 62, September 1978, pp. 2–14.

12. Leslau, 'Sons of Edward IV', p. 12.

13. Anonymous compilation, 'Did the Sons of Edward IV Outlive Henry VII: A postscript', *Ricardian*, vol. 5, no. 64, March 1979, pp. 24-26, (p. 25).

14. J. Leslau, 'A rejoinder', *Ricardian*, vol. 5, no. 65, June 1979, pp. 56–60 (p. 57).

15. E. Cavell, ed., *The Heralds' Memoir 1486–1490*, Richard III & Yorkist History Trust 2009, pp. 116–17.

12. Edward IV's Heir, 'King Richard IV'

1. http://en.wikipedia.org/wiki/Henry_VII_of_England (consulted May 2015).

2. J. Gairdner, *History of the Life and Reign of Richard the Third to which is added The Story of Perkin Warbeck*, Cambridge 1898, p. 267.

3. Sutton D. F., ed., Bernard André, *De Vita atque Gestis Henrici Septimi Historia*, on-line 2010.

4. Gairdner, … *The Story of Perkin Warbeck*, p. 271, citing Bernard André (see above, note 118).

5. Gairdner, … *The Story of Perkin Warbeck*, pp. 267, 274.

6. Gairdner, … *The Story of Perkin Warbeck*, p. 267.

7. Gairdner, … *The Story of Perkin Warbeck*, p. 271, citing 'Speed' (John Speede?) but with no source given.

8. For details of this suggestion, and the reasoning behind it, see Ashdown-Hill, *The Dublin King*.

9. See W. E. A. Moorhen, 'Lady Katherine Gordon: A Genealogical Puzzle', *The Ricardian*, vol. 11, no. 139 (Dec. 1997), pp. 191-213 (p. 207).

10. D. F. Sutton, ed., Polydore Vergil, *Anglica Historia* (1555 version), on-line 2005, 2010 – my emphasis.

11. R. Lockyer, ed., Bacon, *The History of the Reign of King Henry the Seventh*, London 1971, p. 195.

12. 'At the junction with the presently named Shornecliff Road (previously Thomas Street) was the bridge crossing of *St Thomas-a-Watering* over a small brook, which marked a boundary in the Archbishop of Canterbury's authority of the nearby manors in Southwark and Walworth. The landmark pub nearby, the 'Thomas a Becket', derives its name from this connection. It was a place of execution for criminals whose bodies were left in gibbets at this spot, the principal route from the southeast to the City of London'. http://en.wikipedia.org/wiki/Old_Kent_Road (consulted December 2013).

13. A. H. Thomas & I. D. Thornley, *The Great Chronicle of London*, London 1938, p. 289.

14. G. A. Bergenroth, ed., *Calendar of State Papers between England and Spain*, vol. 1, *1485–1509*, London 1862, vol. 1, p. 213, January 1500. http://www.british-history.ac.uk/cal-state-papers/spain/vol1/pp213-216 (consulted April 2015).

15. Sylvester, ed., St Thomas More, *The History of King Richard III*, p. 89, note 6.

16. Sylvester, ed., St Thomas More, *The History of King Richard III*, pp. 88–89.

13. De la Poles, Poles and Courtenays

1. Sutton / Vergil p. 66.

2. *ibid.*

3. Gairdner, ed., *Letters and Papers illustrative of the Reigns of Richard III and Henry VII*, vol. 1, p. 134.

4. Although, strictly speaking, his title in the English peerage had been reduced by Henry VII to 'Earl of Suffolk', once he had left England Edmund described himself as 'The White Rose, Duke of Suffolk'.

5. Gairdner, ed., *Letters and Papers illustrative of the Reigns of Richard III and Henry VII*, vol. 1, pp. 134–36.

6. *op. cit.*, p. 137.

7. Fabyan stated that this was done on the *first* Sunday of Lent, a year later, and the chronology of the Grey Friars' Chronicle does seem slightly muddled (see below).

8. Nichols' footnote at this point reads: 'On the vj. day of May on Tower hill, says Fabyan: they were partisans of Sir Edmund de la Pole'.

9. J.G. Nichols, ed. *Chronicle of the Grey Friars of London*, (Camden Society, Old Series, 53) London 1852: http://www.british-history.ac.uk/camden-record-soc/vol53/pp24-29 (consulted April 2015).

10. R. S. Sylvester, ed., *The Complete Works of St Thomas More*, *vol. 1, English Poems, Life of Pico, The Last Things*, Yale University Press 1963, p. 9.

11. M. Wood, *In Search of the Trojan War*, London 1985, pp. 33–34.

12. This is a manuscript in the *Bibliothèque Nationale*, illustrated in Wood, *In Search of the Trojan War*, p. 22.

13. Nichols, ed. *Chronicle of the Grey Friars of London*: http://www.british-history.ac.uk/camden-record-soc/vol53/pp24-29 (consulted April 2015).
14. The other was Anne Boleyn, who was created Marquess of Pembroke before her 'marriage' to Henry VIII.

Part 4: 'Tudor' = York; Habsburg = Lancaster

14. The Last Lancastrian Claimants

1. J. Gairdner, ed., *Letters and Papers, Foreign and Domestic, Henry VIII*, vol. 6, London (HMSO) 1882, p. 618.
2. J. Gairdner, ed, *Letters and Papers, Foreign and Domestic, Henry VIII*, vol. 7, London (HMSO) 1883, p. 519.
3. M. Waldman, *Elizabeth and Leicester*, London 1946, p. 209.

15. Conclusions

1. http://www.englandforever.org/national-symbols.php (consulted April 2015).

Appendix 1

1. Leicestershire Record Office B. R. II/3/3: R. A. Griffiths, 'Queen Katherine de Valois and a missing statue of the realm', *Law Quarterly Review*, vol. 93 (1977), pp. 257–58.

BIBLIOGRAPHY

Books

André, Bernard – see Sutton

Angelo S., *Spectacle, Pageantry and Early Tudor Policy*, Oxford 1969

Anon., *Prince Henry the Navigator and Portuguese Maritime Enterprise* (British Museum catalogue, October 1960), London 1960

Armstrong C. A. J., ed., D. Mancini, *The Usurpation*[sic] *of Richard the Third*, Gloucester 1989

Ashdown-Hill J., *Richard III's 'Beloved Cousyn', John Howard and the House of York*, Stroud 2009

Ashdown-Hill J., *Royal Marriage Secrets*, Stroud 2013

Ashdown-Hill J., *The Third Plantagenet*, Stroud 2014

Ashdown-Hill J., *The Dublin King*, Stroud 2015

Bacon, Francis – see Lockyer

Bergenroth G. A., ed., *Calendar of State Papers between England and Spain*, vol. 1, *1485–1509*, London 1862, vol. 1 – see also internet

Bruce J., ed., *Historie of the Arrivall of Edward IV. in England*

and the Final Recouerye of his Kingdomes from Henry VI. A.D. M.CCCC.LXXI, London (Camden Society) 1838

Bullen W., & Brewer J. S., eds, *Calendar of the Carew Manuscripts preserved in the Archiepiscopal Library at Lambeth: The Book of Howth*, London 1871

Calendar of Patent Rolls 1452–1461, London 1971

Calendar of Patent Rolls 1461–1467, London 1897

Campbell W., ed., *Materials for a History of the Reign of Henry VII*, vol. 1, London 1873

Cavell E, ed., *The Heralds' Memoir 1486–1490*, Richard III & Yorkist History Trust 2009

Clive M., *This Sun of York*, London 1973

Commynes, Philippe de – see Jones

Crowland (Croyland) Chronicle – see Pronay & Cox; Riley

Davies J. S., ed., *An English Chronicle of the Reigns of Richard II, Henry IV, Henry V and Henry VI*, London (Camden Society) 1856

Davis N., *Paston Letters and Papers of the fifteenth century*, two volumes, Oxford 1971, 1976

De But, Adrien – see Kervyn

Doubleday H. A., and Lord Howard de Walden, *Complete Peerage*, vol. 7 London 1929

Ellis H., ed., *Three Books of Polydore Vergil's English History*, London 1844

Emden A. B., *Biographical Register of the University of Oxford*, 3 volumes, Oxford 1957–59

Foss P. J., *The Field of Redemore* (Newtown Linford 1990, 1998)

Gairdner J., ed., *Letters and Papers illustrative of the Reigns of Richard III and Henry VII*, 2 vols., vol. 1, London 1861

Gairdner J., ed., *The historical collections of a citizen of London in the fifteenth century*, London (Camden Society, new ser., 17) 1876 [Gregory's Chronicle]

Gairdner J., ed, *Letters and Papers, Foreign and Domestic, Henry VIII*, vol. 6, London (HMSO) 1882

Gairdner J., ed, *Letters and Papers, Foreign and Domestic, Henry VIII*, vol. 7, London (HMSO) 1883

Gairdner J., *History of the Life and Reign of Richard the Third to which is added The Story of Perkin Warbeck*, Cambridge 1898

Gairdner J., ed., *The Paston Letters*, vol. 1, London 1907; vol. 4 reprinted Gloucester 1983

Giles J. A., ed., *Incerti scriptoris chronicon Angliae de regnis trium regum Lancastriensium Henrici IV, Henrici V et Henrici VI*, London, 1848

Gregory's Chronicle – see Gairdner

Halliwell J. O., ed., *The Chronicle of William de Rishanger*, London 1840

Hardy W. & L. C. P, ed. Jehan de Wavrin, *Recueil des Chroniques et Anchiennes Istoires de la Grant Bretaigne, a present nommé Engleterre*, vol. 5, London 1891, reprinted Cambridge 2012

Harriss G. L., *Cardinal Beaufort: a study of Lancastrian ascendancy and decline*, Clarendon, Oxford 1988

Hearne T., ed., *Joannis Rossi Antiquarii Warwicensis Historia Regum Angliae*, London 1716

Horrox R. and Hammond P. W., *British Library Harleian Manuscript 433*, vol. 1, Upminster, 1979

Howth, Book of – see Bullen

Jones M., ed., Philippe de Commynes, *Memoirs*, Harmondsworth, 1972.

Jones M., *Bosworth 1485: Psychology of a Battle*, Stroud 2002

Jowett J., ed., *The Tragedy of King Richard III*, Oxford 2000

Kervyn de Lettenhove, Baron, ed., *Chroniques relatives à l'histoire de la Belgique sous la domination des Ducs de Bourgogne*, vol. 1 (Adrien de But, Chroniques), Bruxelles 1870

Kingsford C. L., ed., *The Stonor Letters and papers*, vol. 2, Camden third series, XXX, London 1919

Lockyer R., ed., Bacon, *The History of the Reign of King Henry the Seventh*, London 1971

Maclean J, ed., Smyth J., *The Lives of the Berkeleys*, 3 volumes, vol. 2., Gloucester 1883

Mancini, Domenico – see Armstrong

More, Thomas – see Sylvester

Morley H., ed., John Stow, *A Survay of London* (1598), London 1893

Myers A. R., ed., *English Historical Documents, 1327–1485*, London 1969

Nichols J. G., ed., *Chronicle of the Grey Friars of London*, (Camden Society, Old Series, 53) London 1852 (see also internet)

Oman C. W. C., *England and the Hundred Years' War*, London 1898

Penn T., *Winter King*, London 2011

Pronay N., and Cox J., eds, *The Crowland Chronicle Continuations: 1459–1486*, London 1986

Riley H. T., ed., John Whethamstede, *Registrum Quorundum Abbatum Monasterii Sancti Albani*, vol. 1, London 1872

Riley H. T, ed., *Ingulph's Chronicle of the Abbey of Croyland*, London 1908

Rishanger, William de – see Halliwell

Rotuli Parliamentorum – see Strachey

Rous, John – see Hearne

St Clare Byrne M., ed., *The Lisle Letters*, 6 vols, Chicago 1981

Scofield C. L., *Edward the Fourth*, vol. 1, London 2005

Somogyi N. de, ed., *The Shakespeare Folios: Richard III*, London 2002

Stephen L., and Lee S., eds, *Dictionary of National Biography*, London 1891, vol. 26

Stow, John – see Morley

Strachey J., ed., *Rotuli Parliamentorum*, vol. 3, 1377–1411 (*tempore Ricardi R. II*), London 1771

Strachey J., ed., *Rotuli Parliamentorum*, vol. 5, 1439–1467/8 (*Ab Anno Decimo Octavo R. Henrici Sexti ad Finem eiusdem Regni*), London 1775

Strachey J., ed., *Rotuli Parliamentorum; ut et Petitiones, et Placita in Parliamento*, vol. 6, (*ab Anno Duodecimo R. Edwardi IV. ad Finem eiusdem Regni*), London 1777

Sutton D. F., ed., Polydore Vergil, *Anglica Historia* (1555 version), on-line 2005, 2010

Sutton D. F., ed., Bernard André, *De Vita atque Gestis Henrici Septimi Historia*, on-line 2010

Sylvester R. S., ed., *The Complete Works of St Thomas More*, vol. 1, *English Poems, Life of Pico, The Last Things*, Yale University Press 1963

Sylvester R. S., ed., St Thomas More, *The History of King Richard III*, London 1976

Thomas A. H. & Thornley I. D., eds, *The Great Chronicle of London*, London 1938

Twining, Lord, *European Regalia*, London 1967

Vergil, Polydore – see Ellis; Sutton

Wade J., *Rerum Hibernicarum Annales*, Dublin 1664

Waldman, *Elizabeth and Leicester*, London 1946

Wavrin – see Hardy

Whethamstede – see Riley
Wolffe B., *Henry VI*, London 1981
Wood M., *In Search of the Trojan War*, London 1985

Papers

Anonymous compilation, 'Did the Sons of Edward IV Outlive Henry VII: A postscript', *Ricardian*, vol. 5, no. 64, March 1979, pp. 24–26

Ashdown-Hill J., 'The Red Rose of Lancaster?', *Ricardian*, vol. 10, June 1996, pp. 406–420

Ashdown-Hill, 'Roses with Thorns: The Dangers of Restoration and Interpretation', *Ricardian*, vol. 11, no. 141, June 1998, pp. 297–301

Ashdown-Hill J., 'The Elusive Mistress: Elizabeth Lucy and her Family', *Ricardian* 11 June 1999, 490–505

Ashdown-Hill J., 'Norfolk Requiem: the Passing of the House of Mowbray', *Ricardian*, vol. 12, March 2001, pp. 198–217

Ashdown-Hill J., 'The Bosworth Crucifix', *Transactions of the Leicestershire Archaeological & Historical Society*, vol. 78 (2004), pp. 83–96

Ashdown-Hill J. & Carson A., 'The Execution of the Earl of Desmond', *Ricardian* vol. 15, 2005, pp. 70–93

Ashdown-Hill J., 'Lady Eleanor Talbot: New Evidence; New Answers; New Questions', *Ricardian*, vol. 16, 2006, pp. 113–32

Davies C. S. L., 'A Requiem for King Edward', *Ricardian*, vol. 11, no. 114, September 1991, pp 102–05

Madden F., 'Political Poems of the Reigns of Henry VI and Edward IV', *Archaeologia*, vol. 29 (1842), pp. 318–347

Griffiths R. A., 'Queen Katherine de Valois and a missing statue of the realm', *Law Quarterly Review*, 93 (1977), pp. 257–258

Hayden M T 'Lambert Simnel in Ireland', *Studies. An Irish Quarterly Review* 4 (1915), 622–38

Leslau J., 'Did the Sons of Edward IV Outlive Henry VII', *Ricardian*, vol. 4, no. 62, September 1978, pp. 2–14

Leslau J., 'A rejoinder', *Ricardian*, vol. 5, no. 65, June 1979, pp. 56–60

Moorhen W. E. A., 'Lady Katherine Gordon: A Genealogical Puzzle', *The Ricardian*, vol. 11, no. 139 (Dec. 1997), pp. 191–213

Verkaik J. W., 'King Richard's Last Sacrament', *Ricardian*, vol. 9, (1991–93), pp. 359–360

Warnicke R. M., 'Sir Ralph Bigod: a loyal servant to King Richard III', *Ricardian*, vol. 6 (1982–84), pp. 299–303

Internet

http://dictionary.reference.com/browse/jackanapes (consulted April 2015)

http://www.englandforever.org/national-symbols.php (consulted April 2015)

http://en.wikipedia.org/wiki/Edward_of_Norwich,_2nd_Duke_of_York (consulted December 2014)

http://en.wikipedia.org/wiki/Henry_VII_of_England (consulted May 2015)

http://en.wikipedia.org/wiki/Old_Kent_Road (consulted December 2013)

http://en.wikipedia.org/wiki/Wars_of_the_Roses (consulted

December 2014) http://historypoints.org/index.
php?page=henry-tudor-s-landing-site (consulted May 2015)

http://www.british-history.ac.uk/cal-state-papers/spain/vol1/
pp213-216 (G.A. Bergenroth, ed., *Calendar of State Papers
between England and Spain*, vol. 1, *1485–1509*, London 1862,
vol. 1, p. 213, January 1500 – consulted April 2015).

http://www.british-history.ac.uk/camden-record-soc/vol53/
pp24-29 (J.G. Nichols, ed. *Chronicle of the Grey Friars of
London*, (Camden Society, Old Series, 53) London 1852 –
consulted April 2015)

http://www.historyofparliamentonline.org/volume/1422–1504/
parliament/1426 (consulted February 2015)

http://www.nature.com/ncomms/2014/141202/ncomms6631/
full/ncomms6631.html (consulted December 2014) http://
www.ncbi.nlm.nih.gov/pmc/articles/PMC1043971/pdf/
medhist00024-0104.pdf (consulted May 2015)

ODNB

Richmond C., 'Beaufort, Edmund, first Duke of Somerset'
(consulted March 2015)
and see BOOKS – Sutton

INDEX